To Bob Cannell, to recall
our adventures in the area
of Loma Bonita, Oaxaca
in the winter-spring of 1945

Villa San Miguel, Aptdo 50,
El Sausal, Baja Ca, Mexico
12/3/74

Tom Robertson

Tropical Frontier

PAUL RECORD

TROPICAL
FRONTIER

ALFRED A. KNOPF  Publisher, New York

1969

TO

My friends of the Xucuapan
For their fondness,

And to Robert
For his encouragement,

This book is dedicated.

TO

My friends of the Kucupan
For their fondness,

And to Robert
For his encouragement,

This book is dedicated.

Foreword

T<small>HIS IS NOT</small> a novel. It is a factual account, one might even say an ethnographic sketch, of aspects of life on a modern frontier.

Terrestrial frontiers in this day are few and far between. Nowadays most talk is about the frontiers of outer space, to which one must be projected on the point of an enormous rocket, a concept terrifying to an earthbound type like myself. Consequently I find it consoling that there remain a few nooks and crannies of earthly frontier which one can reach on foot or on horseback, rather than on the tip of a huge projectile.

The frontier of my story is a tiny area, consisting of some four hundred or at the very most five hundred square miles of foothill country in a corner of southeastern Mexico. It is a frontier today and has been one for fifty or sixty years, because it lacks communications. There are no roads, only trails. To get in or out, one must cross a stretch of swampy coastal plain, where the trails wind interminably following what high ground there is along the riverbanks, and even there one comes to crossings where a horse goes belly-deep in mud. The river, which should provide access, surges over its banks in rainy seasons, so that the channel is well-nigh impossible to follow. In dry periods, it shrinks to a driblet so that one must get out, to drag the heavy dugout canoe over the shoals. Behind us, to the south, the rocky façade of the Sierra

Madre de Chiapas inhibits entry. There are times when it is very difficult to get into, or to get out of, this place.

Most of southeastern Mexico is not at all like this. Much of the area has been settled for a long time; many of the settlements were old population centers when Cortés arrived with his gold-hungry Conquistadores. Many places in the old settled area have kept up with the times: Villahermosa, Comalcalco, Coatzacoalcos, and Minatitlán are modern cities, with stores well stocked with up-to-date merchandise, radio and TV, traffic cops on the corners, and a trend toward decent plumbing. But these localities are favored by routes of easy communication: deep navigable rivers, stretches of open firm-soiled savannahs passable year-round, and railroads and all-weather highways.

The little foothill isolate that is the frontier of this tale is called the Xucuapan. This is the old name of the principal river. You will not find "Rio Xucuapan" on any but very old maps. However, the term is still used locally to refer not only to the river but to the whole drainage system of the river and its two main tributaries, from the steep slopes of the Sierra northward to the confluence of the Rio Xucuapan with a larger stream at the edge of the coastal plain.

The letter x is a tricky one in modern Mexican-Spanish orthography. At times it has the value of English h, as in "México," "Oaxaca." Sometimes it stands for an s sound, as in "Xochimilco," "café exprés." Occasionally it represents the sound of English sh, as in "ixtle" (a cordage-producing agave) and "Xucuapan."

In the remote pocket of the Xucuapan live some three hundred pioneer families. They are pioneers because they still, year after year, attack primeval jungle to make clearings for their plantings and pastures. They do not live in villages or hamlets; rather, each family dwells apart,

on its farmstead. Older men, after a lifetime of work,
have houses surrounded by expanses of clearings, open
pastures, and second growth that is the fallow cycle of
farmland. Young men, beginning their career of wresting
a living from the land, make a small clearing far back
in the forest, and build a hut there as a base from which
to battle the jungle with machete and ax. Clearing to
plant crops: maize, rice, beans, and above all pasture
grasses, as well as cacao, coffee, and minor vegetables and
fruits; and tending livestock: cattle, hogs, poultry—that
is the way of life on the Xucuapan.

Deer and peccary roam the woods, often come out into
the clearings. Tapirs wallow in swampy gullies like giant
hogs. Turkey-size curassows hoot from the treetops; tinamou, resembling immensely overstuffed pigeons, scuttle
over the jungle floor. Parrots and howler monkeys compete
with each other at dawn to make the most noise. Now
and then a jaguar roars—men who hear him curse and
look to their weapons, hoping against hope that he is stalk-
ing wild game, not a newborn calf or a domestic pig.
Hunting is not a sport, but a practical way of supplement-
ing a plain diet and of defending domestic animals against
predators. Fishing similarly is important to the diet. The
river and its tributaries teem with panfish, with catfish
whose flesh is sweet and firm in the cool swift waters
that spill from the Sierra, with snook, and with other
species, as well as freshwater shrimp and turtles.

Life on a frontier is never easy. To live under frontier
conditions, to tolerate the lack of conveniences, the hard-
ships, the drudgeries, and the frequent loneliness, certain character traits are required. This does not mean that
there is a special pioneer personality complex: pioneers
differ from one another in many ways as widely as do
their congeners of the old settlements—some are outgoing,

others reserved, even introverted; some are genial and pleasant-natured while others are ill-tempered and rancorous; some are grasping, others openhanded; and so it goes. But there are a few traits that nearly all frontiersmen display in abundance. Among these are a strong sense of personal independence and self-reliance. Noble qualities these may be, but under some circumstances, and when overstressed, they may produce person-to-person conflicts that all too frequently erupt into violence. There is a good deal of violence in this story, because there is a good deal of violence on the Xucuapan. Other factors contribute to such eruptions: the well-known Mexican—or rather, general Latin American—concept of *machismo*, an ideal of manliness that among other things idealizes swift aggressive reaction to the most minimal affront and makes vengeance a duty. But the pioneer, independent to the point where he brooks no man's dominance, so self-reliant that he feels no need for support by the law of the distant settled regions, is especially inclined to resolve his problems by his own hand, that is, by his gun or his machete— the latter supposedly a tool but essentially a weapon, a lineal descendant of the mariner's cutlass of the Spanish Main. Other pioneers—ours of yesteryear, of Old Arizona and Old Wyoming—reacted to stress situations in similar fashion, with Jim Bowie's fighting knife in place of the machete.

The pattern of violence is a very real one. There have been a dozen slayings, many more cases of mayhem, in the decade of my residence in the region; certainly a high index for so small a population. On the other hand, professional criminals have always been very uncommon. The purpose of this story is not to paint a picture of lawless savagery, for that would not be a true picture. The typical pioneer is not a lawless person, but rather one who is accustomed to handling his own problems, whatever they may be.

Technically of course there is Law and Authority, centered in the distant town of Lomas Bonitas, in the offices of the *Municipio*, roughly equivalent to the county seat, and to which this locality belongs administratively. But the authorities in town, try as they may, simply are not equipped to handle affairs in remote districts lacking routes of communication. By the time notice of a crime reaches them and the town policemen obtain horses for the trip, find guides, and eventually reach the scene, the slayer can be several days away. There is a supplementary system: local persons are appointed to formal—and unpaid —posts, such as *Agente Municipal*, and Auxiliary Judge, and control an auxiliary police force and are empowered to handle minor cases and to remit those charged with more serious offenses to the *Municipio*. But these posts are a burden; their holders operate under too many disadvantages to be effective.

To present the situation in better perspective and still get the story between the covers of a single book, two related series of incidents will be recounted. One series concerns the development of a conflict to its fateful climax. The other reports the bringing of law and order to this frontier by a dedicated police officer. The Rule of Law cannot be established in a day; the officer still has not completed the task. But he will. This is an important part of the whole account: the transition from the claw-and-fang rule of the wild to the Rule of Law is a process every frontier must go through; it is as much a part of the conversion of wilderness to the domain of civilized man as is the felling of the primeval forests.

These incidents will be reported as they happened, sandwiched in, so to speak, between accounts of the daily routine of working and living, because that is the way that we, my friends and neighbors and I, saw them occur, in the course of a varying rhythm: the usual sequence of chores and trivial incidents, day after day, interrupted now and then by staccato beats of crisis.

My qualification for telling the story of life on this frontier is that I have lived here on the Xucuapan for more than a decade. I know all my friends and neighbors and how they live, and there are but few corners of the region I have not traversed. I shall appear in the story from time to time, but I am not important to it except as observer and reporter; use of the first-person singular is not intended to vaunt my personal adventures and misadventures, but only to stress the fact that firsthand information is being recounted.

How I happen to be here can best be resumed in a mathematical fashion:

Given: a country boy inordinately fond of animals and green growing things, who had listened avidly to a lot of stories about the Old West as related by old-timers rolling brown-paper cigarettes or spitting tobacco juice so it sizzled in the campfire or down the sides of the pot-bellied stove in the bunkhouse as they yarned of cattle drives to Denver and Cheyenne, of life in a shanty on the Kansas plains when people still wondered whether the Indians would stay on the reservations, of cattlemen and homesteaders, gunmen and bronc-riders;

Let: destiny lead this country boy, as he grew older, to the city, finally to a stultifying desk job where he seemed fated to bore his life away;

Let, again: this dull creature turn to hunting and fishing as an escape back to the green of the countryside— no expensive African safaris or swank Alaskan hunting lodges, just vacation jaunts with friends as restless and dissatisfied as he, to spots off the tourist track they had learned to nose out;

Let, once more: our bored little man learn of the rich and accessible fishing grounds of the coastal rivers of southeastern Mexico, and when there let him hear of a game-filled wilderness, a hunter's paradise, called the Xucuapan. When he got there he found less game than reported, but instead a place that fascinated him, where pioneers battled the wilderness to plant their crops and grow their livestock;

Then finally, let: this lonesome figure become enamored of a sweet-natured country girl named Maria.

How does the equation solve? Well, human nature rarely proceeds by mathematical rules. But there was one such man who walked away from his dull desk job to marry Maria and settle on the Xucuapan.

THIS PREFACE is growing longer than intended. I shall cut it short with two brief advertences.

This tale is about my friends and neighbors. Since it is manifestly impossible to obtain permission from so many persons to write about their doings, I shall use the standard sociological device of altering their names to protect their identities. After all, it is their actions and attitudes that are important here. For the same reason I am taking a few liberties with geographic nomenclature. The name of a person's farm or that of the stream he lives by can identify him as surely as his correct name.

The final explanatory item is that when conversations are reported in colloquial English, as most of them will be, the intent is to indicate that they were originally made in countrified Spanish.

AND NOW we are ready to go to the Xucuapan.

CONTENTS

1	Branding Bee	3
2	Jungle	23
3	Venin	33
4	*Columna Volante*	52
5	Kinship	62
6	The Art of Bigamy	68
7	Patrol	81
8	The Brown Cow	86
9	Hunters' Traverse	111
10	A Trip to Town	160
11	To Live by the River	167
12	Pound of Flesh	210
13	The Ax and the Jungle	215
14	The Red Bull	239
15	Pattern of Violence	246
16	Profit and Loss	271
17	The Owl in the Tree	276
18	Pursuit	284
	Epilogue	317
	Glossary of Spanish Terms	321

Tropical Frontier

1

Branding Bee

THE BRASS-RED SUN was more than an hour high behind the stands of palm trees and scrub on the east bank of the river, the righthand side going downstream, and its heat was already burning through the dawn mists. I slowed the outboard motor and swung the tiller to nose the mahogany dugout into Arroyo Ixtal. My *compadre* Sebastián stood in the bow with a paddle, sounding the shallows and shoving against the banks to help steer, for the *arroyo* was low and narrow between its winding banks in May, late in the dry season. Maria began fussing with our two small youngsters about how to disembark without falling into the creek, while our *comadre* Tomasa did the same with her five. We were arriving after a predawn start. Don Panuncio was giving a branding bee. The whole countryside was invited; almost everyone would be there. We wouldn't have missed it for the world.

At the landing, Silviano, one of my *compadre's* hired hands, jumped ashore with the painter to steady the canoe while the women and small fry got out. They scrambled up the steep bank without mishap. As shallow as the creek was, a fall would not have been dangerous, but it would have been pretty muddy.

Don Panuncio had heard the clatter of the motor and was waiting at the landing. There were not many outboards on the river in those days.

"We've all been waiting for you people," he said, gesturing toward the crowd that stood chatting in the broad *patio* between his house and his general store. He gave Sebastián a hearty Latin *abrazo*, for they are *compadres*, and to his *comadre* Tomasa the more formal greeting of laying his hand gently on her shoulder. Maria he gave an avuncular hug, since he calls her his niece (the genealogical tie is so complex I am not quite sure I understand it). He patted all the youngsters on the head or chucked their chins, calling them by name. Then he enveloped me in an embrace. He reeked of *aguardiente*, raw white sugarcane rum.

"Pablito, how good to see you!" he shouted. "I'm glad you could come to help me."

"Uncle, you know that when you invite me I'll surely arrive."

He laughed. He thinks it is very funny that I call him "Uncle."

"Pablito, it amazes me every time we meet, *por Dios*. I never dreamed, when you came down here a few years ago with that bunch of dudes on that fantastic jaguarhunting expedition, that you'd come back to be my neighbor, then marry my niece and turn out to be my nephew. *Caramba, hombre*, what a deal!" He gave me another hung.

He goes through this routine every time we meet. It may sound dull, but really it is nice, because it is what gave me status—established me, an outlander, in this backwoods community. He knows this himself, of course, which is one of the reasons he keeps it up. For my "Uncle" Panuncio is the local Mr. Big, the local success story. He has more pasture land and more cattle than anyone else on the river, as well as the general store that supplies all but the more distant neighbors. You'd never have thought so to look at him as he greeted us on the creekbank, a tall thin old man with a lean tanned face, Indian-wide cheekbones. A shaggy handlebar mustache dangles under his long beak of a nose. A hank of grizzled hair usually hangs over his forehead, poking from under his huge Tabascan sombrero. His shoulders are broad but rounded from many a long day of slouching in the saddle. This day he was wearing his usual country garb: an old-fashioned collar-less shirt, homemade of coarse white cloth that looks like sugar sacking, flappy pantaloons of the same material, and bullhide *guaraches*. He looked like any peasant farmer of the Xucuapan.

But see him in town, freshly barbered (except for the shaggy mustache), his lean frame covered by a starched white *guayabera*, the many-pleated button-adorned shirt that is the well-to-do townsman's elegance, well-tailored black trousers, shined black shoes, and a black felt hat. He looks like an elderly citified dandy, not at all like a frontier cowman, if you don't notice his bowlegged gait.

One of the reasons, I am sure, that Don Panuncio likes me is that he knows that I understand him, though we never discuss it. I know his coarse country garb and coun-try manners are affectations, like his backslapping and jok-ing and drinking with his neighbors. It is part of his sys-tem of handling the peasantry who might be envious and difficult. But they are all fond of Don Panuncio. "Look at him!" they say. "As rich as he is, he puts on no airs. He's just like one of us." They will do whatever he wants of them—even to paying the big mark-ups for the merchan-dise in his store.

Underneath I know him to be a Tory and an aristocrat. His different dress and manners in town show this. So does his library. Aside from a few works on veterinary medicine there is not one book that treats of a modern theme. What he reads for pleasure (he and I are the only people on the Xucuapan who read at all) is of the grand past, of the conquest of New Spain, of colonial aristocrats. Don Artemio del Valle Arispe, the whimsical historian of the glories of the days of the Viceroys, is represented by many volumes. There are books on the aristocrats in the war of independence from Spain and on the elegant fashionable society during the dictator Díaz's regime. But nothing on the 1910 Revolution, or modern times.

This is of course why he stages branding bees year after year, for there is something of the old grand manner in inviting the countryside, barbecuing a couple of steers, importing quantities of beer and strong drinks, hiring musicians to play through the night—in short, staging the sort of *fiesta* that the *hacendados* of olden days used to give. Don Panuncio is ordinarily not a man to waste a peso, albeit he has many of them. It would really be cheaper for him to hire some extra cowboys to corral, brand, and cut his calves. Actually he does handle part of his calf crop that way, for there are too many for even the lot of us to handle in one day. But he always keeps one herd apart for the branding bee.

Don Panuncio herded Maria and Tomasa toward the house, "where Doña Carmen is waiting for you." To us he said, "Let's go to the store. I have something to show you, and we can have some coffee. You there, Silviano, come along too. I may need you."

Don Domingo Hernandez, all lanky six feet four of him, came running, his spurs clattering. In a region where most men stand a slim wiry five feet six or seven he loomed up like a lighthouse. Not only in height but in coloring and features did Domingo differ from most of his neighbors. His clean-cut, rather handsome features were Spanish, not Indian in cast, his coloring was lighter, and when he failed to shave, his jaws became covered with a dense black stubble, not the patchy, straggly whiskers of those in whom Indian blood predominates.

Grinning his usual happy smile Domingo spun Sebastián around in an *abrazo*, then reached out a long arm to wallop me across the back. "Don Pablito!" he whooped. "Welcome to the cow work! Who is going to catch more of Don Panuncio's wild calves today, you or me?"

"You are, of course." He was an excellent roper, far out of my class. "But maybe I can help you a little."

"Let's get on to the store," said Don Panuncio. "If more people see you two, we'll never have time to have that coffee. Bring Domingo." At the door of the big plank-walled, palm-thatched structure, he fumbled with the lock dangling from a heavy chain until it clicked, then swung the door open. We stepped inside. There in the middle of the floor, looking almost as big as a haycock, was a pile of weapons. In the course of my travels, including a hitch in the navy, I have seen some weaponry. But never had I seen anything quite like this.

There were machetes with and without scabbards, shiny new ones, and old ones filed to needle points. There were daggers, dirks, and old kitchen knives, some with makeshift sheaths for carrying in the waistband, and a number of large switchblades. There were single-shot, repeating, and autoloading rifles, mostly .22s but also some larger calibers. There were shotguns, old and new, and even a few muzzleloaders with their big hammers, along with powderhorns and shotbags. Mixed in the lot were pistols: revolvers and automatics, big ones and some tiny derringer-like .22s and .25s.

[7]

"Have you anything for the pile, Silviano?"

My *compadre*'s hired hand shook his head.

"That lump in your pants pocket?" The lad flushed, then took out a switchblade knife.

"That's a weapon too. Into the pile with it," said Don Panuncio. "See what I'm doing?" he chortled to us. "Last year I spent half the night stopping fights. This time I'm disarming every mother's son. Tomorrow, or whenever they sober up, they can have their irons back. We're going to brand a lot of calves today, eat a lot, and drink more than a lot, dance *huapangos* tonight and drink some more, all with no bloodshed. Even the auxiliary police are disarmed. Incidentally, if you two are packing guns, let me have them. I'll put them in the cash drawer. You might not be able to find them again if you dropped them into that pile of junk." Into the cash drawer they went.

A youngster brought a pot of coffee so black it stained the enamelware cups. Our host poured, lacing the brew heavily with *aguardiente*. "Start the day right, lads. We have lots of work to do."

People came and went, some for instructions, some to report progress. Don Panuncio had the work organized: the cattle to be handled were in the big holding pen, some of them were already being cut into the corral. Branding fires were laid and lighted, with plenty of wood stacked just outside the corral fence. There were many calves to be branded, but there were many of us as well. Some of us would rope, some would throw and tie, some would handle the irons and the castrating pincers. When the branding was done the *fiesta* would begin.

"Pablito, I didn't see any roping horse in that canoe of yours," said Don Panuncio. "Do you want me to tell Jorge to saddle one for you?"

"I brought an extra one, Pablito," said Domingo. "All

saddled and ready. You can use him—he works better than these goats of Don Panuncio's."

"Thanks, both of you. But I sent one down with the boys—ought to be out there now." There was a herd of horses under the spreading mango trees in front of the house. "I'll have a look when I finish my coffee."

Don Panuncio looked down his long nose. "If you don't find him, and are so fussy about mounts, you can work on the ground, throwing and tying."

"*A la jodida.* I don't work afoot in any branding pen except my own."

Everything Don Panuncio owns is big. His main corral is the size of a football field; there is plenty of room to stretch a pony out after a calf, and the calf has space to run. And the calves! Don Panuncio doesn't brand small calves, for his iron is too big. Most of them are yearlings. There are always a few two-year-olds that had escaped the previous year's roundup. The "calves" are always big, and wild, for they are well graded up with zebu—they are of the same genetic mix that produces the rough tough bulls used in Stateside rodeos.

We tightened cinches, unkinked lassos, to move in. Those who were to work on the ground had the fires blazing and bristling with handles of heating branding irons.

Don Panuncio always catches the first one. He entered the corral on a big rawboned gray, cut an animal from the bunch at one end, went after him at full tilt, threw a loop that sang "zingggg!" as it whipped around the calf's neck. The old man took his turns around his saddle-horn to brake the calf to a stop. In moments he had the animal against one of the big forked snubbing posts to be thrown and tied. That was how it was to be done, said his demonstration.

Then the rest of us went to work. There were thirty or forty of us roping most of the time, more than twice as many working on foot. The five snubbing posts were empty for moments only. As soon as an animal was thrown and tied, another roper dragged or drove his catch to the post, flipped his lasso over the fork, hauled his calf up close to be lassoed by the heels or thrown with handropes. Those working on the ground were soon dripping with sweat. We caught and branded all the unmarked calves in the first bunch—the bull calves got the pincers—drove them out the gate, then moved in more from the holding pen. Women, children, and non-cowpunching men crowded around the outside of the corral, watching.

At midmorning women began to bring buckets of *pozole*, lye-leached ground corn in water, which is at once a refreshing drink and a food. Others brought coffee, and platters of *tacos* thick with beef and turkey. There were jugs of *aguardiente*. A few men drank too much and gave up the struggle. They were replaced by others from the crowd outside.

The calves were big and wild. They bucked and bellowed as they felt the rope tauten on them, and fought like furies at the snubbing posts. On untying, some got up full of fight, chasing the nearest tiers and branders amid cheers from the spectators.

There were some hard falls. Agustín Perez's cinch broke as he was snubbing a big red calf, and he hit the ground with a thud. He lay there for a minute or so, but got up before anyone could help him. A new cinch was found. He kept on roping. A few mounts slipped or stumbled, falling heavily, shaking up their riders. A calf, not a very big one, butted portly Don Petronilo, sending him sprawling, the wind knocked out of him. Don Panuncio ran to help him up.

"Come on out of this, old-timer, let someone else wrestle those calves. Let's go have a drink." This was his standard remedy for healing the bumps and wallops of the branding pen—a good stiff drink in the shade of the *apompo* trees just outside.

Most of the ropers, with the exception of myself—I am just run of the mine—were excellent at their craft: Don Gonzalo, Juvencio Gomez, Manuel Sanchez, and many others. A bawling, frightened calf stretching out as he runs, thundering hooves of two or three horses overtaking him, cries of "Take him, Goncho!" or "Get him, Vencho!"—and a long rope zings through the air to drop its loop on the animal's neck. The rope squeals as it brakes around the saddlehorn till the calf is stopped. Another one for the iron.

But the star of the show, as usual, was Don Domingo. His two horses, which he alternated, one cooling out in the shade while the other worked, were big and fast. His skill with a lasso was amazing. Whether the calf ran straight or zigzagged and dodged, it could not escape that whistling loop. Domingo had new ropes, a new buckskin roping glove, and new saddles on both mounts. When he took his turns he let the rope run around the horn till a puff of smoke rose from the tortured wood. The lassos used here are of hardtwist cotton fiber, twenty-five Spanish *varas* long, which is sixty-six feet. That is farther than a man can throw a loop, but it leaves him plenty to slide around the horn when he wants to swank it, as Domingo was doing. At day's end he had worn out one rope and his roping glove, and had burned deep spirals into both hardwood saddlehorns. That is swank, hereabouts.

There was a two-year-old heifer, the gray color called *sereno* ("misty"), with long zebu ears and a zebu hump on her withers, spooky as could be. I was roping with

Domingo. The heifer broke sharply to her left, toward me. "Hang it on her, hang it on her!" Domingo yelled.

She was going to the wrong side for a normal throw. I tried a backhand but missed. Then I slammed my pony into her to turn her toward Domingo, and went to work hazing for him. He was wide to the right—some other animals had got in his way. When we got in the clear and straightened her out she ran diagonally across the corral straight toward one of the branding fires. Domingo was standing in his stirrups whirling a long loop. The heifer was fifty feet from the fire when he snapped his loop about her neck, closer by the time he took his turns and stopped his horse.

A number of men were standing around the fire, watching. Some began to move away as the heifer raced toward them. Some stood their ground, certain that Domingo would stop her in time. He didn't. With a shrill yell he let the rope whistle around the horn till the animal was almost at the fire. Then he stopped her down hard, so that she spun around, then swung like a pendulum at the end of the rope across the fire, scattering branding irons, firebrands, and people. He did it on purpose, of course, as a joke. Most of the men who ran or fell tumbling out of the way got up laughing. But not Benito Cadena. The animal had bumped him and he had fallen hard.

Benito is somewhat taller and brawnier than the average among local men, though nowhere near as big as Domingo. He has the typical facial features showing an Indian strain: wide cheekbones, close-set dark eyes, aquiline nose, thin-lipped mouth, and angular chin. But he has a shock of carrot-red hair and fair, freckled skin. In central Tabasco, where his family came from, there are many blonds and redheads. Local folklore derives such coloration from the Northern freebooters who caroused in the pirate towns on the Grijalva River, in the days of the Spanish Main.

It may or may not be true that redheaded people are quicker-tempered than others. But when Benito got to his feet he was in a rage. He picked up a branding iron, holding it menacingly. It was still hot. Some bits of dry cow dung stuck to the stamping end smoldered, sending up wisps of blue smoke. He stood straddle-legged, eyes mere slits.

"Hijo de tu puta madre," he snarled ("son of your whore mother"—about as vile an insult as the Spanish language can offer). *"Hijo de tu puta madre,* if you don't know how to work in a branding pen, go to the kitchen to make *tortillas* with the other old women."

Domingo's face went bleak. His gloved hand loosened its grip on the lasso, his knees relaxed slightly. He was going to let the heifer go as he spurred his horse to ride Benito down. Both had been disarmed, but angry men can always find weapons.

There was utter silence in the corral. None of us, inside the corral and out, watching the two confronting each other in hate, seemed to be able to breathe. Then someone giggled, a loud hysterical giggle that bounced absurdly through the thick tense quiet. That broke it. We all began to laugh and hoot and shout in nervous glee. Domingo tightened his rope about the saddlehorn to work the heifer against a snubbing post. Benito turned away, assembling his branding irons and scattered fire.

This happened several years ago. It was the first turn of the wheel along the track.

THE AFTERNOON SUN was scorching but low in the western sky as we branded the last of the calves.

"Four hundred forty-six head," Don Panuncio announced. "Twenty-three more than last year. You boys keep improving—" he looked down his nose the way he does—"and soon you'll qualify for full cowboy wages."

We gave a jeering shout, for we know it is his conceit to pretend he is saving great sums by giving the *fiesta* instead of hiring cowboys to do the branding.

"If you're going to wash up, hurry it up, then come along to the house. We have lots to eat, and to drink too," he said.

We headed for the river. Ropers, tiers, branders, pincer operators, all were dripping sweat, coated with dust, and smeared with cow dung. Hollywood to the contrary, no one comes out of an honest day's work in a branding pen neat and tidy and smelling like a rose. I found my hands, Juanito and Feliciano. We bathed ourselves and the sweaty horses, rinsed out the dripping saddle cloths. The river was full of other men doing the same. The water was barely cool, but still refreshing after the long day. We went to the house, hung up our saddles, hung out the saddle cloths on the yards and yards of rope stretched out for the purpose, then turned the tired ponies loose to graze. Good wife Maria, like other good wives for their husbands, had brought me a change of clothes.

We were hungry enough to eat an ox—we ate two barbecued ones, stacks of turkeys in *mole* sauce, tubs of rice and the flavorsome black beans of the tropics. There could not possibly be enough plates for the multitude, so we ladled out our servings on hot *tortillas*, laced them with a sauce of tomato, chopped onion, chile pepper, a touch of ground garlic, and plenty of the fragrant herb *silantro*. There was *aguardiente* to wash the food down with, but not many wanted it. There was *pozole* and coffee, mountainous stacks of beer, and soft drinks for the women and children. The launch that was supposed to bring the ice for the beer and soft drinks had broken down—somewhere down by La Ceiba, they said—but no one cared. Mexican beers, among the best in the world, are palatable even *al tiempo*, at air temperature, and kids brought up without refrigerators are happy with tepid soft drinks. We stuffed ourselves, lounged about, and no one said very much.

BLACK IS ABSENCE of light. Black is black. When one reads "the soft black of the tropic night" one wonders how absence of color could conceivably have qualities of hardness. But there really is a difference in the black of a tropical night from that of deserts or northern countries. Probably it is the atmospheric humidity that produces the soft velvety quality.

The night was black with whatever distinctive character of black a tropical night has. Polaris, tiny and fuzzy, hung at about seventeen degrees above the indistinct horizon. A sea breeze began to work its refreshing way inland.

Don Panuncio got up from his hammock to rout out the musicians. Guitars and their miniatures, the *jaranas*, twanged as they were tuned up, then began to throb in rhythm, the rollicking rhythm of the Veracruz *huapango*, as the singers shrilled in strained falsetto:

"*Para bailar la bamba*
Se necesita
Una poca de gracia,
Y otra cosita . . ."

"To dance the *bamba*
One must have
A bit of grace,
And something else too . . ."

I don't know what the verse means, if it means anything, but the tune is catchy and it is fun. Flickery coal-oil lamps hang on posts about the *tarima*, the planked dance platform six feet wide by eight long. The dancers, a pair

at a time, stamp their heels against the platform in time
to the music, making it boom like a great drum. The man,
hat cocked over one eye or tilted to the back of his head,
dances with his hands dangling at his sides or stuffed in
his pockets, his torso rigid, all the action and energy in
his feet and legs. The woman holds her skirts wide, shuffling her feet in intricate patterns of stomps and steps.
In the central part of Veracruz state a bolt of wide blue
ribbon is thrown across the platform and, to the rhythm
of the *bamba*, the dancers kick it into a complicated bow
knot without missing a beat. No one around here knows
how to do such fancy steps, but we still take turns on the
tarima making it resound in time to the twanging strings.

OUTSIDE the strings vibrated, the falsettos reached
new heights, the dance platform boomed accompaniment
to *La Bamba, La Chachalaca, Pájaro Cú, La Marcelina*—
the whole repertoire. Inside the store we sat around the
haycock of machetes, knives, and guns by the light of a
coal-oil lamp. Don Domingo sat on the counter dangling
his long legs; he had taken his big spurs off at last. "El
Güero" ("The Blond") Roberto, looking like a fat Dutch-
man trying to disguise himself with a Tabascan sombrero,
sat on an upended box. His ancestry, like Benito's, goes
back to central Tabasco. Short, somber Don Concepción
—"Don Chon"—sat on a chair tilted against the wall. He
is not really as somber as he first appears, but cannot forget the discipline he learned during his career as a revolu-
tionary before 1910, then with the Carranza forces to
1916, when he was mustered out with the rank of captain.
This is frustrating for him, as there is little discipline on
the Xucuapan. Cadaverously lean Don Amaranto slouched
against the counter chatting with my *compadre* Sebastián
and short, ruddy-faced Don Salvador Ordoñez. There was

Don Antonio Palma from down near the fork of the river, his brother Don Silvestre, who lives on the tributary (we call it the "other river"), and Don Cayetano Garcia. And, of course, Don Panuncio. This is the Establishment.

All are considered cattlemen, although there is a long stretch from Don Panuncio's three thousand head to Don Amaranto's twenty-five—and I mean twenty-five cows, not thousands. Quantity is not the criterion. There are other people who have more cattle than Amaranto, more than Sebastián and old Don Concepción, but are never included in these sessions. Don Margarito Lopez, for example. The members of the Establishment are linked by an intricate network of kinship ties and the sacrosanct *compadrazgo* relationship. I, a small operator and an outlander, was there because Don Panuncio wanted me there.

Outside, people were drinking beer and *aguardiente* between dances. Don Panuncio opened a bottle of a good Spanish brandy, but he served it as he would *aguardiente*, filling a water tumbler and passing it around loving-cup fashion.

"There is some news," he said. "Don Chon and I have some news for you."

Don Concepción took the ball. "This is something that must not be noised around. As the gossipy *comadres* say, 'In strict confidence, *comadrita*.' But this is for real. This is only for us here."

"My *compadre* Chon and I," said Panuncio, "went to the state capital a few days ago. We talked to a lot of people, including the Governor. About our problems here on the Xucuapan. Everybody knows we have some."

"Chucho Ortiz is our biggest one," said Don Antonio. "That *hijo de la chingada* stole a pair of mules from me—"

"Yes, yes, *compadre* Salvador, we know about that."

Don Panuncio was taking the floor. "But this is more than just rounding up Don Chucho. We are going to bring a *Columna Volante* in here. You all know what that is."

"I don't, Don Panuncio," I admitted.

"It's a force of state police, equipped and authorized to move anywhere—they have horses, vehicles, special trains if necessary. The *Columnas* are supported partly by the state and partly by the Cattlemen's Associations. They are mainly set up to work with cattlemen, hunting down rustlers, but they can do other police work too."

"That sounds good," said I.

"You're damn right it's good," said El Güero.

"We also talked with the officer who'll be in charge— Don Juan Pereyra. They say he's a good man, and he looks it. He says he will get a special order to apprehend Don Chuchito dead or alive."

Don Chon broke in, "This officer is going to straighten out some other things too. He's going to collect a lot of illegal firearms, like those my *compadre* assembled in this pile."

"From cattlemen too?" Don Amaranto asked.

Don Panuncio grinned. "We figure it depends on who the cattlemen are."

"Don Manto is worrying about that antique Parabellum he packs," chuckled El Guero. Everyone laughed. Don Amaranto is known to be a great worrier.

"Who has the glass?" asked Don Panuncio. "It probably needs refilling." He poured it full of brandy to start it on another round.

"The only problem is that the local Cattlemen's Associations have to make token payments to maintain the force. Nearly all the funds come from the state and from the Regional Association, but we have to put up this token payment as show of good faith and cooperation. It isn't a large amount, and we have it in the treasury. But we don't want to bring it up in open meeting. For obvious reasons."

"For the obvious reasons that several of Chucho's relatives are members of the Association," Don Chon put in.

"They are good people, all of them," said Don Salvador.

"Surely," put in Don Sebastián. "But you know perfectly well they aren't going to vote funds to catch their kinsmen. And if they're outvoted it will be just as bad— that's when bad feeling starts."

"It's because of them that Chucho has lasted as long as he has," growled Don Cayetano. "No one wants trouble with them. Otherwise somebody would have applied Article 16 to the *cabrón* long ago." (Article 16, because 16-gauge is the most popular shotgun caliber locally.)

"That's why we wanted to talk this over here," Don Panuncio continued. "We here can decide to turn over the funds. At the end of the year we'll just write them off. The associations at Lomas Bonitas and San Francisco don't have this sort of problem, so they are making their contributions publicly. That gives the *Columna* three local associations to look after, and yet it will look as though the downriver ones—Lomas and San Francisco—brought the police force in."

"We have to do it this way because it's the only way to bring law and order to the Xucuapan," Don Chon added. "I mean real law and order. The town police never accomplish anything here, and this unpaid auxiliary police force has never worked out right."

"Never will," said Don Amaranto. "I've been through it many times, as *Sub-Agente* and as Auxiliary Police Chief. You get an order to arrest someone. You round up your local auxiliaries: half of them are relatives or *compadres* of the criminal, the other half are afraid he'll take revenge on them when he gets out of jail. What do you catch? Nothing."

"That's how Chucho got his start," El Güero chimed in. "That's why he killed José—José was in charge of the auxiliary police who disarmed him and tied him up for being drunk and disorderly at a *velorio* Don Ramón was giving."

"Macheted him from behind, then hacked the body all over," said Don Silvestre. "I helped Don Pastor bring the body home. It was pretty bad. But what Don Manto says is right. One accomplishes little, wastes a lot of time and money, and all the pay he gets is that his neighbors start to distrust and dislike him."

"We all know that," said Don Chon. "That's why we need real professional police. We never had this opportunity before to bring some in, so now we're going to do it, even if we have to do it this way, sort of privately." He said "privately," not "highhandedly," but his meaning was clear: the other seventy voting members of the Association were not to be consulted.

"Law and order have to come to the Xucuapan," Don Panuncio said. "And we are going to bring that law and order in. We have now decided that point."

"The only other thing," put in Don Chon, "is that we here will also see to it that the police troop is provided with food, shelter, fresh mounts if they need them, while they are working here."

"That's pretty obvious, *compadre*," Panuncio retorted. "I'm sure everyone here sees the need for that. That's part of our cooperation. Now that everything is settled, who needs another drink?"

We polished off the brandy, then went out into the cooling night to join the dancing and singing. Strings throbbed, falsetto voices chanted, heels drummed the planks.

"Pajarito eres muy bonito
Y de muy bonitos colores,
De muy bonitos colores,
"Pajarito eres muy bonito
Pero más bonito fuera-a-as
Si me hicieras el favor
De llevarme esta carta
A la dueña de mi amor."

"Little bird you're very pretty,
And of very pretty colors,
Of very pretty colors,
Little bird you're very pretty.
But you'd be even prettier
If you would do me the favor
Of carrying this letter
To the owner of my love."

The immense black night surrounded the little patch of yellow flickering light from the coal-oil dips ringing the platform. The dancers changed off continually: another man stepped onto the platform and the male dancer stepped off. The women did the same—it reminded me of tag dances at country dances back home. Men from the audience relieved the hoarse and finger-weary musicians.

Someone shouted *"Bamba!"* and the the music stopped abruptly. One of the dancers recited a verse. Most of the verses are old standards, known to everyone. By slight changes they can be made to allude to some person present; some flatter, some are derisive, some amorous. The audience cheered, the musicians struck their chords, the heels drummed again until dawn. Only small children got any sleep.

There were tubs of black coffee ready at dawn as the party broke up. Spiked if one wished. It had taken us three hours bucking current in the canoe to reach my *compadre*'s farm. Don Sebastián wanted us to stop off, but I decided I could stay awake just barely another hour and a half, the time it would take to get home.

Doña Chabela, our cook, who has been with us so long that she runs the place too, was at the landing, glowering about how long we had taken to get back. She grumbled until I poured her a stiff slug from the bottle Don Panuncio had slipped into my *morral* "for the road." Then I climbed into the hammock and slept until dusk. Country parties are strenuous.

2

Jungle

It was a rare day on the farm, indeed a rare sort of day for any farm: there were no urgent chores once the milking had been done and the hogs and poultry fed. There was, *mirabile dictu*, no fallen fence to fix, no newborn calf to search for in the tall grass pastures, no injured animals to be treated. The pasture weeding was being done on the basis of contracts, so much per hectare, each contractor working a long or a short day as suited him, so there was no overseeing to be done.

Feliciano asked for the day off to go fishing with Don Bernando.

I said to Juanito, "Let's go have a look in the jungle to see if we can find a better trail to the Jó."

His wide round catface broke into a grin. He likes such tasks. "*Bueno!* Which horse shall I catch for you?"

"Any. It doesn't matter—we'll have to leave the ponies at the edge of the woods anyhow."

"We can leave them at the big *zapote mamey* tree. There's good shade there."

The Jó is a small creek, named after a little blue heron in I don't know what Indian tongue, behind the first range of ridges flanking the river. To us the name also means about sixty acres of pasture where the stream runs through a broad flat alluvial valley ringed by virgin rain forest.

The old trail to the pasture, over which we move the cattle when they feed in there, is a mile-long, roundabout route across the steep ridges. In the rainy season when the red clays are watersoaked this uphill-and-down route is difficult. An unshod pony slips and slithers, clawing like a frantic cat to climb the side of one ridge, then bunches his feet and squats, his tail dragging in the mud, to skim down the other side. My idea was to search for a more level route, skirting the ridges where they drop off into a narrow strip of swamp that is the source of a tiny stream we call Aguamiel ("Honeywater").

Juanito knew what I meant, because we had discussed the plan many times. Every time a horse fell on the steep climbs and descents we cursed and vowed to find a better route. This was the first good opportunity we had had to do it.

"Why don't you take the shotgun, Don Pablo? We might see some game in the woods."

"Good idea."

I shoved a buckshot load in the port barrel, for deer or peccary, and a load of number 4 shot in the other, for small game and birds, then put a few additional cartridges of each in my button-down shirt pockets according to the same system, buckshot left, birdshot right.

We rode to the big *zapote* tree to leave the ponies in the shade with loosened cinches.

"Take off your spurs, Don Pablo. They will make an awful noise in the woods."

I obliged, hanging the offending articles on the saddlehorn. We went into the primeval forest, Juanito in the lead. His machete flashed as with little apparent effort he lopped off branches of undergrowth and little trees to pick us a narrow path through the tangle on the jungle floor.

EVERY FOREST has its distinctive character. The open sunny yellow-pine forests of the eastern slopes of the Oregon Cascades are quite unlike the somber dense tangles of giant fir and spruce and hemlock of the British Columbia coasts (even though botanists might point out that both consist principally of conifers). The deciduous forests of the eastern United States, which produce such a spectacular show of autumn leaves, must be very different from western forests to walk through, to hunt in, or to chop down. The jungle here in southeastern Mexico has a character of its own—its own personality.

This jungle is a rather pleasant place, not at all a dank and gloomy mansion of horrors, or a "green hell," as some jungles have been depicted. Its colors are soft neutral ones for the most part—browns and grays of tree trunks, dull yellows and browns of fallen leaves, quiet greens of underbrush and epiphytes, and, above, the canopies of branches. Many of the giant trees and the lianas that net their tops together produce blossoms of vivid hues—bright yellows, reds, blues, and lavenders—but these floral displays are high above the jungle floor, out of sight behind the ceilings of branches and leaves. One standing on the forest floor sees them only after they have fallen, wilted and faded till they nearly blend with ground coloration. The only way to see such colors as they really are, if one cannot fly over the forest in a plane, is to stand on a high cleared hill overlooking an expanse of jungle. There, looking down on the forest roof, one sees in vivid contrast to the green leaf-mass great patches of the gaudy yellow blossoms of the *guayacán* trees, the pink to lavender flowers of the *macuiles*, streamers of the scarlet-flowered liana called *uña de iguana*, and splashes of various shades of blue of other trees and vines. But down inside the jungle, on its floor, the gaily colored blossoms of a few bushes and plants are not enough to modify the prevailing pattern of grays, browns, dull yellows, and quiet greens.

Two outstanding features of this jungle are the way it encloses one, closely and completely, horizontally and vertically, and its silence. The enclosure is produced by the endless number of huge tree trunks, exaggerated by the enormously flaring buttress roots; the closely spaced, slim straight trunks of the young growth fighting its way up between the old trees toward the light; dangling strands and loops of lianas; and underbrush mixed with scattered leafy plants. All this is what shuts one in horizontally. You can move about in the jungle, with a little difficulty in places where the undergrowth is dense, with ease where it is sparse, but nowhere can you see far in any direction— you are walled in by trees. One way to define this enclosure is to point out that the jungle cannot properly be photographed from within. Even a wide-angle lens cannot get enough coverage to capture what the forest really looks like. Obviously, I do not mean that one cannot take a picture of a section of the trunk of a single tree festooned with epiphytes and lianas, as a sort of symbol of the whole, but that is not the same. The nearest approach to a true picture is one taken from the outside, at a point where the forest has been cross-sectioned by a new clearing.

The vertical enclosure is formed by the lowest canopy of the young replacement growth, an irregular mass not far overhead that sometimes merges into another intermediate layer above. The high canopy of the big trees far above one senses rather than sees, except when deliberately trying to find breaks in the lower layer to spy through. It is almost a complete cover, for the crowded branches of the forest giants are knit together by lianas. One might expect the jungle with this multiple roof to be very dark, but actually a surprising amount of light filters through. In the dry season, February through May, when the big trees shed their leaves—they do not all do so at once, but each of the many species takes its turn— the jungle floor is a place of moderate shade and myriad patches of bright strong light.

Daytime light in the jungle, incidentally, has some tricks of its own. On a bright clear day in the dry season, like the day Juanito and I went into the woods, the sunlight that comes through forms small dazzling-bright patches against the background of shade that break shapes up into random patterns of light and dark, just the way camouflage designs are meant to do. One must *learn* to see under these conditions.

JUANITO AND I had been in the woods for about three hours, casting back and forth like bird dogs. With visibility so limited, it was difficult to pick the sort of level-ground route we wanted. Some of our attempts led us into the swamp, others into marshy extensions of it in gullies between the ridges. When we worked back up the gully to find a firm crossing we had to go back to correct our approach. We had started with simple blazes to mark our route. Then we made double ones, then triple for the corrections. It was sticky hot, for there is no movement of air in the jungle. We walked quietly, making as little noise as possible among the litter of dead leaves, and we spoke in low tones. Suddenly Juanito froze.

"The deer, Don Pablo, the deer!"

I saw nothing. "Where? I don't see him."

"There, right in front of me! Left of the big *guapaque!*"

I had the gun at the ready, my finger loose before the rear trigger. I stared. In front of us was a flimsy screen of undergrowth. One could see through it, most places. I could see the trunk of the *guapaque* tree, ten yards away. But lopsided rectangles, triangles, and halfmoons of dazzling yellow sunlight bounced off the foliage, off the tree trunks, off the deer in blinding contrast with the patches of shade. I could distinguish nothing.

"Where? Where is he?"

Juanito thought he was blocking my view. He sank into a squatting position so I could shoot over him.

"There, right in front of me! Left of the big *guapaque!*"

"I don't see him!"

Juanito could stand it no more. He jabbed his arm forward to point, with a hoarsely whispered "There!" The abrupt motion startled the deer into flight—as soon as he moved I saw him. "Going to cross in front of the *guapaque!*" I thought—swung the muzzle fast toward the tree—fired—just as he cut back sharply to his right, ducking behind the huge trunk. He kept going. We could hear the thumping of his frantic bounds, the rattling of the brush as he drove through it.

"*Dios de la vida*, you missed him! You shot way in front of him! Look where you hit the *guapaque.*" Juanito was disgusted.

"I thought he would cross in front of the tree."

"You should have shot him standing. He was right in front of us. *Qué bruto*, how my ears hurt—that thing makes a lot of noise right over one's head." He had got a good dose of the muzzle blast where he was squatting.

"You just don't understand that you know how to see things in these woods better than I. I'm trying to learn. Well, he got away. Let's get going."

"I'm thirsty." He was still a little surly. "I want to drink *pozole*."

He had a *morral* slung over his left shoulder with our joint ration of the leached and ground maize, a pellet the size of an indoor baseball, ready to be mixed with water in the tree-gourd dipper that accompanied it.

"Let's go back to that little gully we just crossed. There's water there, a little way below our crossing—I saw it."

THE SILENCE of the jungle is impressive. I do not mean that there is no sound at all, but rather that most sounds are small ones, the hum of mosquitos, the distant shrill of a cicada in the upper canopy, the chirp of a small bird. And there is a soundproofing effect that mutes even these noises, produced by the leafy masses overhead, the layer of dead leaves underfoot, and the fibrous barks of tree trunks and vines and brush of the enclosing forest wall. There is something compelling about the quiet. One lowers one's voice even when not hunting. The few noisy denizens of the forest belong for the most part far off: up on top of the upper canopy; their occasional descents create a shocking din. There is a big brown jay, *peya*, who has all the bad manners and vituperative stridency of his bluejay and whiskeyjack cousins, plus more volume because of his larger size. When he, or several of him, discern you from above, then dive to lower-canopy level to shriek jaybird curses and insults at you, the disruption of the quiet is disconcerting and unpleasant because you have become attuned to the quiet tranquillity of the forest. As one walks along hearing even the rustle of leaves in the roof of the jungle a hundred feet above that denotes a breeze not even felt at ground level, the gay raucous shouts of a flight of parrots passing high overhead give one a start. The howler monkey makes quite a racket, especially at dawn. His doleful braying yell, however, is in a minor key, and unless he is very close at hand the soundproofing of the forest moderates his noise. Infrequently the booming thunder of a jaguar's roar rings through the woods. But jays and parrots, howler monkeys and jaguars, and the few other leather-lunged creatures are exceptions. Most of the animals of the jungle rarely break the quiet.

WE SQUATTED on our heels under a five-foot-through *marote* tree at the edge of the rivulet, swilling down the insipid but refreshing *pozole* and smoking cigarettes. The smoke drifted faintly toward the east, where we had left our horses.

"What air there is is in our favor," whispered Juanito. "We might find another deer."

"Maybe."

"That was a big one. You should have shot him."

"How the *chingada* could I shoot him when I couldn't see him?" I was weary of this theme. "Let's go."

We tossed our cigarettes into the water. The dead leaves on the ground were very dry.

"I think we ought to bear a little to our left," Juanito whispered.

We climbed out of the gully and went on. Under a big *ahosh* half a dozen curassows were feeding on the tree's sour-sweet big-seeded fruit. Juanito saw them just as they alerted to the rustle of our footsteps among the leaves. As he pointed, they lifted with the ponderous wingbeats that remind one of buzzards getting airborne.

The jungle is a poor place for wing shooting. I saw the birds just after Juanito did, as they were flapping their wings about to rise, but through a tangle of underbrush too dense for a shot. My chance would be when they cleared the underbrush and before they went through breaks in the lower canopy, a narrow space.

I glimpsed a big black male flapping upward behind the brush. When he came into the clear I took him. It was not a difficult shot. Curassows are slow fliers and the distance was not great. He flipped in the air, then tumbled with spread wings. But Juanito thought it was splendid, for no one else around here wing-shoots. The curassow made up for the deer I missed, in his estimation.

He gave a small muted whoop of pleasure, then crouched and pointed. "A hen, Don Pablo! Up there in the *chalté*. She lit on the thick limb out to the right."

I peered. I could just make out a small bulk that had to be the russet hen curassow, partly screened by the tip of a branch of a neighboring tree. I broke the gun, slipped the buckshot load replaced after missing the deer into my shirt pocket, and loaded two rounds of number 4. It was a long shot for my upland double, and the screen of twigs and foliage was just right to disrupt the shot pattern. I decided to work to my left to clear the branch.

I moved rapidly past a thick tree, relocated the bird, and without taking my eyes off her began to shuffle to the left, slipping the safety off. In just a couple more steps I would clear the interfering branch for my shot. Just as I was shifting my weight to take the next step, a hand clutched the back of my shirt and yanked me violently backward. By luck I got my finger off the trigger in time.

"The *nauyaca!*" Juanito screamed.

I looked down at the ground, to my left where I had been about to step. There was the deadly fer-de-lance, all five feet of him, loosely coiled, his head raised about a foot high, his bright yellow throat and belly gleaming, flickering his delicate forked tongue in my direction. Along his back in the coils I could see the staggered black

V marks, a sort of reverse of the diamond pattern of his rattlesnake relative, against the dull gray and reddish-brown background color.

The reptile had sensed but had not determined the source of the invasion of his privacy. Then he tightened his coils. The tip of his tail, erect, began to vibrate like a rattler's but there were no rattles to give warning. He was about to attack. My stomach seemed tied in a knot, my pulse hammered in my ears. Then I was looking down the midrib of the shotgun, squeezing the trigger.

At four feet, muzzle to target, a load of birdshot is a solid ball. This one caught the snake on the nose, ripping his head into shreds of skin and flesh and bony attachments hanging from his neck. The impact flipped him backward about a yard, where he thrashed violently for some moments, they lay quiet, just the tip of his tail twitching.

The knot in my stomach unwound. Sweat began to stream from me. My knees felt rubbery.

Juanito was blubbering, "I didn't see him! He was hidden under the leaves! I didn't see him till he coiled and raised his head!"

"You saw him in time, Juanito, thanks, many thanks! Heaven save me, I would have stepped right on that thing if you hadn't grabbed me!"

My knees were very unsteady. "Let's have a smoke." I watched the snake's tail twitch. I couldn't take my eyes off it, recalling the superstition I had heard as a youngster that a dead snake's tail twitches until sundown.

After a while Juanito said, "The hen curassow flew off when you fired."

"To hell with her. We have the male, anyhow. Pick him up and let's get out of here."

3

Venin

I DO NOT HAVE any horror of snakes in general. I am afraid
of the fer-de-lance only. Most of my neighbors feel the
same way. This is not a phobia or other psychic aberration
but good practical common sense. For *Bothrops atrox*, the
fer-de-lance, is a very unpleasant component of our landscape.

The local name of the reptile, *nauyaca*, is said to derive
from the Aztec *nauyac-coatl*, "four-nostril serpent," in reference to the pits on the nose, for the fer-de-lance is a pit
viper, close kin to the rattlesnake, the copperhead, and
the water moccasin. An unpleasant family, the lot of them.

A herpetologist once told me that there is but a single
species and single variety of fer-de-lance. My Xucuapan
friends and neighbors distinguish three varieties: the yel-
lowhead, with yellowish head and vivid yellow throat and
underside, like the one that gave me the scare out in the
woods, a run-of-the-mill variety whose head is the same
grayish to russet brown as back and sides and whose throat
and belly is a dirty ivory white, not yellow. The third is
called *rabo de hueso*, "bone-tail," like the second in color
but with the tip of the top pinched out to a thin spike.

All have the distinctive black *V*'s down their backs. Local naturalists argue for hours as to which kind is most deadly.

The fer-de-lance is an aggressive beast. True, sometimes when aroused from sleep under a shady bush in midday heat it may be sluggish, lethargic. But with the cooling effect of late afternoon, as the sun hangs low in the western sky and shadows lengthen, the snake becomes active. From then on through the night, for the reptile tends to be of nocturnal habit, it will advance to attack where a rattlesnake might crawl away or stay coiled sounding its warning signal. This does not mean, of course, that the fer-de-lance is completely innocuous by day. People have died from bites received when the sun was at midheaven.

Not all fer-de-lance bites are fatal. My Red Cross manual estimates that in the United States between 10 and 15 per cent of untreated rattlesnake bites are fatal. My guess would be that casualties from fer-de-lance bites run a little higher, precisely because of the more aggressive nature of this serpent. Not only does it attack, but it strikes again and again until it pumps its poison sacs empty. The more venin, the more lethal the effect. Years ago, on a fishing trip along a river down near the Tabasco coast, I met a man who had eleven pairs of big ugly scarpits on his right leg between ankle and knee. The snake had struck him eleven times. It was a large one too, for the breadth of the pairs of scarpits—the distance between the reptile's fangs—was wide. This man did not die, so he related, because he had the good luck to meet his misfortune (that's the way he himself expressed it) not many yards from a camp of oil geologists. They had an abundant supply of antivenin in their medical kit, shot him full of it, and so he survived.

The fer-de-lance uses its venom in its food quest, to kill the frogs, mice, birds, and other creatures it eats. Perhaps the reptile is a heavy feeder, so that only rarely is it found with its poison sacs brimming full. At any rate, I know many people who have been bitten who have survived with no treatment other than the useless folk remedies—teas of herbs whose leaves bear patterns similar to those of the serpent, ointments of hot oil and garlic, and the like—which means the dose of poison was too small to be fatal.

These household remedies, biochemically worthless, do have a psychological utility. They make the victim feel that something is being done for him in his agony, for all who have been bitten by the snake insist that the pain is excruciating as the toxin surges through the bloodstream. Compounding agony is fear. The venin contains certain enzymes—so reports a manual I have on the subject of snakebite—that attack the blood, reducing its viscosity, and damage the walls of blood vessels. Hemorrhage results. The diluted blood seeps into the saliva and urine, dribbles from nose and ears, leaks through the skin in red droplets. The victim knows he is in peril as the pain surges from his bitten leg into his vitals, and as his heart races wildly, then slows until he feels clammy cold. Suddenly his own organism seems to be betraying him when his blood bursts its bounds, flushing into his mouth, trickling from his nose, sweating through his skin. Terror seizes him. Faith in the curative powers of the treatment being given, even though the medicines are physiologically worthless, can keep the snakebitten patient out of shock. Shock kills too.

Fortunately, there is an effective antidote to fer-de-lance poison, the antivenin the oil geologists gave to the man with the eleven pairs of fang marks. It consists of a serum

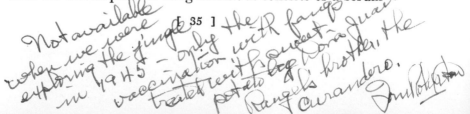

made from antibodies created in the bloodstream of horses through a controlled series of injections of the reptile's venom. The serum, by neutralizing the venin, relieves a great deal of the pain, so it is very helpful even in less serious cases, and of course it is the only really effective remedy when the snake has injected a lethal dose of poison into his victim. I always keep several kits of antivenin on hand.

I WAS STILL a newcomer on the river. After a long day of clearing bush three of us loafed on the front porch, smoking and making small talk. It was not very intellectual conversation; we had put in a hard day's labor, taken a dip in the river and changed our sweat-soaked clothes, filled up on *tortillas*, black beans and rice, and fiery chile sauce of the wild chile *amash*, delicious in flavor but flame-hot, washed down with copious drafts of *pozole* (the day was too hot for coffee). I threw a palm-fiber mat, a *petate*, on the floor and sprawled on my back, shirtless. The sweat tickled as it dribbled down my ribs. Manuel and Meregildo thought the bare cement cooler.

"We can finish that patch of bush tomorrow," I said, "if we hit it like we did today." Trying to stir up a little pep talk, keep up interest in the work.

"We can if we don't run into any more wasp nests," said Manuel. "Christ, those big red *carniceros* hurt when they jab that stinger into you. A man can take only so much of that."

"Enough of them sting you, you'll come down with fever," put in Meregildo.

"You can make torches with rags soaked in coal oil," I said, "and go burn them out in the night, if you remember where the nests are."

"And get stung to hell in the dark."

"They can't sting in the dark," Manuel put in.

"They don't, anyhow. They fly into the flame—the light attracts them," I tried to explain. "I burned out a whopping big nest in that *guásimo* tree in front of the house. They buzzed all around me but not a sting did I get. They flew into the torch and died."

Meregildo said, "*Bueno*, if I can keep awake long enough, I'll try it. I saw big nests in that patch of *tanai* and in the *guayaba* tree. Go with me, Manuel?"

"If you can make it, I can."

"I'll get you two some rags and a bottle of coal oil as soon as I can assemble enough energy to get up."

We relaxed quietly, sticky with sweat, waiting for the evening breeze. I was thinking that as soon as the cool came, I would go down to the river for another plunge— the river water here in the foothill country stays pleasantly cool until late May.

Meregildo, who had seemed to be asleep, lifted his head. "I hear somebody running."

Manuel turned over. At that time one could see a long way down the trail toward the Arroyo del Carmen—I hadn't yet built the henhouse and pen that now block the view. "Here he comes. It's Don Guillermo. Something's the matter—he's in a hurry." A figure came trotting up the trail toward the house, the shotgun slung over his shoulder jouncing against his back.

I sat up. It was Don Guillo. Short, stocky. Quiet. I didn't then know him well—thought him a stolid lump— really he is quiet because he is a little shy. He works hard but is always in hard luck. His well-planted corn grows tall—a sudden wind squall uproots it. Or cutworm attacks it. When he does make a harvest, cholera kills the hogs he intends to fatten. Once, later on, I persuaded him to inoculate the few animals he had left—brought him the vaccine from town at cost, helped him with the chore. A jaguar killed the inoculated hogs, including the only good brood sow he had. There is no known anti-jaguar vaccine but buckshot injected into the jaguar. But Guillermo never complains about his outrageous fortunes.

I was amazed to see as he came near that he was crying.

"The snake! . . . Bit Chala!" he gasped.

"Who?"

"Chala. My wife. She's dying. Have you a medicine for it?"

"What kind of snake?" I knew that there are rattle-snakes down below in the savannahs, and coral snakes everywhere.

"*Nauyaca!*"

"Yes, I have some . . ."

"Please, Don Pablo, come cure her!"

We went into action, I assembling the equipment: serum, hypodermic syringe, needles, cotton, alcohol, the metal dish to boil the syringe in. Meregildo and Manuel saddled mounts for me and for themselves, and one for Guillermo. Dusk was falling by the time we reached Guillermo's thatched hut.

There were a lot of people there, relatives of Doña Chala and her husband. It had been some hours since the accident. News travels. Kin assemble, to aid if they can, or to witness the demise.

I heard fragments of low-voiced conversation:

". . . all those weeds in the *patio*."

"A thicket, that's what it is. Could be full of snakes."

"The lazy bastard. If he'd kept the *patio* clean she wouldn't have been bitten right in front of the house."

". . . his fault. If she dies we should . . ."

Obviously, Doña Chala's kin.

Doña Chala was sitting on a rustic bed of poles covered

with an enormous strip of *jolocín* bark, tough but spongy, as a mattress. She was propped up with a pile of pillows and a gunnysack stuffed full of cornhusks. Her face was muddy-gray and streaming with sweat. She moaned softly, "Ai-i-i, ai!" In one hand she clutched a piece of rag into which she spat bloody saliva, and with which alternately she daubed at her nose. A tiny trickle of blood leaked from one nostril. On the dirt floor beside the bed was a litter of other rags saturated with blood and spittle.

Her injured foot was stretched out in front of her. It looked horrible (although since then I have seen worse). Foot, ankle, and lower leg to the knee were swollen until the taut skin shone, feverish red, green, and purple.

The syringe had been sterilized, armed. I drew the solvent into it from one of the two little bottles of the antivenin kit, broke the seal on the other, jabbed the needle through the rubber cap, squirted the solvent on the dry yellow powder that was the antivenin, all just as the instructions said. I had never done this before. To my horror the powder did not dissolve, just broke up into lumps that floated in the solvent. I shook the bottle violently. The lumps of powder gradually dissolved, but a thick froth, obviously impossible to inject, formed. I set the bottle down, hoping the form would settle. Meanwhile I pretended to adjust the needle on the syringe.

Don Guillermo's mother, Doña Felicitas, and his sister arranged the patient meanwhile, turning her over and covering her with a sheet so that only the area to be injected was exposed. They knew the routine for intramuscular injections. The crowd of relatives filled the room, watching.

The froth in the bottle subsided after what seemed a long time, leaving a clear yellow liquid, I drew the solution up into the syringe, then carefully squeezed out the air bubbles. My hands trembled. I had observed intra-muscular injections, but I had never driven a hyperdermic needle into living flesh before.

There is a vast difference between seeing and doing. The needle looked enormous. How tough is human hide? How hard must the needle be thrust to penetrate human flesh? There was a moment in which I thought I couldn't do it. Then I bolstered up my courage, steadied my hand, and stabbed the lady in the rump with the needle. Doña Chala flinched convulsively and moaned louder. Clearly, nature had not blessed me with a light hand for this task.

The antibodies are almost as rapid in their action as the venom they neutralize. Soon the seeping of blood ceased. Doña Chala's pulse rate steadied, and she reported the pain was subsiding. Her gray pallor faded into the normal light brown of her face. In an hour she was out of danger, almost comfortable, though the wounded leg still pained. I began to assemble my gear to go home.

"What do I owe you, Don Pablo?" Guillermo asked.

The question obviously had to come; the reply I had decided in advance. "The serum costs forty-seven pesos sixty centavos. Let's say forty centavos for cotton and alcohol. Forty-eight pesos even."

"And for your time and trouble?"

By local standards I could have charged any reasonable amount, fifty to a hundred pesos more. Guillermo would have paid. But I couldn't do it. I'm not a doctor. All I know is a little rough and ready first aid, and one can't in conscience charge for that. I remembered how my hand shook as I held the loaded syringe. So I established the precedent.

"That costs nothing, Don Guillermo. After all, we're neighbors. I don't charge a neighbor for a small favor. Just pay me for the serum."

"I don't have the money for the medicine right now, but

I'll bring it in a day or two. Or I can work it off, weeding pasture or clearing bush if you still have some to clear."

"Come to the house tomorrow or the next day, and we'll arrange it."

THERE HAVE BEEN fourteen snakebite cases since. Most of the victims probably would have recovered without treatment, but the antivenin eased the terrible pain and speeded the cure. Three of the list surely would have died. One of those was my *compadre* Candelario.

Past midnight on a murky black night—the wisp of new moon had set early—Candelario's lank taciturn wife called in front of our house, "*Compadre! Compadre* Pablo!"

Maria nudged me. "It's *comadre* Chana!"

Struggling toward wakefulness, knowing it must be an emergency, I mumbled as loudly as I could, "What is it, *comadre?*"

"Your *compadre* is snakebitten. Bad. Have you the medicine?"

"Yes. Wait just a moment."

I dressed. Maria lit the coal-oil lamp and opened the door. Doña Chana stood there with her fourteen-year-old son Francisco. Both their faces shone with sweat in the light that beamed out the doorway, showing they had hurried over the two miles of trail between our houses, but they showed no emotion.

"Come in, *comadre*," Maria said. "How did it happen?"

"He was trying to jacklight a *tepescuinte* at the big breadfruit tree, with Francisco. They found nothing. On the way home the snake struck him. Four times, on the ankle." The *tepescuinte* ("agouti") is a sort of twenty-pound gopher.

"GOOD MORNING, *compadre*," Candelario said. "Old coldbelly got me this time."

It was obvious that he was dangerously ill. His steady voice was the only good sign—he was not going into shock from fright. But his pulse that now raced and pounded, now fluttered, the gray of his face, the bleeding, the vilely colored lump that was his foot and lower leg, all proclaimed that he had taken a heavy dosage of venom—a fatal dose, if it could not be controlled. By this time I had seen enough fer-de-lance victims to be able to appraise their condition.

"We'll fix you up in just a little while, *compadre*. Does it hurt a lot?"

"The pain . . ." He clenched his jaws, then spat into a faded bandanna that was assuming a new shade of red. "The pain . . . I never imagined anything could hurt so much."

"You're going to hurt in a different place, *compadre*," I said, readying the syringe. "They all say I have a heavy hand with this thing."

He tried to grin. "That's all right, if it kills the big pain."

"Just turn over, and you'll see." Doña Chana and the boy had to help him. He was very weak.

I didn't bother to boil the syringe to sterilize it, just wiped the needle with a bit of cotton moistened in alcohol, and injected him with two units of antivenin, twenty centimeters. A minor infection could be cured with antibiotics a few days later, if need be. But he could die in a short time from the venom—too much time had been lost already.

We sat and waited. This is the rugged part of the procedure. I checked his pulse from time to time. Gradually it seemed to be steadying. The pallor of his face slowly altered to a tone closer to his normal bronze. After half an hour or so he said, "The pain is sort of sliding back down my leg. It doesn't come up into my belly any more."

I heaved a sigh of relief—I'd weathered another crisis.

Both my Red Cross manual and the instruction booklet put out by the people who manufacture the antivenin emphasize that a snakebite patient should under no circumstances be given alcoholic beverages. But I have searched both authorities in vain for a like rule for the first-aider. So I took a hearty drink from a flask I'd had the foresight to bring along.

"Sorry, no booze for you, *compadre*. Two or three weeks from now, when you're back in shape, I'll buy you a drink."

He chuckled, plainly more comfortable. "I can wait. You take mine for me."

His mother, Doña Luisa, brought me a *jícara*, a dipper made of tree gourd, full of hot black coffee. I spiked it a little, sat sipping it. Time passed slowly. I was wondering if it would be safe to go home when the relapse began. The pain in his leg was becoming intense again, surging upward. His pulse once more turned irregular, and there was blood in his saliva again.

The instruction manual, which I know by heart, says that in severe cases the antivenin may have a greater effect injected intravenously. I fumbled the needle into the big vein just below the crook of his elbow. That controlled it. The danger symptoms subsided. By dawn it was clear that Candelario was safe. I went home. The manual also says that as many as five or six units of antivenin may be used if necessary. But this time three had to do the trick. Because three was all I had.

As MIGHT BE expected, where people live with and worry about a creature like the fer-de-lance, they have a vast store of information about it. Some of the lore is factual, some is fantasy, and it is sometimes difficult to separate the two. One trait my neighbors insist is true is that the reptile aggressively approaches light, such as that of a flashlight. Whether it is activated by some automatic reaction, a tropism, that attracts it to the light, or whether it sees the light as an enemy to be attacked, I do not know. But I do know that the belief caused Candelario to hack blindly at the sound of the snake that struck him rather than search it out with the flashlight he carried.

Don Noë was on his way to our house early one night. He and Juanito had arranged to borrow my small canoe and a harpoon to go night-lighting panfish. The river was low, it was the dark of the moon, and the bluegills and their relatives could be found dozing in the shoal nooks and crannies along the riverbanks. As Noë was rounding a turn in the trail just this side of a streamlet we call the Arroyo del Mico, his light fell on the Thing, coiled in the middle of the track, and poised to strike. It had sensed his approach. It was a huge fer-de-lance, the biggest I have ever seen. Next day I measured it—nearly seven feet.

The snake relaxed its coil toward the light source, Don Noë's flashlight. He was too close to dare try to jump back; he dropped his flashlight as gently as he could to the ground, to his right, and drew his machete. As the reptile slithered toward the light, head raised menacingly, he slashed through the neck.

When Don Noë told the tale on his arrival, I asked him what he would have done had the flashlight gone out when he dropped it on the ground. He just laughed. On reflection I realize it was a pretty silly question.

THE FER-DE-LANCE sings. Or at least so everyone says. Several times I have heard a sweet, high-pitched trill, similar to but distinct from the tree frog's song, and have been told, "Listen! That's the *nauyaca!*" Usually one hears the call at night—I could never bring my interest in natural science to sufficient pitch to go dashing off in the dark to look for poisonous snakes. The fact is that I regarded the story as a bit of folklore, mainly because after much questioning I had not found anyone who had seen the reptile in the act of producing the sound. Some people told of having heard the sweet musical call, and the next day, or several days later, finding a fer-de-lance near the place from which the call had come. But no one claimed to have seen the reptile in the act, until some years ago Don Mario told his yarn.

Don Mario, short and chunky, short-necked, with a Mayan profile—he comes from over in Campeche—has a parcel of land down toward the savannah, poor soil that does not yield well. He has formed the habit of coming to work for me, a month or two or three, to earn a little cash when his own chores are few. I gather that these periods often coincide with those in which his wife leaves him, as she frequently does—he says he is very fond of her, but "has the habit" of beating her when he is drunk. Mario is a hunter and an excellent woodsman. Like many such he is not above drawing a long bow at times to make a good tale better, but this one I almost believe.

"Yes, I've seen it," he said one evening as we sat sipping coffee—unspiked, I might add. "I've heard the *nauyaca* sing many times, but once I actually saw him do it. Have you a cigarette? I left mine in the bunkhouse in my other shirt."

I gave him the cigarette, knowing he lied. He had no cigarettes, nor other shirt either. He was just back from a trip to town; the rags he wore were all he brought back. I'd paid him three months' wages when he left; he got drunk on the way to town, squandered and otherwise got separated from his bankroll and few possessions, was thrown into the pokey overnight, managed to borrow a few pesos to pay his fine, and got back to the farm in five days, including nearly four days of travel time. We are proud of Don Mario; it isn't everyone who can do it that fast.

"*Sí, señor*, I am one of the few people who has really seen the cold-bellied beast sing. There was no mistake, because it was broad daylight and he was right close to me, not much farther than across this table. I was hunting deer in a bamboo thicket, on Don Hilario Gonzalez's place down on the Arroyo Zanapa. There was about ten hectares of old tangled bamboo there—he's cut it down since to plant pasture, but then, eight or nine years ago, it was a tangle you could barely crawl through. A lot of deer laid up in the thicket in daytime. I'd seen tracks and bedding places and all. So one day I took an old 16-gauge to go in to get me a deer. It was a dark, overcast day, raining, not hard but what we call *chipi-chipi*, a steady little drizzle— just right for hunting in the bamboo, for all the leaves on the ground were moist so made no noise when one stepped on them or crawled over them.

"I walked a little, crawled and wriggled a lot more. After a while I heard a noise that might have been a deer moving around in his bed, ahead and to my right. I began to crawl toward the sound, and then I heard the song of the *nauyaca*, right above me. I didn't move. For the moment I couldn't. I thought the snake would kill me right then. But nothing happened. I began to turn over, very very slow, to see where the thing was. Finally I was looking straight up, and there he lay on a branch of bamboo, sort of spraddled out over the little side branches. And right while I was looking at his yellow belly, the snake sang again. He—"

"How did he do it?" I interrupted, excited. "Did he coil, or raise his head?" My imagination pictured the reptile rearing up like a Hindu fakir's cobra. At the same time, logic warned me that if Mario's fer-de-lance performed too spectacularly the tale was not to be believed.

"He did nothing but sing. Didn't move, just lay there. Didn't even open his mouth. But I could see that his throat puffed up a little, and sort of vibrated as he sang. I could see everything he did, *por Dios Santo*, he wasn't much more than a meter above my face. I could have counted his belly scales. The noise was very certainly coming out of him, and his throat puffed out—not far like a frog's, but just a little, and it vibrated."

"What did you do, Don Mario?" Six-year-old Pablito's eyes were wide, shining with excitement. He has been brought up on yarns like this rather than fairy tales. "Did he try to bite you?"

"Was it a great big snake, Don Mario?" asked Pablito's sister Rosamaria.

"No, he didn't bite me. He wasn't real big, Rosita, kind of medium, about a meter long. I knew he couldn't strike me where he was; what I was afraid of was that if I startled him he might fall off the branch and land on top of me. As I was trying to work the shotgun around to poke it up through the branches without making any noise, he slithered out along the branch, crossed to another, and was out of sight before I could draw a bead. I wanted to kill him for the scare he gave me, but he got away. I got up and went out of the bamboo—I didn't feel like any more hunting that day."

This is the sum of my information about singing snakes. While the voice of the turtle may be a myth, there are reptiles that make noises: alligators make grunting and bellowing sounds, and the little gecko lizards of Guam and other places in the western Pacific produce a racket out of all proportion to their size. So maybe the story is true. But even if the fer-de-lance sang like a nightingale, it would be an unpleasant creature as long as it had those long fangs and sacs filled with venom.

WE WERE IN Don Panuncio's store, he, Don Domingo, and I. Don Domingo sat on the plank counter, jingling the spurs at the end of his long legs against the woodwork. I leaned against the counter, near him. Don Panuncio was on the other side, pouring.

Don Domingo was ragging me. "Don Pablito, Don Pablito," he chanted, "I hear you're losing money hand over fist on your medical business."

"What medical business? I don't have any."

"That's my point. You have one, but get nothing out of it. You cure as many people as that old Doña Josefa over at Arroyo Prieto. She is getting rich, or at least well off, and you are losing money."

"That damned old witch . . ."

"Witch isn't the right word, Pablito," broke in Don Panuncio, gently. "At least not the way we use it around here. Doña Josefa is a *curandera*, a healer."

"Witch or *curandera*, she's a charlatan. Her worthless brews of weeds! Lately she's taken to prescribing big doses of penicillin, so I'm told. She'll poison someone one of these days. And she gouges more out of the poor fools that go to her than a real doctor in town would."

Domingo said, "She's making pesos hand over fist. They had nothing when they moved to the *arroyo*, she and that lazy husband of hers. Now they have some pasture and fifteen or twenty head of cows, all from the concoction of herbs and weeds that she peddles to the suckers."

"You want me to operate the same sort of dishonest racket?"

"No, because it wouldn't be the same. You read books, you know infinitely more than she does. You brought that serum for *nauyaca* bite that none of us knew existed. You sutured up that machete cut on Santos Lopez's arm. She couldn't have done that—she'd have put herbal poultices on it till his arm rotted off."

I tried a diversion. "That was something that had me worried. I tried to pull the cut together with adhesive tape, but the tape wouldn't hold. So I got out the vial of veterinary suture, and a veterinary book that tells how to do it, and followed instructions."

This should have produced laughs. To use animal materials and methods on a human being is somehow disparaging to the person, and comical. But Domingo persisted.

"It was a good job. Nearly as good as a doctor in town would have done. I saw it later. How much did you charge him?"

"Nothing. *Caramba*, I'm not a doctor. I have no right to charge for such things."

"A doctor in town would have charged him two or three hundred pesos. So would Doña Josefa for her worthless herbs. You lost even the materials you used. You're a pretty poor businessman."

"Like hell. I figured up all the materials: suture, merthiolate, bandage, and all. Came to twenty-eight pesos. Santos paid me."

"The difference between bare costs and three hundred, eh, Don Panuncio?"

I picked up the glass of *aguardiente* stirred up with brown sugar and lime juice, the classic Veracruzan *torito*, and gulped. I was a bit fed up with the discussion. My defense of course was a matter of ethics, which I didn't want to go into—and so long as I didn't, I had the losing side of the argument. I could sense that Domingo was leading up to something; that was why he would not be diverted.

"That snakebite serum, how much do you get for it?"

"What it costs. Forty-seven sixty. Lately I've been adding in something for freight to make an even fifty pesos."

"There you are. That's what I'm telling you: you're just not a good businessman. That's why the yokels here on the river laugh at you behind your back. They figure you're a sucker. Do you think they appreciate your consideration? *A la chingada!* You ought to soak them three or four hundred for each kit. Who wouldn't pay that much to save his life?"

"That would really be gouging."

"A man has to have a commercial sense to get along in this world. You're losing thousands of pesos that you could make. What's the matter, don't you like money?"

"I like to make a peso as well as anybody, but not that way."

"How many bottles of snakebite medicine did you put into that worthless bastard Benito Cadena?"

"Four. That lad was in bad shape—worse than my *compadre* Candelario. There was one time I accomplished something—he surely would have died without the serum."

Domingo's grin faded, and his voice grated a bit. "You really did something that time, for sure. You should have let the *hijo de puta* die. It would have been a great improvement on the Xucuapan. That red-headed scum!" Then he grinned again, jeeringly. "Four injections! I'll bet you're still waiting to collect the cost of them, after nearly a year."

"That's not so. Benito has paid me back more than half. He rode over the other day to bring me ten pesos."

"That's what I mean. That's how they play you for a sucker. Last week Benito shot an ocelot; he sold the hide to El Teco Gilberto for one hundred eighty pesos. So he gives you ten. Big deal."

"Well it was something. How much did he pay you? I

hear he owes you money too." This was a low blow, but my annoyance was growing.

"Not a centavo." The voice grated again. "If I'd known about it in time I'd have taken it all from him—and he knows it. He kept away from me. But you let him and the likes of him make a fool of you. Sets a bad example for . . ."

Don Panuncio interrupted again, busily stirring *aguardiente* into the brown sugar and lime juice. "Mingo, quit nagging at Don Pablito. He has his own way of doing things. If I could do this stuff he calls 'first aid' I'd do as you would—I'd make it pay. But he has a different kind of conscience. And it's all right. A lot of our neighbors, just as you say, don't appreciate what he does. But a lot more of them do. Pablito has a lot of friends on the Xucuapan because of it. Furthermore, all this pointless chatter is causing us to get behind in our drinking. I've just mixed a formidable *torito*. Try it."

We drank up, then talked of other things.

4

Columna Volante

ONE AFTERNOON Feliciano, Juanito, and I set out to tend to some calves we had staked out. In temperate climes it was autumn, but there is no autumn here, just a time of pleasant weather, variable in length, once the equinox has passed and the sun is not directly overhead, and before the wet cold *nortes*, spawn of Arctic storms that roll down the Mississippi Valley and across the Gulf of Mexico, arrive to drench us. Some years the sticky heat of the dog days lasts beyond September; occasionally the *nortes* begin early and come frequently, but in normal years there is a lot of pleasant weather, warm and sunny but not really hot, from late September to early December, with only an occasional one-day *norte* to disturb the pattern.

We had already put in a day's work. But there were the calves to be tended to. The tender umbilicals of newborn calves are subject to screwworm attacks, so we usually catch them as soon after birth as possible and tie them in the shade of a tree with a wide loop that slides around and around and does not get tangled up. The calves are then easy to check daily, to paint their bellies with a repellent that drives away the screwworm flies. Calves running loose spend much of their time curled up asleep in the shade. They hide easily in tall grass pastures; one can ride and ride and not find them. So we stake them. Mama cow brings her baby its breakfast, lunch, and supper in her full udder.

Just on the other side of the Arroyo del Carmen a column of horsemen appeared, silhouetted against the sky where the trail crosses the high ridge. There were eleven horsemen and a lead horse. As we approached each other, I recognized Josefino Aguilar in the lead. Obviously he was the guide. He is a lean, malarial-yellow man in his mid-twenties, a poor relation of Doña Carmen, Don Panuncio's wife. He rides for Don Panuncio. They say he is a good cowhand. He was leading a packhorse with an open-mouthed gunny sack hanging on each side, from which protruded barrels of rifles and shotguns. Confiscated weapons. Josefino grinned at me but did not speak. He was frightened.

Behind the packhorse was a man mounted on a handsome big bay. The man was short and slightly paunchy, but he sat the horse with ease. There was about him an air of authority that left no doubt but that he was in charge of the group. He was without doubt the *Comandante* Juan Pereyra, of the *Columna Volante*.

He wore a military-type cap, the kind with a bill, faded, slightly mended khaki shirt and trousers. About his waist was an ornate alligator gun belt with a gold buckle, clip carriers, and a lowcut holster from which protruded the decorated butt of a .38 Colt automatic, hammer cocked, resting on the thumb safety, the way such arms are carried here.

It was his face, not his dress—not even the fancy gun and belt—that was striking. A wide flat countenance with heavy squarish jowls. Deep-bronze skin color. Out of the dark face looked a pair of pale-gray eyes, the palest and coldest I had ever seen.

A flash of recall brought back to me where I had seen that color before. It was years back, aboard a convoy ship sailing the Great Circle route below Greenland. Radar picked up a pip too large to be a submarine, or even a ship. Flag hoists went up, blinkers flashed, ordering course changes. We were on the side nearest the iceberg; we manned the rail, staring in fascination at the huge chunk of ice that had slid into the sea from Greenland's glaciers. The mass, looming above the dark-gray sea and outlined against the pale gray sky, was whitish-gray, faintly streaked with darker but luminous grays, cold not just because one knows that ice is cold but because the pale grays were themselves frigid colors. That piece of polar ice was of exactly the same tones as the eyes of Don Juan Pereyra, who, so Don Panuncio and Don Concepción had told us, was to bring law and order to the Xucuapan. He reined in the big bay to sit there expressionless, looking me over, forcing me into making the first move.

Situations like this take far longer in the telling than in the acting out. In the same glance I had seen that behind the *Comandante* were five men, like him with military caps and khakis, rifles slung over their shoulders, pistols strapped around their waists. There followed four mounted soldiers in the dark field green of the Mexican Army. Two carried the ancient but reliable Mausers, two carried Mendozas, an automatic weapon that is the Mexican Army's equivalent of the BAR. I have been told it is a smooth-operating arm.

I spurred past Josefino and the nag with the confiscated weapons, self-conscious of my own pistol but trying not to show it, and held out my hand to the man with the ice-gray eyes.

"I'm Pablo Record, at your orders. You must be the Commander of the *Columna Volante*. I'm glad to see you here."

He took my hand in a limp cold handshake, dropped it. "Juan Pereyra Méndez. *Comandante* of the *Columna*."

He didn't use any of the expressions of courtesy, like "at your orders," or "to serve you."

"You must have set out early, and I know there are no restaurants along these trails. I'd like to invite you and your people to a meal."

"That would be all right. We had only coffee before daybreak," he replied in a flat tone.

I turned to Feliciano and Juanito. "Take this *morral* with the screwworm dope. Tend to the calves, and look for the yellow cow and the black one with the crooked horn that are coming due—you know the ones I mean. I'm going back to the house with these people." I led the column. The *Comandante* addressed no word to me, so I had none for him. He seemed unnecessarily unpleasant.

As they were tying their mounts in the shade, loosening cinches, straightening saddle cloths, I hurried in to tell Maria. "This is the *Columna Volante*. Fix up some food for them—I invited them to eat."

"How many?"

"Eleven."

"Eleven! *Virgen Santísima!* What'll I give them?"

"I don't know. Stew up a couple of hens, maybe. They haven't eaten all day—just had coffee before dawn."

"That old white turkey hen! She doesn't lay any more. She'll be enough for them. Doña Chabela! Put some water on to heat, and start grinding *nixtamal*—we have to make lots of *tortillas!*"

Don Juan and his troop were relaxing on the porch. A diversion seemed in order to help pass the time while

Maria threw the meal together. You understand me, I'm sure—did you ever, with no warning, bring eleven people home for your wife to feed?

"Don Juan, it's a warm day, If you think a drink would freshen your people up, I'll stir up a *torito*."

"Thanks, that sounds good." Then he turned to his men. "Don Pablo is inviting us to a drink. Usually I don't permit drinking during a patrol. But this time we'll accept. However, if there is any one of you who can't handle his liquor, don't take it."

I went into the house to assemble a half-liter enamelware cup, brown sugar, limes, the jug of *aguardiente*, and got busy. I was squeezing limes when I heard the bark of a pistol. When I reached the door there was nothing to see: Don Juan was walking back toward the porch, Maria headed toward the kitchen door carrying a dead turkey hen by the legs.

In the kitchen plucking the turkey she told me what had happened: "I was running after the turkey hen— the old bitch wouldn't let me catch her. Don—what's his name—Don Juan, came over, saying, 'Please, *señora*, let me help you. It's too hot to run so. Which bird are you after?'

" 'That white one over there!'

"What a draw! I just barely saw his elbow jerk and he fired and the turkey hen was flapping around on the ground shot right through the head. Better than in the movies! But doesn't he have the most frightening eyes?"

Don Juan's manner changed as he sipped the drink. "Nice place you have here, Don Pablo."

"Thanks. I'm trying to civilize the jungles. But it's a tough chore."

"Don Panuncio told me you do well at it."

"That was nice of him. I only wish I could do it the

way he does. How is he? Did he spike your coffee this morning?"

"He wanted to a couple of mornings ago, but I didn't let him. Last night we stayed with your *compadre* Sebastián."

I said, "Oh!" and dropped the topic. If he had visited my *compadre*, he had left the main trail from El Ixtal. They must have turned off on the trail just below the crossing of Arroyo Santa Lucia to cut across to the Arroyo del Tigrillo, where Don Chucho Ortiz lived or, rather, where he hung out when not running stolen livestock over into Chiapas or rustling Chiapanecan animals down into the coastal country. It seemed inappropriate to pry into this topic with Pereyra. (Later, I heard via the grapevine that while the *Columna* was at Don Panuncio's ranch an uncle managed to send word to Chucho, who took to the woods just in time. The patrol painstakingly stalked and surrounded an empty hut.)

As we chatted, I puzzled over his change of attitude. He obviously knew a great deal about me; Don Panuncio and my *compadre* must have briefed him him on me as well as on other neighbors. Yet at first he had been distant, unfriendly, almost as though I were on his "wanted" list and he was planning to order me to surrender. Now he was relaxed and pleasant. Perhaps he had been probing for something—I still don't know what—and was now satisfied with what he had found out. In any case, it wasn't the sort of thing to quiz him about.

The *cazuela*, the big pottery stewpan in which the turkey had been stewed up, was scraped clean, along with the standard accompaniments of black beans, rice, *tortillas*, and chile sauce. Don Juan was effusive in his thanks.

"What a wonderful meal, Doña Maria! Delicious! We're grateful to you for taking so much trouble."

"It was no trouble, Don Juan."

"Don Pablo, I hope you know how lucky you are—there just aren't many women who can put together a meal for eleven hungry *diablos* so fast, and flavorsome too."

Maria said, "It would have taken a lot longer, Don Juan, if it hadn't been for your marksmanship."

"Oh, that! Sometimes I get off a lucky shot." But the way he said it made plain that he was a little vain about his skill with a gun.

While his people were readying their mounts, he said, "Don Pablo, do me a favor. Lend me a pair of good gunny-sacks, and let me leave these with the weapons here. I'll pick them up on the way back, or send for them if I go out by some other trail."

"Glad to, if you have a list of what you have in those sacks."

He eyed me speculatively. "You're right. I have it here," gesturing toward a notebook in his shirt pocket. "Do you want to check them off?"

"No. All I wanted to know is that you have a list. I'll get you the new sacks."

Which I did. Josefino lugged over the sacks of confiscated arms. I tossed them into a corner in the storeroom.

LATE IN THE AFTERNOON, four days later, Don Juan and his party rode into the *patio*. A *patio*, down here, is simply a yard, a fenced-off tract surrounding a house, not a space hidden in and surrounded by the house itself as in highland Mexico. The party was mud-spattered and sweat-streaked. The ponies were gaunt.

"*Hola*, Don Pablo!" Don Juan swung off the big bay horse. "We're back to cause more bother."

"Not the least bother, Don Juan. You know you are in your home."

"Genaro, put my horse in the shade. Loosen the cinch. You, Tomás, you Pancho! Help the prisoners dismount and tie up their horses."

I realized why the party seemed larger. There were two men with their hands handcuffed behind their backs. I didn't know either of them, nor the horses they rode.

It is not easy for a man with his hands bound behind him to get off a horse. All he can do is to fall off. But with the policemen's help they dismounted. As they did, the late afternoon sun glistened on the nickel-plated handcuffs.

"Some out-of-state customers. They're way up on the 'wanted' list over in Chiapas. I think I can swap them for something useful," Pereyra said.

I didn't understand what he meant for some time.

"Josefino," he called, "bring those birds and the *morrales* over to the house." To me, "Is Doña Maria in? I'd like to speak to her."

"There she is on the porch."

Josefino came by with two turkeys slung over his shoulder by the cord that tied their feet together, and carrying a couple of *morrales* that clinked glassily.

"Doña Maria, here's a turkey hen to replace the one we ate the other day," Pereyra said. "We sort of had to decommission her, through military necessity. And another one, if you'd be so kind as to cook her up for us now. We haven't eaten very well since we left here. *Por Dios*, those people upriver didn't even want to sell us a dry *tortilla*. Don Pablo, here's a bottle to replace what we used up, and another if you'd like to stir us up a *torito*. We need it. I collected this for evidence, but I have plenty left."

I sniffed the *aguardiente*. It had a sweet clean smell. "Good Heavens, did you knock over Don Armando's still?"

"I did. He was on my list. I had to."

"He made the only decent *aguardiente* on the river."

"He's been making it for thirty years. What he owes the state in liquor taxes amounts to a small fortune. They know all about him in the capital. I tore his still all apart."

"And poor old Don Armando?"

"I should have taken him in, but I didn't. He's being turned over to local authorities, meaning his *compadre* Don Concepción. A small fine—I talked it over with Don Chon. But he'll make no more cane juice for a while."

I was interested in watching how he treated his prisoners. I had expected he would be harsh, even brutal. But he was not. He had their handcuffs changed to front soon after they dismounted, and taken off while they ate, after the patrol had finished.

He stood watching in the kitchen as one of them swabbed his plate with a piece of *tortilla.* "Doña Maria, is there a little of that good stew left? No? Well, maybe a plate of rice and beans. This lad has been laying out in the woods, not eating too well—he can use some nourishment. No, don't you serve him—I will . . ." and with the smooth movement of an expert waiter he set the full plate in front of the prisoner. He served, I noted, with his left hand. His right was never far from his gun.

When their horses cooled out, the patrol unsaddled and turned their mounts out into the little pasture above the corral; there was plenty of feed and water, and it would be easy to find the animals in the morning. The troop and prisoners were to stay in the other house, which serves as granary, warehouse, toolhouse, and bunkhouse as needed. Don Juan set up a watch over the prisoners. He himself would stay in the big house, on a cot in the living room.

We sat sipping coffee. He chatted mostly with our youngsters, telling them of marvelous Mexico City, its monuments, its traffic, its zoo out at Chapultepec Park with the long-necked giraffes and the popcorn-eating hippopotamuses—he kept them starry-eyed till long after their bedtime. During the night I heard that rusty hinge on the front door (one of these days I'll fix it) squeak several times as he went out to check on the watch over the prisoners.

5

Kinship

I HAD SOME BRANDING to do. I mark small calves with a cheek brand, which I don't stamp in too hard—they are marked, although when they grow it doesn't always show well. But the brand is always there. Then the next year I put the big iron on them, on the thigh.

There were a few good-sized heifers too; I had been trading steer calves for heifers, a process that reduces immediate cash income but over the long haul builds up the herd. Four I had got in a swap with Don Margarito were well graded up with zebu—they were tall, rangy, sereno-gray with humps on their withers, and inevitably wild.

I don't of course stage a branding bee the way Don Panuncio does. Feliciano, Juanito, and I were going to handle the job, with no barbecue and no *huapango* after. We rounded up the little herd late the previous afternoon to put them in the holding pen behind the house. During the night cows lowed to their errant calves. Maria said, "How happy the house is with the sound of the cattle—not lonely and sad as it is when they are away in the back pastures."

At dawn we saddled, gulped down some black coffee,

then moved the cattle into the corral. I lighted the fire for the branding irons. Juanito and Feliciano were to take turns, one roping, the other throwing and tying. I was going to help with the tying and handle the irons and the castrating pincers.

We caught and cured two elderly cows with screwworm infestations and branded three yearlings. A little cloud that had been floating up there no bigger than a man's fist since sunup suddenly zoomed across the sky showering buckets of rain. The rain squall didn't last for much more than five minutes. The cloud broke up and the sun shone again. But the cattle were steaming wet, and the corral was an expanse of slimy red clay. And I was disgusted.

"Don Pablo, it's not good to brand now," said Feliciano. "That wet hair will steam and make an awful burn instead of a clean brand."

"I know it," glumly.

"Shall I keep on roping?"

"No. We'll knock off for a while. Leave your horse in the shade. It doesn't look like it will rain more. Let's go eat some breakfast while the animals dry out."

The cattle dried out, but the red clay of the corral did not. We slipped and slithered and got spattered with mud. I had to steal a little of Maria's kitchen firewood to get the branding fire going again. Everything was in a mess.

Feliciano roped a big yellow calf, a long yearling. He pulled the animal to the snubbing post. Juanito neck-yoked him. As I went to help catch his hind feet to throw him, he kicked me on the thigh. I saw the kick coming, but when I tried to move away my feet slipped on the slimy clay and he caught me full. He was a big husky animal, and it hurt. I walked about reciting a lifetime's collection of vulgarities and rubbing my thigh, about to decide to turn the cattle loose until a better day, when I heard someone say, "What's the matter, Don Pablo? What happened?"

It was Benito Cadena, looking over the corral gate. With him was his brother-in-law Felipe Reyes.

"That *hijo de la gran puta* calf just kicked me. I've a mind to butcher him and make him into beefsteaks."

"That would be good. He's big and fat, there should be beefsteaks for all of us."

Felipe said, "*Buenos días*, Don Pablo."

I remembered my manners too. "Good day, Don Felipe. Good day, Don Benito. May you both have a very good day."

"And you a better one," said Benito.

"Where are you traveling?"

"Homeward," Benito answered. "We've been visiting my uncle Modesto over on Arroyo Bravo."

"I didn't see you go in."

"We went in by the other trail, behind Don Domingo's ranch. But it's terrible, that trail. So we came out this way."

I had an idea. "Look, if you two are not in a hurry, why don't you stay to help me? The way the corral is, the three of us can't possibly finish today, but if you give us a hand, we'll get through early. I'll pay you wages."

They looked at each other.

"Let's help Don Pablito."

"Sure, let's. But I don't have a lasso," said Felipe, "nor do you."

"That's no problem," I said. "I have a couple of new ropes you can use."

They let down the gate bars to ride into the corral. Felipe mounted a chunky buckskin pony. Benito rode a long-legged little sorrel with a white-striped face. The pony was not badly shaped or ugly, he was just spindly, with long legs holding up a small barrel, little narrow rump.

Had he been mine I'd have christened him "Daddy Long-legs." He might have weighed five hundred pounds after a good feed of corn. Benito's saddle was an old frame, the horn cut deep with lasso burns. The off stirrup had been improvised from liana. For a cinch he used a strip of *majagua* bark, tied directly into the cinch ring, with no latigo or thong. I eyed Benito's outfit with misgivings, thinking of those rambunctious heifers.

"I can lend you a pony, Don Benito, and a saddle too if you want it."

"Thanks, Don Pablo. But I'll use this horse. The practice will be good for him. And don't worry about the *majagua*. It'll hold anything in the corral. All I need is a lasso rope."

I went to the house to get the lassos.

"You two pair off with Feliciano and Juanito. They know the cattle. Two roping, two throwing and tying, in turns. I'm handling the irons and the pincers."

Never have I seen anything quite like that puny, skinny pony of Benito's. He was quick of foot, at least in a corral— I don't know how he'd be for roping in the open. Benito went for the big heifers. He had no roping glove. No matter how tough and callused a man's hand may be, one of these hard-laid cotton ropes will burn it like a hot iron if the roper lets it run through his hand to slide it around the horn. So Benito stopped the heifers down hard. They hit hard, too. The sorrel pony spraddled his gangling legs and slithered over the slippery clay, but he held. Benito helped him a lot, of course, throwing his weight to one side or the other as a counterbalance. But no matter what kind of a catch, ahead, or crossing to right or left, the skinny pony braced his long legs and held.

We finished early in the afternoon. We sat on the porch while Maria got dinner. I had concocted a *torito*. As a rule,

I don't drink with the help, but this was a special occasion. We had all pulled and hauled and sweated and had been spattered with the same mud and cow dung under the same hot sun. We sipped and relaxed.

Benito said, "What's the matter, Uncle Pablo? You're very quiet."

"I'm thinking. I'm trying to decide whether that thing you ride is the biggest little horse I ever saw, or the littlest big horse. Incidentally, when did I get to be your uncle?"

The redhead grinned. "It's obvious. Doña Maria is Don Panuncio's niece, isn't she?"

"Well, yes. I don't quite understand the genealogy, but they agree on it."

"That's the thing: it's simple. My great-aunt Petrona, half-sister of my grandmother, was a niece, kind of, sort of, one step removed, but a niece just the same, of Don Panuncio's mother's mother, Doña Domitila Sanchez. So that makes Doña Maria my aunt and you my uncle."

I pondered this argument for a moment. "I would hardly say it was real close. But since you figured it out, it's all right with me, nephew."

Maria called us to eat. Afterward, Benito and Felipe cinched up their ponies to leave. Benito didn't want to take the twenty-five pesos, which is standard cowboy wages hereabouts; finally he accepted fifteen, leaving ten for the snakebite serum account.

Felipe said, "We're on our way. Many thanks for everything."

"Thanks for the help. May all go well with you."

"*Adiós*, Uncle Pablo. And many thanks," said Benito.

"Thanks to you. May you go with God, nephew."

FELICIANO, JUANITO, AND I lounged about. There was

nothing to do until time to bring in the three milch cows and the night horse. The cattle had slammed into a corral post, breaking it, but it was too late to go to the woods to cut a new one. That could wait until tomorrow.

Feliciano sniggered. He has a dirty mind—I guessed that he had thought of something nasty. I knew it would be about Felipe and Benito, for his nose was a little out of joint—they had outroped him, outdone him in throwing and tying. They were far better cowhands than he.

"What's the joke?" I asked.

"I was just thinking. Those two, Benito and Felipe, are brothers-in-law. Not only that, but they are the mostest brothers-in-law on the river." He said *los masísimos, más* plus the superlative suffix *-ismio,* which is as incorrect in Spanish as "mostest" is in English.

"How do you mean 'mostest'?"

"As I figure it, they are triple brothers-in-law."

"Triple? How can that be?"

"Felipe is married to your nephew Benito's sister."

"I know that. The time I got lost, when Don Severiano chopped down the big timber across the trail to El Ixtal, of all the spiderweb of trails around it I took one that took me to Felipe's house. His wife is not only redheaded too, she is the image, female version, of Benito."

"*Bueno.* That's one. Then Benito is married to Felipe's sister Agustina. That's two. That makes them double brothers-in-law. Then he is also married to Felipe's other sister Clara. That makes the triple. Three times one is three."

"Arithmetic like that will curdle such brains as you have, if you work at it long enough. Besides, it's none of my concern how many wives my nephew has."

6

The Art of Bigamy

BIGAMY IS AN INTERESTING CUSTOM not only in our little
backwoods corner but in the older, settled parts of southeastern Mexico. By "bigamy" I do not mean the business
of having a wife and a mistress or mistresses. I mean the
situation in which a man has two women who are publicly
recognized as wives. Mexican law, of course, does not
sanction such goings-on, but since most country and many
small-town marriages are what society calls "common
law"—without benefit of either priest or judge—public
opinion is what counts. When a neighbor introduces his
"wife" at his house or at a *fiesta*, even, I, boorish as I am at
times, cannot possibly say, "Is this a legal wife or just a
shack job?"

As all sociologists and demographers know, bigamy, or
"polygyny," as the professors call it, cannot be a popular
practice unless women outnumber men in the given society.
There are no precise statistics available to me to prove it,
but it seems possible that there may be fewer men here, in
view of men's more hazardous occupations: felling big
timber, handling wild cattle, traveling the rivers in unstable canoes, and going armed to *fiestas* where liquor
flows freely.

There are a number of bigamous families here on the Xucuapan. When mention is made of them, most men snigger vulgarly, "How can one man handle those women?" However, this is not the snide remark it is intended to be, but is, rather a profound query into human behavior. How *does* one man do it? Observation makes clear that it is not as easy as one might imagine. Many of my friends and neighbors have tried and failed to maintain a bigamous household on a permanent basis.

Bigamy was old Don Paco's downfall ("Paco" is a nickname for Francisco). He raised seven sons and three daughters with Doña Concha. He brought his sons up to be useful, hard-working men. With them he extended his cacao orchards until he had a productive grove of nearly ten thousand trees, so old-timers on the river tell me. The husbands of his two older daughters also worked for him. He slaved along with his sons and sons-in-law from sun to sun on his way to affluence. With a production of five tons of cacao a year, even back when cacao brought only a peso a kilo, he had a good income, for in those days a peso had a lot of buying power. Nowadays, with cacao selling at five to six pesos, such a quantity produces worthwhile income by country standards. Buyers paddled and poled huge canoes up the long, winding river, competing bitterly to buy Don Paco's thick russet cacao beans.

Don Paco had been having an affair with Doña Anastacia for some time. This was before my time as a resident on the river, but the gossip-derived time schedule checks: their eldest daughter, Juana, is a year or so older than Elodia, Doña Concha's last child. Then Don Paco made Doña Tacha (for Anastacia) his second wife, socially speaking. He built a house for her, set her up as spouse. Doña Concha, her sons backing her, went to the local authorities and then to the *Municipio*, the county seat. Under Mexican law, common-law wives, like Doña Concha, have clearly defined rights, and bigamy is regarded as antisocial behavior. Don Paco was ordered to appear. When it was obvious that he had no legitimate defense—that the charges were true—the authorities stripped him of his lands and orchards, dividing them up among his first wife and her children. They left him only the worst small tract, where he lives in poverty with Doña Tacha to this day.

Don Pastor, Don Guillermo's father, was another. He had cattle, a small herd of forty or fifty. When he took Doña Felicitas, his first wife's younger sister, to wife, the two women wrangled constantly. They were a dozen years or so apart in age, perhaps too far apart for the peck order to have been established. Finally the elder was driven out. But she too made the trip to town, where she was awarded the cattle for herself and her numerous children. Don Pastor has had nothing since, except Doña Felicitas and a second brood of offspring.

More recently, there was Don Dolores ("Lolo"). His wife, Clementina, and my Maria came to be good friends, though it was a long and at times muddy hike for Doña Clementina from their house to ours. Don Lolo became wildly enamored of Ramona, Don Chema's daughter. He was still fond of Clementina and of their three baby daughters, so he decided to set up a *ménage à trois*. Doña Clementina told Maria about it:

"He says he still loves me, but he is going to bring my cousin Ramona for his second wife. If I don't take it, he says he will beat me with the flat of his machete like I've never been beaten before. So I told him I'd agree. But that's a lie, Doña Maria. When that slut walks in the front door I go out the back."

She was as good as her word. When Lolo brought his new wife home, Doña Clementina was gone. He went to her father's house, a pistol in his waistband, in a storming rage. His father-in-law, Don Lino (the name is really Tranquilino, but no one ever seems to have time to say all that), was sitting quietly with a 16-gauge shotgun across his knees. His two elder sons, Doña Clementina's brothers, were slouching about, one with a .22 autoloading rifle in the crook of his arm, the other fiddling with the safety of a .380 automatic. Don Lolo did not find out anything regarding Clementina's whereabouts. Next day her brothers took her and the three little girls over the long trail to the railroad, to take the train to town.

Though not pertinent to the present argument, for the sake of closure I report that I know where Clementina is. She is washing dishes in a cheap restaurant in Coatzacoalcos. Lately she has taken up with a tinsmith, who doesn't make much money but who is kindly to the little girls. He is related to the Palma family on our river. Not long ago when I was in town they invited me to supper— coffee and rolls—after Clementina got off work. I filled them in on the latest news from the Xucuapan. Don Lino, later on, was pleased to have news of her.

The point of this—and I could cite several more examples—is that bigamy creates complex situations that not every man can handle.

Of the several bigamous families that are stable arrangements, there are but two that I know well enough to report on—to be able to isolate the factors producing stability. A story like this one must be completely honest to have any worth at all. The novelist can invent details to carry his plot. But the reporter of fact must define what it is that he knows to be true, what he guesses at, and what the gaps in his knowledge are. For instance, I know Benito Cadena pretty well, but always away from his house. I have no idea how he manages his two wives. Nor do I know how Don Diego, our cook Chabela's double son-in-law (to apply Feliciano's arithmetic), handles the two sisters he has been married to for more than twenty years. There are others I don't know about, Don Gabino over on Arroyo Arenal, for example. But I do know about two of my neighbors. One is my *compadre* Santiago.

Years ago my *compadre* took as his common-law wife a girl from San Fermín, far down the river. She, Doña Cornelia, became very ill carrying their first child. She sent for a cousin of hers, Doña Carlota, to come help her with the daily chores—laboriously grinding lye-leached corn on the *metate* (that was before the metal handmills had become popular), making *tortillas* and *pozole*, shelling corn for the poultry and hogs, washing clothes, sweeping and scrubbing and carrying water—all the tasks that fall to the lot of a country woman. In those days Doña Carlota must have looked very much like her daughter, our god-child Elvira, slim, with shiny black hair, an oval face, and bright almond-shaped eyes. Santiago made Doña Carlota his wife too.

He built a separate house for each wife, on two plots of ground about half a mile apart. He has maintained his two households in absolute equivalence. Hard worker and good provider, when he planted an avocado or orange seedling in one *patio*, he planted one in the other. When he bought a kilogram of sugar for one house he bought the same amount for the other one. The same with dress goods, or whatever. He makes a fetish of equal treatment. When he buys sugar by the fifty-kilogram sack, he brings it to my house (I have a scale) to weigh it out into two exactly equal parts. He saved his money until he could buy two milch cows, one for each house.

He has twenty-one living children from his two wives. The kids travel back and forth from one house to the

other, work and play together; it took me a couple of years
to learn which ones belonged in which house. Don Santiago distributes the same affection and the same discipline
impartially among them all.

The youngsters are the payoff. The older ones are now
young adults, some of them recently married. They are
all nice people, well mannered, hard-working, decent. We
know them well, because we are close neighbors and visit
back and forth often. I am not competent to analyze the
moralistic aspects of the bigamous situation, but I can
say this: my *compadre* has made a success of raising his
double family, a success that any man can envy.

CHEPE JOLOCHE is another breed of cat.

First of all, Chepe Joloche is not a name, but a nickname that translates roughly as "Joe Cornshucks." He is
short and wiry, with quick black eyes in a lemon-brown
face. His buttocks stick out because of a strong curvature
in the lumbar region, giving him a slightly effeminate
waddle when he walks. There is nothing else effeminate
about Chepe.

He can be smooth-spoken and pleasant when he chooses.
One comes to learn though that the courtesy and pleas-
antry is a hollow shield. Underneath is malice and complete amorality. Don Pastor moved out, selling his parcel
of land (all his first wife had left him), and his plantings
for a song, because of Chepe. They had a run-in over a
minor problem: at this date I can't even recall whose hog
damaged corn in the other's *milpa*. Don Pastor, middle-
aged but still rugged, told me. "That little bastard Chepe.
I'll tell you the truth, Don Pablo, I'm afraid of him. If he
was the kind who would stand up in front of you with
machete or gun saying, 'Let's see which one of us dies here,'
I'd stand up to him. But he's not. He'll wait behind a yel-

lowwood tree to salt a load of buckshot in your back. I'm too old to stand the strain of peering behind every tree as I go down a trail. That's why I'm leaving. I'm going over to Arroyo Bravo." Chepe was about sixteen then.

There is no professional labor force in the Xucuapan, only neighbors who hire out when they are caught up on their own work. The competition among those of us who need hired labor for clearing and weeding pastures is keen indeed. Yet even where labor is a seller's market, Chepe has trouble finding work. We all know that, hired by the day he arrives late and, if not watched, slips away early in the afternoon. He rarely finishes a "contract," an agreement to clear or weed a specified tract for a fixed sum. When the job is half done, he tries to collect for it, "in advance," then leaves it. He and I had some jangles before we learned to coexist. It is no fun to squabble with Chepe; one thinks about the yellowwood tree.

I broke a rule of several years standing a while ago: I lent Chepe a couple of hundred pesos. Our coexistence involves the understanding that, besides not hiring him, I do not lend him money. I buy fish and game from him occasionally. I also lend him carpentry tools, for, curiously enough, he is not only good with tools, but careful of them and very punctilious about returning them. I lent him the money this time because his four-year-old Carlitos was very sick. It was some sort of dysentery that did not yield to household remedies or even to those in my medical kit. The little boy, gaunt and pallid instead of his usual chubby brown self, probably would have died without medical attention. It seemed terrible to refuse, even though Chepe is the poorest credit risk on the river.

I made a little speech. "Here's the money, Chepe. And here's a note to Dr. Barradas—he's a good doctor and a friend of mine, maybe he'll give Carlitos a little extra attention. But when you come back, if you don't have a way to raise the money to pay me back, you will pay it off in work—weeding that corner of the Amate pasture from the orange trees to the fenceline. And all of it. Or we're really going to lock horns, you and I."

"Don't worry, Don Pablo, I'll start on the weeding job as soon as we get back."

Antibiotics cured the child in short order. I heard they had returned with him. A few days later I rode to the Amate pasture. From the high ridge I could see an expanse of weed-free grass in the corner Chepe was to weed. It struck me that for once he had been bearing down hard on the job. I rode down for a close look. There I found Chepe's wives, Carmela and Lupe, skirts hiked up so as to brush fewer ticks from the grass, swinging machetes like goodfellows amid the head-high clumps of elephant grass.

They were embarrassed to be found so, not because of their tucked-up skirts, but because unlike the highland custom, women down in this region do not work in the fields. I complimented them on their progress, vainly trying to keep from leering at their long well-rounded legs. Chepe, they told me, was down along the creek, trying to shoot an iguana in the bamboo thicket.

They are sisters, Carmela and Lupe, daughters of Don Noë and the late Doña Julia. Those two people, plain enough to look at themselves, produced eight handsome children, six of whom are the best-looking girls along the river (one can see that little Florinda and Anita are going to grow up to look like their elder sisters)—tall, high breasted, well buttocked, with slim waists and straight Indian backs. Oval faces with satiny bronze complexions, big dark eyes, small full-lipped mouths, noses a little shorter and straighter than usual in this region, and thick, waist-long black hair.

Chepe married Carmela when she was scarcely fourteen. When he formally asked her parents for her hand, they set a *plazo*, an engagement period of two years. A *plazo* hereabouts is not quite as rigorous as the Biblical period of bridegroom's servitude, but almost. Chepe pretended to accede. He was courteous to his future parents-in-law and helped Don Noë in his fields. Then he let himself be caught in bed with Carmela on a night when Noë and Doña Julia returned late from a visit to a dying relative. He did it deliberately, of course, for he had his shotgun at hand—when he rolled out of bed he picked it up, then said, "Good morning, father-in-law." He knew Don Noë didn't have a gun. So they were married. Doña Julia slaughtered two of her few hens for the wedding feast, to which only a few close relatives were invited. Chepe had cut almost a year and a half off the two-year engagement.

Lupe is about eight years older than Carmela. She had been married to a lad from town who used to work occasionally as a cowhand for cattle buyers, driving bunches of steers from the back-country ranches. He mistreated her, so she told Maria, and was a poor provider. So she left him, several years after their elopement, to return to her parents. She had not been home long when she took up with Chepe, leaping, in her graceful, long-legged way, from the frying pan into the blazing fire. For slothful Chepe is not much of a provider either. The three, and the babies, of whom there are now seven or eight or maybe nine, live in a small house *en campana*, which means that it consists solely of the framework that supports the thatch roof, with no sidewalls. Sleeping quarters are on the *tapanco*, a sort of attic made of poles laid over the beams. Such a house is cool in warm weather, for the breezes waft through, but so does the rain when the *nortes* howl and when the summer thundershowers boom out of the eastern sky, drowning the cooking fire in the middle of the dirt floor. Chepe has never found time to build the usual *fogón*, a raised clay-filled box on which the kitchen fire is laid. If the girls weren't so good at catching panfish in the creek, at snaring iguanas, and, rumor has it, at snitching a few ears of corn from some neighbor's *milpa*, they'd often go hungry. As for treatment: Chepe's recipe for managing his women consists in liberal applications of the flat of his machete.

Cinchar is the colloquial verb meaning to beat with the flat of a machete. The springy twenty-eight-inch blade bends across the victim's back, leaving an angry red welt, then a green and purple bruise. And when you are on the receiving end, empty-handed, you stand and take it. Your aggressor has the drop on you. If you offer resistance he has only to turn his wrist the slightest bit to give you the edge. I have been told there are laws in Tabasco specifically prohibiting *cinchando*, but it is done all the time.

Carmela, young and malleable, has adjusted to Chepe's regime. Her mother used to beat her too, and her father is not a much better provider, not that Don Noë doesn't work, but his liking for *aguardiente* cuts heavily into his take-home pay. But Lupe, a woman with a mind of her own, has had a harder time living with it.

She ran away one time, hiking to our house with her youngest baby under one arm and a *morral* containing her other dress and the worn-out shoes that were her souvenir of life in town.

Maria told me of the visit—I was back in the hills looking for a newborn calf that the cow had hidden with malicious skill.

"Doña Maria," she said, "look what that *cabrón* has done to me." She plunked the baby into the hammock, and unbuttoned the top of her dress to slip it off her shoulders. Her upper arms, shoulders, and back were a mass of welts and bruises. "I'm through with him. I'll take no more of his beatings."

Maria murmured condolences and smeared her back with a soothing ointment, then sent her on her way to her father's house. Lupe tried to walk mostly on the short grass and weeds alongside the trail, but Chepe found her tracks early next morning. He hid in a thicket near Don Noë's house.

Presently Lupe came out with a bucket of *nixtamal*, maize boiled with lye, to wash in the river. The cooking with lye loosens the tough integument, and repeated washing and rinsing leaves the kernels bland and hominy-like, ready for grinding to make *tortillas*.

There is a long gravel bar in front of Don Noë's house, a little more than ankle deep at low water. Lupe walked down the steep bank and waded out into the stream. As she dipped water into the bucket, to begin washing the maize, standing straight-legged, bent over at the waist, Chepe circled through the brush to avoid being seen from the house. He descended the embankment, moved stealthily behind her.

The current is swift over the bar. The water shouts and sings as it bounces over the coarse gravels, so Lupe did not hear his approach. She did not hear the hiss of steel on leather as he drew his machete from its scabbard. Then he hit her across the back with the flat of it, hit her hard so that she went sprawling face-down in the water. The bucket upset. She sat up.

"*Madre de Dios!* Don't kill me, Chepe, don't kill me!" The mischievous current rolled and tumbled the bucket away downstream. She didn't notice the loss.

"Get up." The machete glinted as he held it high.

"Who's in the house?"

"My father. He's fitting a new ax handle. Please Chepe, don't hit me again."

"Your brother?"

"Only the little one. Manuel isn't here."

"Go get the baby and your things. We're going home."

When they entered the house, Chepe carried his machete unsheathed and kept his left hand in his pocket. Lupe's father knew what was probably in the pocket, Don Eulalio's cigarette-pack-size .25-caliber automatic, one of those Czech models with the double-action first shot. Eulalio is married to one of Chepe's sisters and is one of the few people who likes him—everyone knows he lends Chepe the gun occasionally.

"Good morning, father-in-law. I've come to take my wife home."

Don Noë smiled foolishly, to conceal his rage. He is no coward, but the unfinished ax handle and the bit of glass he was using to plane it down were not enough armament.

It is plain that special types of personality are necessary to make a success of bigamy, but they are not necessarily all alike.

LITTLE TRINIDAD, when he was about seven years old, explained something about bigamy. He is the only male among neighbor Rufino's eight offspring and is our Chabela's favorite grandchild; she brings him to our house now and then to play with our youngsters. Trini is a couple of months older than our Rosamaria, half a head shorter, with a mop of unruly wiry black hair, vivacious beady eyes, and a chubby, deep-bronze face. Like most children raised on the precept that small fry should be seen but not heard, he is tongue-tied in the presence of adults but chatters like a rainsoaked parrot with his play-mates.

When I came in from the pastures, Maria did not wait for me to come to the house but ran to meet me under the spreading *guasimo* tree where I tie my ponies.

"That Trini!" she laughed. "He's really something! Listen to what I just heard him say . . ."

The youngsters had been playing cowboy. They had hackamored the patient dogs, lashing them close together to make a *mancuerna*, the way bronco steers are lashed to lead and fight them down jungle trails. On their stick horses they had dragged and hazed their *mancuerna* round and round the house until the weary dogs dropped in the shade, tongues lolling, refusing to budge. Tying their stick horses to the cornerpost of the porch, with much exchange of advice about loosening cinches and straightening saddle cloths, the children squatted on their heels, cowpuncher fashion, in the shade of an orange tree. Maria passed unnoticed behind the tree on some errand, just in time to hear Rosamaria say, "Trini, when you grow up are you going to get married?"

"Married? Me?"

"Yes, are you going to have a wife?"

"Have a wife? I should say so—I'm going to have two, maybe even three of 'em!"

Bigamy seldom works out well around here, but males who plan on it from the age of seven are likely to keep trying.

7

Patrol

Don Juan Pereyra made another patrol two or three months after the first one. The winter rains had started, the trails were foul. Locally there had been some speculation that perhaps he would travel in good weather only; perhaps he chose the time to demonstrate otherwise. A *norte* was blowing when he came. Most of the *arroyos* were swimming-deep. He and his men were outfitted with plastic bags to protect arms and ammunition, so they arrived with their weapons dry but were themselves soaked and shaking with cold. When the *nortes* roll in, dumping all the moisture they have picked up crossing the Gulf, the thermometer may read no lower than the mid-forties. But when you have been out in the weather all day, dripping wet and lashed with the wind, you feel so cold that you are amazed the mud puddles aren't freezing over.

When the troop rode into the *patio*, Maria put a bucket of water on the kitchen fire and began fanning the blaze. There wasn't a drop of liquor in the house to help cut the chill. But plenty of coffee proved just as good; they gulped it down scalding hot. Then Don Juan and his men went on.

Slogging through rain and muddy trails and brimming *arroyos*, the patrol picked up Don Rodolfo Palma, who had returned after several years of self-exile—fleeing from justice after killing Don Arnulfo Méndez in a machete fight. He came back when he learned that Arnulfo's two brothers had died; he thought he had nothing more to fear. No one had told him that times were changing on the Xucuapan. Don Juan also confiscated more illicit weapons. With his party he cut over on a hunter's track to the upper course of Arroyo Bravo, where he disarmed, among others, Chabela's son-in-law Diego.

Doña Chabela pretended to be enraged when she heard the news. "That white-eyed *diablo*. I'll make no *tortillas* for him next time he shows up here." Then she chuckled. "Too bad he didn't take Diego's machete too." Maybe Diego uses his machete the way Chepe Joloche does.

But Don Juan did not find Chucho Ortiz.

NOT MANY DAYS after, Don Juan rode from town to Don Panuncio's ranch at El Ixtal with two of his policemen. When he left, he took with him a young man named Crisóforo Hernandez, from far upriver. No one knew what crime Crisóforo had committed. Imaginations ran wild, and gossips hinted at lurid misdeeds. The fact is that he went not as a prisoner but as a guide.

It is only sixteen or seventeen miles from our house to the railroad, but the trip involves crossing the river, a swamp and a couple of deep *arroyos*. We used to take the train to town occasionally, during the driest part of the year, when one can ride across the gravel bar in front of Don Noë's house without getting wet. Then they changed the train schedule, so that we would have to set out at three in the morning, traversing the worst parts of the trail in the dark, so we rarely travel that way.

From our flagstop station the rail line swings south-easterly, roughly paralleling the river, so that some miles on, at a station called Pozo Azul, the distance to the river is about the same as here. There is a trail from Pozo Azul that comes out well above Don Amaranto's place—I have never traveled it but am told it is good even in rainy times, traversing mostly level high ground, with no really sticky stream crossings. Don Juan went to Pozo Azul by train, a special train: locomotive, a cattle car for the horses, and a caboose. He disembarked and, with Crisóforo as guide, appeared suddenly far upstream, to make a sweep from there down. He was plainly demonstrating that he could patrol the Xucuapan, any time, in any weather, and by any route. No one could predict when or from what direction he might appear with his troop.

THE NEWS spread like wildfire—Don Juan had finally caught up with Chucho Ortiz, over in Chiapas. He didn't bring him in alive.

That Don Juan was able to operate in another state proved several important points. First, that he had sufficient prestige and official backing to make such a complex arrangement. Second, it demonstrated that times were changing: not many years ago, states were very jealous of their rights and would not permit entry of an out-of-state police force, but of late there has been increasing interstate cooperation in such matters. The fact that the Cattlemen's Association sponsors the *Columnas Volantes* certainly must be a factor. Perhaps the taking of the Chiapanecan prisoners on the first patrol helped set the stage for the project.

Whatever the official arrangements, Don Juan went to Chiapas as he had to Pozo Azul, by special train, the horses in a cattle car. At a flagstop along the line, he

[83]

rendezvoused with a *Columna* from Chiapas. Don Chucho was on their list too. The joint force rode to a remote spot in the jungle high on the rocky slopes of the Sierra Madre de Chiapas, to a hut in a small clearing.

The versions we received of what happened varied considerably in some respects, in others were surprisingly consistent. All agree that Don Chucho and two of his cronies were in the hut and that they replied to the surrender order with gunfire. One of the trio, a Chiapanecan, was seriously wounded. Then, according to one tale, Chucho slipped out the back door of the hut to run for it. The clearing was small. He had a pistol in either hand, firing as he ran. Don Juan, so the story goes, snatched a Mendoza from a soldier who was firing ineffectively, and put a burst into the fugitive.

Another version was that Don Chucho surrendered, along with his unwounded companion, then, near the edge of the forest, tried to escape. As in the previous version, Don Juan seized the automatic weapon and cut him down just as he reached the edge of the clearing.

The third variant of the story was related chiefly by relatives of the slain bandit. Old Don Ramón, his eyes misty with tears, said, "It must have been awful, horrible, Don Pablito. Law and order, they call it—but what kind of law is that, tying poor Chucho to a tree to tear him apart with one of those machine-gun things. Chucho wasn't really bad, just a little mixed up. He was family to us, you know."

Just a little mixed up. Two cowardly murders, from behind. Rumor reported another in Chiapas. A career of stealing livestock. Not many: two or three or four head at a time—whatever could be hustled over the jungle trails. But the total must have been considerable over the ten or twelve years of his thieving. But there was nothing I could say to Don Ramón, a good neighbor, whom I like. Nor could I tell him that his tale sounded very improbable. I just shook my head sympathetically. I had sat up a few nights myself, in previous times, when gossip related that Don Chucho had expressed admiration for a big bay mare I had and for my chunky blue roping horse.

LOCAL CUSTOM begain to change. People rarely went about with firearms—those who still had them—except when they were going hunting in the woods. They didn't carry them along the main trails lest they meet the *Columna Volante* around the next turn. At a *fiesta* downriver, Epifanio Guerrero and Julio Vasquez fought with machetes—Epifanio fled leaving his adversary seriously wounded. Next day he voluntarily surrendered to my *compadre* Sebastián, to be sent to the authorities in town. He said he would rather do it that way than to wait for Don Juan to capture him.

8

The Brown Cow

As I HAVE BEEN an avid reader of whodunits for years, it occurred to me to consider whether some incident here on the Xucuapan could be presented in mystery-story fashion, an almost perfect crime whose perpetrator was identified through the observations and deductions of some jungle Sherlock. But the stories can't be told in that fashion without distorting the facts. The incidents just don't happen that way. There are no perfect crimes, or even near-perfect ones, in a sparsely settled rural region. Even if there are no eyewitnesses, the identity of the culprit or culprits becomes general knowledge in a short time.

There are many reasons for this. Country people are observant, unlike the anonymous, bustling city crowds with their unseeing eyes and their indifference that enable the criminal to come and go as he pleases. Moreover, everyone knows everyone else and his affairs: business dealings, friendships, amours, and rancors. If grizzled old Don Ramón Jiménez is seen riding up the trail, the odds are that he is going to visit his son Constancio, who is married to one of Don Margarito's daughters. That is the old man's only important interest upriver. If young Pedro Perez is

seen headed in the same direction, it is logical to suppose
that he is going to visit his elder sister, Don Elias's wife,
or to the house of Don Armando, the ex-*aguardiente*
maker, whose daughter he has been courting for about a
year. If people do not arrive at their normal destinations,
the gossips buzz: "Where *did* he go? Why?"

A traveler passing unseen leaves tracks, conspicuous because even main trails have sparse traffic. Prints of bare
feet are distinctive, easily recognizable—I have learned to
know those of most of my close neighbors. The plastic
boots and shoes that have become popular recently have
a great variety of distinctive treads. Even the tracks of
one's neighbor's saddle horses are known. Not long ago
I went to see my *compadre* Natividad. There was no one
home; the house was closed up tight. I did not dismount.
There was no point in leaving a note, for no one in the
family can read. Next day he came to my house. "I saw
the tracks of your big roan in the *patio*, so I figured you
wanted to see me, *compadre*."

If a person stays off the trails, cutting through the woods
on foot, that would also be known. Men cruise the forests
a good deal, hunting, looking for timber for house construction and repair, collecting lianas for lashings, or looking for a bee tree. A track through the woods would be
followed until a recognizable print was found.

"I saw Don X's track, cutting straight through the jungle way in above the forks of Ceiba Creek. What do you
suppose he was doing in there?"

All this nosy information—who went where, who did
or did not visit his *compadres* and relatives—passes
through the grapevine, along with other news: who has
had a falling-out, and why; whose wife left him; who
wants to buy or sell maize or beans or rice or livestock;
and everything else that happens. The grapevine is a re-

markably effective communications net, funneling all information through to Don Panuncio and Don Concepción. Knowledge of everything that goes on is of great usefulness to the two old men in managing the Xucuapan. This information system makes the storybook kind of detection superfluous.

To prove it, there was the Case of Domingo's Brown Cow.

At first this anecdote may seem to belie what it is supposed to prove, for Don Domingo actually did a piece of efficient detective work. But the point is that he had no need to do it—except for such personal satisfaction as it gave him to solve the problem—for all the information was brought to him.

She was a big young cow, dark-brown, with high, lyre-shaped horns. She had grown long and tall and wide and fat, but did not get with calf. Don Domingo, convinced she was barren, resolved to sell her for beef. Keeping a barren cow is uneconomic; one needs cows that calve every year without fail. Domingo had five or six hundred head of cattle and, like any good cowman, knew them all by sight. He had selected a lot of animals to offer for sale, and the brown cow was high on the list.

It was a period when Domingo was spending only part of his time at the ranch. He had bought a small place on the outskirts of town, moved his wife and children there to put the youngsters in school, and commuted weekly in his big canoe and outboard. He brought in quantities of provisions, and took to town loads of produce; he was building up quite a business with the Arroyo Bravo people. They live too far from El Ixtal to buy at Don Panuncio's store.

Under the circumstances, Don Domingo should have had a *mayoral*, a foreman, to care for the cattle and supervise other work. Instead, he hired several teenagers, and left them to run the place. Most of them were irresponsible, or did not know how to work without direction, so he was constantly firing some and hiring others. Some lasted a month or two, some a week.

"It's a mess, Don Pablito," Domingo told me one day when we met in town. He and Don Juan were sipping cold beer; they called me over to join them. "Life on the ranch has turned into just one long headache for me. Every time I go there those kids have made a mess of something. Last week they let a couple of calves die—one that got tangled up and choked, and another that they didn't bother to find in the pasture."

"Two calves! That's really bad luck."

"Not bad luck, it's the kids' damned laziness! I was going to fire them all, right then, but I didn't have anyone to replace them."

"You ought to get a good reliable man, a *mayoral*," Don Juan said. "That's not a good system, leaving your animals in the care of those kids. Hire a good man, pay him good wages, give him authority to supervise, and even to hire and fire those boys."

"The trouble is that I can't find a man like that."

Rumor had it that he couldn't because he wouldn't pay the kind of wages a competent, responsible man deserves —and can get almost anywhere.

"How about that Don, Don what's-his-name, the oldish fellow with the three boys, who works for you?" I asked.

"Don Antonio? He's reliable enough, honest and hard-working, but he's no cowhand, not much use with animals. He won't even get on a horse if he can avoid it— he'd rather walk."

"You'd better find someone," Don Juan insisted. "You'll end up with some trouble, leaving your cattle with no decent care. You have big pastures; if the kids don't ride them regularly, someone could steal half your herd without your knowing it."

"*Por Dios*, Don Juan, you're scaring me! But now that there is no Don Chucho, I don't think there's much danger."

"I'm telling you there is. You're just inviting someone to do it—some poor devil who needs a few pesos pretty bad. That's how they get started . . ."

LATE ONE AFTERNOON a few weeks later three young men, none of them seasoned criminals, went to Don Domingo's lower pastures to steal a beef. They were Emeterio Palma and the brothers Carmen and Andrés Gomez. Emeterio went by canoe, the brothers on horseback. They knew that Domingo was in town and that the three lads who worked for him were probably swimming in the cool Arroyo del Zapote, over a mile away, and in any case rarely entered the lower pastures when their employer was away. Nor did the horse-shy Don Antonio and his sons. Emeterio and the brothers had announced to neighbors that they would have fresh beef to sell next day. They planned, they said, to butcher a cow of Emeterio's

They found the brown cow, big and fat, lying chewing her cud but a few feet from the riverbank. She was not wild. She lay quietly while Andrés rode close to shoot her in the forehead with his .22 Llama. The cow rolled back dead. The three skinned the carcass, butchered it on the hide to avoid spilling blood on the ground, quartered it, and loaded the meat, liver and lungs, the emptied rumen, even the tongue, into the canoe. The rumen contents, the head with its recognizable horns, the hide with its brand and distinctive color, and the small offal they threw into the river. There is a deep pool just out from the bank there. They worked fast, but dusk was shading into night as they covered the stolen meat with banana leaves and placed a few stubs of banana cuttings on top of the load. They cut some branches to sweep over the site of the butchering to blur their tracks and to straighten up the crushed-down grass and weeds. Carmen embarked in the canoe with Emeterio, to paddle downstream more rapidly as his brother led his horse.

For inexperienced thieves they had done considerable planning. They had even left one of Emeterio's cows tied to a tree near his house, so that any passerby could see her apparently waiting to be sacrificed. She was gentle, could be led like a horse, so after unloading the meat, while the brothers washed the blood from the canoe, Emeterio took her to a small back pasture where no one was likely to see her.

But despite their elaborate precautions, they made many mistakes. Of course Emeterio had been seen on the open river. Perhaps because of the dusk they overlooked some blood spilled when they rolled up the hide. They spilled a bit of the rumen contents close to the riverbank—the material dries yellow, strawy, and conspicuous in the sun. And they left some tracks in the moist clay by the water's edge, where they loaded the canoe.

Don Juan's dire prophecy had been nagging at Don Domingo, and he decided to return this time a few days earlier than originally planned. That night he stayed at Don Panuncio's house, to set out at first light next day.

From the river next morning Domingo could see several men busily slicing and hanging fresh beef under a shed next to Emeterio's house. Although cattle raising is the principal local industry, few people butcher; fresh beef is a special treat. People travel for miles to buy it.

Domingo steered slowly to the landing under the *gua-*

tope tree, coming alongside Emeterio's canoe. "What did you kill, Don Emeterio?" he shouted.

"An old cow, very fat. Do you want some meat?"

"Is there some good meat left?"

"Lots of it. Not many people have arrived yet. The backstraps are nearly complete."

Don Domingo disembarked, made his canoe fast, then climbed the slope to the shed.

"*Hombre*, Don Emeterio, that's good-looking beef! Good color, and fat. You must have some wonderful pastures back in there."

"Pretty fair. Not as good as yours, of course. How much meat do you want?"

"How much does it cost?"

"Six for *carne con hueso*"—meat with bone,—"ten for *pulpa*"—boneless muscle tissue.

"So high? I was going to buy five kilos."

"Have you *aguardiente* in the canoe? I'll trade you, at a bottle per kilo."

"But the *aguardiente* costs twelve pesos a bottle."

They finally settled on three bottles of liquor and twenty pesos for the fifty pesos' worth of meat. Later on, Don Domingo sourly related that he thought he was getting a bargain—at wholesale, the standard twenty-six-ounce bottle of *aguardiente* cost him five pesos.

"Shall I salt it for you?" Emeterio asked.

"No thanks, I think not."

"It's going to be hot today."

"I'll be at the ranch soon—I'll keep some out to use fresh and salt the rest myself."

"Well, after all, Don Mingo, it's your beef," Emeterio said with a broad grin. "I'll fix it any way you want it."

Later on Domingo remembered the remark, with ire. "That *hijo de la chingada!* He had the guts to tell me right to my face that it was my beef!"

But at the moment the cattleman departed content.

A mile or so upstream he saw his *compadre* Ramón Montalvo weeding pasture along the riverbank. He stopped at a little sandy beach. *"Buenos días, compadre.* How about a drink to take the sting out of the sun's heat?"

"Compadre, may you have a good day. The sun isn't hot yet, but a drink would be enjoyable. I'll come right down." Don Ramón scrambled down the steep bank. They drank and chatted.

"Don Emeterio killed a fat cow—very nice beef. I bought some of it. Aren't you going to send for some, *compadre?"*

"Has he started to cut it up already? I heard he was going to butcher, but I figured the meat wouldn't be ready till nearly noon."

"It's nearly all cut up now. He killed the cow late yesterday."

"He couldn't have. He went upriver by canoe yesterday afternoon. Your *comadre"*—Ramón's wife—"was washing clothes by the river and saw him."

"He saw her?"

"Yes. He greeted her—they're kind of cousins, you know. He said he was going up to my namesake, Don Ramón Jiménez, to get a load of banana cuttings."

"Banana cuttings? Plant bananas this time of the year? Don Emeterio is too good a farmer for that. Everybody knows cuttings won't root in the dry season."

"That's what I thought too, when she told me. He came back a little after dark. I was bathing behind my canoe when I heard paddles and low voices. I kept still to see who it was. The canoe was loaded, low in the water. I recognized Don Emeterio. The one in the bow looked like one of those Gomez boys—the tall one."

"Must have been Carmen. Andrés is short."

"It was Carmen, then. I could see he was tall."

"So it couldn't have been the Gomez boys who helped him slaughter the cow—yet they were helping him cut up the meat early this morning. Andrés couldn't have done it all by himself."

"It's a long hard job for one man."

"There's something wrong about this, *compadre*," Domingo said slowly. "That beef was killed yesterday. One shoulder they hadn't cut up was all dry and shiny outside, from hanging up overnight."

He started the outboard and continued on to Don Prisciliano's house. Don Prisci was not at home—he leaves for his fields at the crack of dawn and doesn't return till the afternoon shadows are long. His house is set on a little knoll that commands a view of nearly a thousand yards of river; his wife spends her time watching who passes by. Not a fish can jump in that stretch without her seeing it.

After greetings and inquiries for Don Prisciliano, Domingo asked, "By the way, Doña Marcelina, did the Teco Julio go by yesterday afternoon? I was supposed to meet him at the ranch."

"No, Don Domingo. Not one canoe with motor passed yesterday. The only person I saw was Don Emeterio, who went paddling upriver."

"When did he go by?"

"The sun was about so . . ." She indicated about two hours above the western horizon. "I didn't see him come back—must have been in the night."

It was then, as Domingo related the tale later, that he recalled something: when he was bargaining with Don Emeterio he had not seen a fresh cowhide. Hides are worth money. The canoe-borne peddlers will pay forty or fifty pesos for fresh-salted hides, and the price is even better in town. Some men sun-dry a hide, then give it a crude lye cure so that it can be cut up into *guaraches*, thongs, cinch straps, and other leather items useful on a farm. If Emeterio had killed an animal of his own, the hide should have been in sight, salted and rolled up and hung in the shade, or spread in the sun.

With Juan Pereyra's warning ringing in his memory, and the clear hints that there was something out of line about Emeterio's beef peddling, Don Domingo felt ill at ease. He did not yet know that he had been victimized, but his nerves were taut, his senses alert. Thus, reaching his own lower pastures, he at once saw the scuff marks on the hard clay of the bank where someone or something had slid down.

He steered in close. There was the mark of a canoe's bow in the soft mud of the shallows, where the craft had been pulled in close to the bank. On a ledge by the water were tracks—two sets of narrow-toed, high-heeled shoes with smooth soles. Andrés and Carmen had been wearing riding shoes. Emeterio had left several recognizable prints of his wide, splay-toed feet. Grimly Domingo climbed the bank, cursing under his breath. What he saw left no doubt: the spatters of half-digested rumen contents, the black patch of dried blood, the grass and weeds where the cow had been slaughtered not yet straightened up.

The outraged cattleman returned to his canoe. As he went on upstream, he thought the situation over. He knew what had been done and who had done it. What he needed to know was which animal had been slaughtered.

The three boys at the ranch, who had heard the approach of the motor, were pretending to be very busy repairing a fence behind the house. Don Domingo sent one of them to bring Don Antonio and his boys, another to bring in the horses. The provisions were unloaded and stowed in the warehouse. While the boys saddled up, Domingo took time to salt the meat he had bought. His choler rose as he did so.

He made no explanations, saying only that they were going to round up the herd in the lower pasture. The boys, without initiative by themselves, worked well under supervision. They combed the pasture, ferreting out the cattle from the patches of thicket where they were hiding from the sun. Two of the lads started the assembled herd toward the corral. Domingo and a youth named Fernando made a last swing along the edge of the river.

They came to the place of the slaughtering. Fernando, a bright youngster, looking about, understood what had happened. He got off his pony and began searching in wide circles, bent almost double at the waist. Presently, fifty or sixty yards downstream, he squatted on his heels.

"Don Mingo, come over here. I have something."

"What is it?"

"You'll have to come see—I can't bring it to you."

Domingo walked toward him.

"The other day, it was three days ago, Carmen and Andrés came to the house. They asked for you. Claimed they wanted work. We said you probably wouldn't be back from town till the middle of the week."

"Checking up on me."

"I wouldn't know about that. But Andrés was riding an old long-barreled gray pony. Long ago that pony split his hoof, bad, but it healed. But the split makes the front of his hoof grow out in two lobes—looks like he has two toes. Here's a two-toed horse track."

"What hoof was it?"

"Right front."

"This is a right-front print."

"That's what I was talking about, *patrón*."

A few minutes in the corral were enough for a man

who knew his cattle well to identify a missing animal. There was a red cow absent too, one that had stayed hidden, asleep in some shady nook. But her calf was frisking in the corral, with a full belly that showed he had suckled that morning. Obviously his dam had not been slaughtered the day before. It was the barren brown cow that was missing.

Felipe Reyes was waiting for Domingo at the ranch house. He was nervous, embarrassed: he was playing the role of informer. Why is not altogether clear. He was not a kinsman or good friend or henchman of Domingo's. Apparently he wanted to ingratiate himself. He owed Don Domingo a substantial amount of money—more than he could pay—for provisions, and Domingo had been pressing him.

"May I speak to you in private, Don Domingo?" he asked.

"Surely." Domingo guessed it would be about the cow. They walked to the shade of a big spreading tamarind tree behind the house.

Felipe squatted on his heels. "I don't like what they are saying about you. It's not right," he continued virtuously, "you bring us provisions and things, and they make fun of you."

"Who are 'they'?"

"Why, Don Emeterio and those Gomez boys, Carmen and Andrés."

"What did they say?"

"They were laughing about selling you the meat you bought this morning. They were kind of high on the *aguardiente* you gave them—they were saying you paid a good price to eat your own beef."

"My own beef?" Domingo asked blankly, pretending not to understand.

"Your beef. It was your cow they butchered. Don Emeterio laughed till he rolled on the ground. He said he told you plain that it was your beef, and you, *de pendejo*, paid him just the same."

Domingo cursed bitterly, then controlled himself. "You're a witness, Felipe. If it's the truth that you heard them say those things."

"I heard them, all right. And more, too."

"You'll have to come into town to testify for me."

Felipe was frightened. "I couldn't do that. They'd kill me. You know that."

"You can do it in private, like now with me. You just tell your story to the *Agente del Ministerio Público*." The *Agente del Ministerio Público* is the public prosecutor.

"I can't, Don Domingo."

"You'll have to. I'll see that they don't know. I need a witness. And I'll remember the favor when we settle accounts."

Felipe assented, but reluctantly. He saw that he had put himself into a trap.

That evening the *compadre* Ramón paddled up in a little sliver of a canoe that slid easily over the water. He also came to give information. But his informing had a different motivation from that of Felipe. *Compadres* have an obligation to help and defend one another.

"I hate to bring bad news, *compadre*. But the story is going around that it was your beef that was sold this morning." He told essentially the same story as Felipe's.

Domingo started downriver early next morning. He took Fernando, who had identified the peculiar horse track. He was surprised, though he should not have been, to discover that Don Panuncio already knew most of the facts. (Later he learned that Don Chon and Don Salvador as well had learned of the incident.)

"What are you going to do, Mingo?" the old man asked.

"Throw the bastards in jail. I'll teach them to steal my cattle."

"I wouldn't be so rough on them. Why don't you send for them, talk to them first? Make them pay for the cow — a good stiff price, enough so it hurts. But not jail. They're not really bad. They just took a fool notion. None of them has ever done anything like this before."

"No, *por Dios!* I'm going to give them a lesson they won't forget. It would set a bad example to let them off easy—others will start stealing cattle too."

"Well, you know what you're doing. Just remember we all live here together on the Xucuapan—even if you now live in town part-time."

Domingo straightened up to his full height, slapped his hands against the butt of his pistol. "I'm not afraid of those thieving rats," he growled.

"That isn't quite what I meant," Don Panuncio retorted.

LOOKING BACK on the sequence of events it is clear that Don Domingo's sleuthing had been unnecessary—a waste of time, in fact. The time spent working out the tracks, quizzing neighbors, rounding up the cattle to determine the missing animal, might better have been put to doing something useful, fixing fence, for example. Don Panuncio or Don Chon, understanding the efficacy of the grapevine, would have gone about their routine chores until gossips clarified not only who, but when, how, and even why. But Domingo was young enough to be impatient. He was possessed too of a hairtrigger volcanic temper, but its eruptions of rage ordinarily were brief. He was, normally, a lighthearted man, not an angry one.

What one remembers most about Don Domingo, besides the kink one got in one's neck looking up at him, was the wide smile, the flash of white and gold teeth, that was his usual expression. Even blows of outrageous fortune—mishaps of the sort that leave other men soured and depressed for days—he laughed away.

There was the expensive Brown Swiss bull that he had shipped down from Puebla state. Brown Swiss are small and chunky cattle, with great resistance to heat, ticks, and tropical diseases. Crossed with zebu or zebu-graded stock, their calves are said to grow large and meaty, heavier than the lanky zebu. And gentler than the nasty-tempered Indian cattle, too. Domingo's imported Swiss bull had been in a pasture but two days when four old zebu bulls in an adjacent division smashed through the fence to fight him and kill him.

"Don Pablito!" he whooped from his doorway as I rode up. "You came just in time! You're just in time for the wake!"

"Wake?" I was caught off guard—but it had to be a joke of some sort. "Who is the late lamented?"

"My Brown Swiss bull, may he rest in peace."

"No! How could that happen!"

"It just happened all right! Get off your horse, and I'll tell you while you have a drink in memory of the departed. Paco, tie Don Pablito's horse in the shade."

I dismounted, checked the cinch—it was trail-loose—gave the leadrope to the youngster. Domingo and I shook hands, slapped each other on the back—we were not *compadres* but it seemed that we would eventually have entered into that mutual-esteem relationship. Then Don Domingo gave me a play-by-play account of the bullfight, four against one. Domingo and Josefino—"I borrowed him from Don Panuncio for a few days"—tried fruitlessly to break up the fight. "Those bulls were fight-crazy. They smelled the blood—they'd cut the Swiss bull some and he was bleeding—they charged anything that moved near them."

"Look at my leg," Josefino said. His right lower leg was obviously swollen under the rag bandages that held the curative herbs in place. "That *hijo de puta* black-faced bull hooked me. If he'd got my pony under the flank and flipped him he'd have killed me."

"It was rough," said Domingo. "I was in trouble a few times too. The blackfaced bull that hit Josi in the leg got away with his rope, and I broke mine trying to hold the little white bull. We couldn't do anything—I couldn't shoot the zebus—got too much of an investment in them."

"So you sat watching them kill your latest investment," I said.

He laughed. "There was nothing else we could do. But it was a great spectacle. You don't see a fight like that every day—the little Swiss bull was valiant. He'd lock horns with one, then the others would hit him in the side, knocking him down. But he kept getting up—he didn't quit until he was dead. *Macho, muy macho*, that little Swiss bull. It was worth some money to see a fight like that."

I groped to try to relate this sporting enthusiasm to Domingo's economic views. "But the Brown Swiss did cost you a lot, didn't he?"

"He did. But we tried, and could do nothing about it. No one was to blame. It was God's will; one should not complain about such things. So at least I enjoyed the fight."

"It was God's will." I heard Don Domingo use the phrase on another occasion. That time he was sitting on the gunwale of my canoe, stripped to his shorts. He had been diving in search of various effects—he grinned that a full bottle of *aguardiente* was the most interesting item— that had gone to the bottom when his big canoe hit a sunken snag and capsized. Over the canoe, which he had righted but lay with gunwales awash, was a well-made cover of poles, lashed with tough lianas laced through holes drilled through the gunwales. This was a *guacal*, or crate, for containing hogs—inside it were a dozen drowned hogs Don Domingo had been taking to market, a ton and a quarter of pork on the hoof, he estimated, between five and six thousand pesos' worth of porkers if they had arrived to Lomas Bonitas alive.

"What miserable luck, Don Domingo," I ventured.

"It was no one's fault. I was sober, steering carefully. The *cabrón* snag just didn't show on the surface. The *guacal* was too well made to break loose and let the animals out when I righted the canoe—my machete went to the bottom. It was God's will; one mustn't complain."

I helped him pull the head of his outboard motor to dry out the cylinders so it would start, while we waited for his *compadre* Chon (he had sent a message with a youngster) and some helpers. He planned to butcher the hogs to render out the lard. "I can salvage something out of this disaster, anyhow." As I went on my way I marveled at his resignation. Of course he was well-to-do enough so that losses on the order of that of the bull, and of the hogs, were not critical to him. But with his acute interest in money—a sort of gamesmanship centered on making profit—his calm acceptance of these accidents seemed to me remarkable.

But the affair of the Brown Cow was different. It was not, to Domingo's mind, a manifestation of God's will. It was a misdeed of man, a deliberate offense, a personal affront. It was an act of human malice. To make things worse, there was the business of his having bought the meat from his own cow, and then having been ridiculed for such stupidity.

Don Domingo sat glowering as the outboard purred along taking him to town. Mechanically he swung the tiller to round curves, to avoid floating logs and clumps of lush green water hyacinth with their spikes of sky-blue flowers. The shadows stretched longer and longer to the east until they swallowed the whole landscape as the sun dropped out of sight. Everything became black shadow— the riverbanks and trees and their reflections on the water— streaked with a murky silvery sheen that was the open river. Mechanically he steered the winding course, avoiding driftwood and hyacinth clumps that now showed dead black against the shimmering black of the water but not really seeing them, thinking only of the revenge he would take.

His wife, Doña Cristina, later told one of her *comadres* that she had never seen Domingo in so savage a temper as when he arrived that night. The news soon spread. He stormed into his house speaking to no one, and cuffing his children, of whom he was so fond. When Doña Cristina offered to make him a supper, he roared at her not to bother him and slapped her, he who never before had raised a hand to her in their dozen years of marriage. Then he sprawled fully dressed across the bed, to sleep or more likely to torture himself with the bitter gall of his rage.

Next day, his temper apparently controlled, he was waiting for the *Municipio* offices to open. There an official letter was drafted for him to take to the *Agente del Ministerio Público*. Our *Municipio* offices are busy and understaffed; sometimes it takes days for a letter to go through the mill. But he knew how to speed things up.

He tipped the girl typist, teased and flirted with her a bit, all with his big happy smile. Tall, handsome, merry, he was found by many women difficult to resist. The plain little typist did his letter, then took it in for the proper signatures and seals, before even touching the previous days' urgent correspondence.

After a brief visit with Don Quintín, the *Agente del Ministerio Público*, he used the same tactic to get the arrest warrant typed up. The order was addressed to the *Comandante* of the *Columna Volante* and stamped "Urgent." Don Domingo took it to Juan Pereyra personally. Just before noon Don Juan and eight of his mounted policemen set out for the Xucuapan. By noon of the next day he had his prisoners.

One error occurred, which can probably be attributed either to Domingo's impatience or to the thrilled confusion of one of the typists—the name of Felipe Reyes, whom Domingo had cited as a witness, somehow got into the list of culprits. Don Juan arrested four prisoners, not three.

Felipe was the last of the group to be taken. He was shocked, terrified, then angry. He was about to offer resistance, the only one of the four who came near to doing so, but Don Juan dissuaded him, talking to him as one does to soothe a frightened horse. The three actual thieves freely admitted their guilt, but insisted Felipe had no part in the affair.

"You have to come with me, Don Felipe, for your name is on the arrest order. It looks as though there has been a mistake; if there has, it'll soon be straightened out if you keep calm. Just take it easy. We'll just take a little ride to town. Come along quietly—if it's some sort of error you'll be back home in a couple of days."

The prisoners were in jail two days four hours. Don

Domingo had been notified, but took his time about appearing. Seventy-two hours is the maximum under the law that a person can be held without formal commitment to trial, for which an interrogation in the presence of material witnesses is usually required. Before he had time to tell Domingo of the mix-up, Don Juan had been ordered on another urgent mission down toward San Miguel.

The interrogation room is divided into two parts by a grill of vertical steel bars seven or eight inches apart, with three horizontal stabilizers. On one side is a desk and chairs, for the *Agente*, accuser, and witnesses; behind the bars is a small cubicle for the accused. Domingo was as astonished to see Felipe appear with the three thieves as Felipe had been at being arrested.

"Don Felipe, why are you . . ."

Felipe exploded into fury. "You miserable double-crossing bastard! Why did you do this to me?" His voice rose to a scream. "Why? Why?"

He clutched the steel bars to shake them, tear them apart, only succeeding in shaking himself in violent jerks. Sweat streamed down his flushed face, saliva dribbled from the corners of his mouth. A caged wild animal, no longer a person.

Andrés told me of the scene later. "I was scared of him, Don Pablo—nothing had frightened me up to then, but he scared me. I wanted to get out of that little room behind the bars—get away from him. I'd never seen anybody go crazy before."

"*Mierda!* You're nothing but *mierda!*" Felipe screeched. "Just because I owe you a few pesos you have me dragged off to jail! I'll pay you back your filthy pesos, and I'll pay you back for this too. When I get out I'll get you, *hijo de su chingada madre*—in the guts so you die screaming!"

"What you owe me has nothing to do with this!" Domingo shouted to break through the verbal flood. "I didn't intend for you to be arrested—I don't know how that happened." His voice thickened with anger; he smiled but it was not his usual happy smile, it was more like a snarl. "I just wanted you here as a witness, to squeal on your neighbors, the way you did to me at the ranch."

The danger of the statement penetrated Felipe's frenzy. His fellow prisoners had been staring at him in alarm, but now their expressions changed. It had not occurred to them that he might have been the informer.

"You lie! You lie!" screamed Felipe, still trying to shake the steel bars. "I don't know what they did, if they did anything. I was at Don Panuncio's store the day you say they killed your cow. It's your lousy pesos you're worrying about, you tightfisted . . ." and he loosed a torrent of invective and obscenity, a Devil's Litany of filth and vileness.

Some tall lanky men are loose-jointed, a trifle slow in reaction time. Don Domingo was cat-quick. He lunged, reaching a long arm between the bars, clutching at the slobbering Felipe, to maul him, yank him against the bars to hurt him. But he felt a hard hand on his arm. It was Don Quintín.

"Stop it, Mingo! This is an office of the law—no violence, no nonsense here."

"But you heard . . ."

"Stop it, I tell you. We're friends but if you disrespect the law, on the other side of the bars you go."

"But you heard what he said, didn't you? No man can say such things to me and live!"

"It means nothing, Mingo."

"Nothing? It means something to me. And he threatened my life, too—didn't you hear him?"

"Look, Mingo, all that means nothing. Sit down and

I'll explain." Don Quintín eased him back toward his chair. "Town characters, bums and drunks and petty crooks, think it's funny to go to jail. But some of these backwoods people go frantic when they're locked up. They yell all kinds of foolishness. After a bit they get it off their chests and talk sense. I go through this almost every day. Don't pay any attention to it."

"That's easy for you to say; it wasn't you he was calling . . ."

"Shut up, Don Domingo, or I'll stop this right now. If the complaining witness doesn't cooperate with the law . . ."

"All right. I'll keep still." But Domingo's voice still grated.

"Let's get this straightened out first. Mingo, you're not accusing this Don Felipe of cow stealing?"

"No. I wanted him . . ."

The *Agente* interrupted. "What do the other accused say? Which of you is Don Emeterio Palma?"

"I am."

"What about this man?"

"He had nothing to do with it. We, the three of us, butchered and sold Don Domingo's cow. We admit it. Don Felipe wasn't with us. He came next day, to buy a half kilo of stew meat. I don't know how he squealed on us."

"He didn't." Don Quintín believes in preventing, as well as correcting, crime. He knew Don Domingo's deliberate accusation could lead to more trouble. But he guessed wrong on the course the trouble would take. "Don Domingo just said that because he was mad. I've been over the case with him: what 'squealed' on you three—what gave you away—were the tracks you left on the river's edge, loading the meat into the canoe."

"We don't deny we did it. But Felipe wasn't with us."

"In that case the prisoner should be freed. I'll write an order for it, so we can get on with this thing about the cow."

"Wait a minute." Don Domingo's vindictive streak would not be calmed. "Felipe didn't have any part, so far as I know, in stealing my cow, but he owes for another crime. You might as well make the most of the chance, now you have him in possession."

"What crime?"

"He wounded another man with a machete—Amado Contreras."

"When was this?"

"A couple of years ago—nearly three now, on the Día de la Santa Cruz, the third of May. I know, because it was at a *fiesta* I gave on the night of the second to dawn on the third."

"Was this reported? It was your duty to report it, if it occurred on your premises."

"To the local authorities. I had no way of knowing if they reported it to the *Municipio* or not."

Felipe gradually realized what was being done to him. He began to scream again. "More of your lies! That was all settled! Don Ignacio was *Agente Municipal* then—he fined us fifty pesos apiece—said it was a minor affair, and even—our wounds were about the same. Amado cut me a little bit on the shoulder, here"—he ripped his shirt loose to reveal a small scar—"and I cut him on the forearm. We'd been drinking the *aguardiente* Don Domingo was peddling at the *fiesta*. It wasn't us—it was the *aguardiente* that made us fight. They stopped us and that was it. Don Amado and I had no trouble afterward."

"If blood was drawn it was a serious offense," Don Quintín proclaimed. "In that case . . ."

"Blood there was in plenty," interrupted Domingo. "They bled like stuck hogs, the both of them, but Amado bled more."

"Where is this Don Amado now?"

"Dead. He drowned last January. Capsized his canoe in a big freshet."

"Well, if it happened that long ago, and the injured party is dead, there's nothing much to it. If there were someone to file charges, formally, I'd have to take action, but without a complainant there isn't anything for me to do."

"I'll file the charges." Domingo's voice rasped with poorly controlled temper.

"You! On what grounds?"

"It happened on my premises, didn't it? I could have been implicated."

"You can do it, legally, Don Domingo." Don Quintín stared at him. "But are you sure you really want to?"

"Of course I am," Domingo snarled.

THE WAY the thing worked out, with Don Quintín braking Domingo's desire for vengeance, the cow thieves were not even committed for trial. They agreed to pay Domingo for the cow and the administrative costs, such as the travel of the *Columna*. The cow turned out to have been the most valuable animal that ever ate grass in the Xucuapan, at least according to the price Domingo set on her, but the thieves paid for her just the same—stayed in jail until their relatives raised the money. Domingo wanted to charge them for another cow he had lost some months previously, but Don Quintín wouldn't permit him to do it.

The one who came off worst was Felipe Reyes. He was charged with something that corresponds to "armed assault." Don Quintín apparently talked it over with the judge, so Felipe was let off with a minimal fine. But he stayed in jail awhile. His relatives are poor or improvident: they had difficulties in raising money even for the small fine. His brother-in-law Benito finally scraped together most of the amount.

Gossips' tongues clacked along the river. The high value Domingo put on his cow was regarded as a good joke—it evened things up for having been sold his own beef. It would have been better, people said, had he arranged the settlement on the Xucuapan instead of taking it outside, to town—Don Panuncio or Don Chon could have presided at the settlement, keeping it in the family as it were, without the *Columna Volante* and the *Agente*. But Domingo was sort of half a townsman now, since he had moved his family to town. What was most criticized was the treatment of Felipe. It was generally recognized that Felipe's arrest had been an accident, but the bringing of the old, once-settled charge was resented, no matter what language the distraught prisoner had used. Or so went the local consensus. Then other things happened to give the gossips something to roll their tongues over: Don Pedro Reynosa's long-suffering wife, Maricarmen, chased her temporary co-wife (also her niece) out of the house with a machete; one of my cows had twin calves, both of which survived. As time went by, people tended to forget about the brown cow. But not all of them. Not Felipe.

9

Hunters' Traverse

THE *norte* had been driving in water-drenched clouds for more than twenty-four hours, forming a low overcast that let no glimmer of starlight through. There had been no twilight; when the sun that had grayly lighted the day dipped below the western horizon, no atmospheric reflections of light filtered through. The night went black, dead murky black as though someone had slammed a door shut.

But, for all their violence, early fall *nortes* are short-lived. The heavy downpour had slacked to a drizzle in late afternoon. But it was a wet drizzle, soggy and wind driven, which soaked one through. My *compadre* Candelario and wiry little Don Alberto were dripping water in great puddles on the porch from their saturated denims when I went to the door.

"Come in," I said, after the inevitable interchange of "*Buenas noches.*"

"No thanks, we'll get everything wet."

"It doesn't matter. Come in out of the wind. Are you going hunting in this vile weather?" Don Candelario had asked me if he might hunt the near pastures.

"This is just the night for it," said Alberto. "In this kind of small rain the deer come out into the open pastures to play and caper all night long."

Candelario said, "We're certain to find a deer tonight. But we need a flashlight bulb. Our flashlight dropped, broke the bulb." He used the reflexive form *se cayó*, "it dropped itself," blaming the flashlight rather than telling me which of them had been clumsy. "Can you lend us one?"

"I'll look. Maria," I called, "can you warm up some coffee for my *compadre* and Don Alberto?"

The coffeepot had been on the kitchen fire. She served them big cups of the steaming black liquid while I found a spare flashlight bulb. "Here it is—it's the last spare I have. I hope it works."

Don Alberto took the flashlight apart, replaced the bulb, reassembled the lantern, tried it, shining the light into the shadow under the table. "That's a good bulb," he said. "Nicely centered. That's just right for jacklighting."

"Where are you going to hunt?" I asked.

"Where I told you, *compadre*," Candelario answered, "in the Pará grass along the edge of the cacao orchard, and then over in the Playas pasture. You told me there are no cattle in either place."

"No, there are no cattle there. Can you cross the Arroyo del Carmen? It was rising when I crossed late this afternoon."

"It won't be up to the bridge yet. Don't you want to come along?"

"Thanks, I think not. I was wet all day. I put on dry clothes when I got home, and I'd rather stay dry."

"This will be a good hunting night," said Alberto. "There are sure to be deer prancing around the pastures."

"No, you two go. I'll wish you luck. If you kill a big one, I'll buy some meat."

"Good. We'll sell you a quarter."

They went out into the dark, Don Alberto with the light, and my *compadre* carrying his single-barreled 16-gauge slung over his shoulder, muzzle down.

Passing through the gate shutting off the small pasture below the house, they slanted eastward through the knee-deep Pará grass. Alberto took the lead, swinging the flash from side to side in rapid arcs. The wind and the faint hiss of the drizzling rain covered the small sounds they made, the rustle of the grass against their sopping pant-legs, and the faint squishing of their bare feet on the muddy ground. Nearing the orchard fence they turned faces into the wind, due north.

Alberto's light caught a reflection. He steadied it on two red spots, incandescent ruby red in the night. "Owl," he muttered.

"I know, said Candelario curtly. "Keep the light off him. Let him eat the rats and mice that chew up my *compadre*'s grass."

Beyond the orchard, near the far corner of the pasture, two oval yellow-green lights gleamed, reflecting the flash-light's beam. Deer! Don Alberto froze, steadying the light. But the deer turned his head away and disappeared into the blackness. His eyes reflected only when he looked directly into the light. In vain Alberto swept the light in the direction he seemed to have gone. They heard little splashes as he trotted through a shallow puddle, then nothing but the drizzling rain, the shush of windswept palm fronds.

"*Jívaro*, the *hijo de puta*," Candelario said. "Been shot at before at night."

The pair saw nothing more as they turned westward, hunting the edges of the bamboo thickets that flank the *arroyo* between the two pastures. The drizzle increased, the wind felt raw and cold. At the main trail they went through the pasture gate to the flooding stream, now roiling and swirling, ugly in the flashlight's beam.

"It will be over the bridge before long."

"We can go back the long way around. But we should get a deer soon."

Just over the hill from the stream, where the ridge drops off into the wide flat plain of the Playas pasture, a pair of yellow-green eyes flashed from the blackness.

"Deer!" Alberto breathed. "This is ours, he's quiet."

"He's too far. Let's move up on him."

Candelario was abreast of Alberto now, gun at the ready. They inched forward, slowly, soundlessly, testing their footing at each step. The deer stood quite still, fascinated by the disc of bright light, partly blinded by it but feeling safe in the shelter of the thick darkness. He could not know that his own eyes, great yellow-green reflecting mirrors, were betraying him.

The hunters closed in until the light outlined the deer's head and neck, which showed grayish, less black than the night. The buck lowered his head, then raised it, trying to peer behind the beam.

"Now!" Alberto murmured. "He's nervous; he won't hold much longer."

Candelario leveled the shotgun, silhouetting the bead against the dimly lit patch that was the deer's neck, and squeezed the trigger. A great yellow flame erupted, leaving him momentarily blinded. Don Alberto had shielded his eyes with his free hand, could still see.

"You hit him," he shouted. "He's down!" Then he sprinted forward, drawing his machete while Don Candelario tried to pry the swollen cartridge case from the chamber of the gun. But Alberto did not have to machete the deer. The animal was dead. Three buckshot pellets had hit its neck, two lodging in the vertebrae. Two others had penetrated the breast, a sixth had lodged in the shoulder. The heavy-choke 16-gauge held a good pattern.

Don Alberto poked the fat sides of the deer with the tip of his machete. "He's fat. And *por Dios Santo*, he's a big one."

Candelario was digging a couple of rolls of *mecate*, strips of a tough, flexible bark used for tying and lashing and making tumplines, out of his pockets. "He's all right. Let's get him tied up; you help me get him on my back and I'll carry him the first haul."

They lashed the deer's legs together, crossed tight across his belly with a tricky tie that left a loop in the middle for a tumpline. They rolled him over to tie his head to his underside so it would not flap about. Candelario squatted, slipped the tumpline over his forehead, and, with Alberto lifting and steadying the deer, rocked forward and rose to his feet in one motion. The carcass weighed well over a hundred pounds.

THERE ARE TWO KINDS of deer in the forests of southern Mexico. One is the tropical deer, a pygmy, beautifully formed but tiny—eighteen to twenty inches high at the shoulder when full-grown. The male has unbranching black spikes, for which reason it is often called *cabrito*, "little goat," as well as by its proper Nahau name of *mazate*. The other is a big deer, like the one Candelario and Alberto killed, very like the whitetail deer of temperate zones. Perhaps it is a whitetail. Most are sorrel red, though some vary to a buckskin yellow, others to a dark seal brown. Many males grow sets of symmetrically branched horns, rather small but neatly formed. Others, however, have deformed horns, gnarled branchless lumps. The right horn of this particular deer was a blunt stub five inches long and nearly an inch and a half thick, lumpy and malformed; the other was a short tapered spiral twisted low and flat close to the animal's skull. Perhaps such deformities are caused by mosquitoes and biting flies while the horns are developing and still tender. But insects plague deer in northern climes too, and misshapen horns are rare. My *compadre* Candelario considers such deer a separate species. However, it is a strictly academic problem here on the Xucuapan, for we are interested in venison, not trophy heads.

JACKLIGHTING is probably not a very sporting way to hunt deer. But here, where the animals spend most of their daylight hours in jungles or in the tangles of second growth, which a man cannot penetrate without hacking his way through with a machete, or in the thickets of savagely thorned bamboo, the only effective way to hunt deer is to take advantage of the times when they come out into the open. Don Mario, he of the singing snake, is the only person I know who crawls on his belly under the thorny bamboo in quest of deer—and he doesn't do it as often as he tells about it. (I have tried it several times, but each time a lizard skittering across the mat of dry bamboo leaves sounded so much like a snake that I quickly got up and hacked my way out with my machete, warning away any deer that might be around.) The only practical way to hunt in such places is with dogs, and no one hereabouts has dogs big enough to overtake and pull down a deer or well trained enough to drive deer out into the open.

LATE ONE AFTERNOON I sat on a hillside trying to look as much like a tree stump as possible. The real stump that I leaned against was weathered to a tawny gray, so my faded khakis would be indistinguishable from it in the failing light of dusk. A few spindly bushes in front of me completed my camouflage. Deer came out into this section of pasture from the jungle's edge, for the ground was littered with fresh tracks every morning and here and there shoots and leaf buds that deer like were nibbled off. But neither early in the night nor late had I been able to "shine" one's eyes, though I had prowled the ridges for several nights. Don Rufino, to whom I posed the problem, suggested that perhaps the deer came out to play and browse for short periods about dusk.

We needed meat. No one had killed any game for some weeks; the river was high, so fishing was poor. Maria had gone through her repertoire of things she could do with chicken: stewed fricasseed, in tamales, until we couldn't stand the thought of another chicken dinner. She had begun to complain gently about the dull diet of black beans, rice, and eggs. I wanted to kill a good fat deer.

I had come early, to be in place long before deer were likely to appear. My pony was tied to a *nanche* tree, bridle off so he could graze a bit, on the other side of the ridge— I would not have to worry about shooting him in the bad light. Smeared with insect repellent, I sat back against the stump, rifle across my knees. I even had a book to read, one a friend had sent me from the States that I had been saving for a special occasion. It was a scholarly discussion of the life of the Ancient Hunters of North America, how they hunted mammoths and huge bison and other creatures. It was all very erudite, but as I read I began to wonder if the author had ever sat on a side-hill, rifle on his knees, mosquitoes and biting gnats buzzing about his ears, waiting to see if game would come out of the forest. I decided he had not, so I laid the book down, moving carefully. I did not have to be rigidly still; I could move gently, no more brusquely than the leaves that danced on the branches of the trees to my left and the weeds and bushes that swayed before me from the light northerly breeze.

Sitting in a blind bores me. I would rather be moving about. But this time there were many things to watch to help pass the time. An iridescent green hummingbird darted back and forth, saw a long red blossom, hovered in front of it with his wings making a blur of motion while he probed for small insects. He then reversed the pitch of his wings to back away, remained poised in the air while he turned his head from side to side looking for other flowers, and darted off. He was hunting too. But he could cover more ground than I could.

A large green grasshopper, of the kind that are excellent bluegill bait, came sailing from somewhere to land on one of the skimpy stalks of bush in front of me. He climbed busily up the stalk, testing with his mouth parts as he went along—I was close enough to see him moving them—didn't like what he found and took off in a long jump with whirring wings, down the slope and over the little bench below.

A flight of yellow-headed parrots came over, shouting happily on their way to their roosting place. I noticed they crossed low over the ridge behind me. I could hammer them with the shotgun from a blind on the ridgetop. Two of those parrots yield about as much meat as a hen, are tastier, and the kids like them because they are game. But I dropped the idea when I thought about looking for downed green parrots in the green grass. It would be better to get up on the ridge before dawn and get them on the way out—they probably flew the same course to their feeding grounds in the mornings, so I would have plenty of daylight to search by instead of fighting the dwindling twilight.

A two-inch ribbon of big fat black ants, the kind we call *pepegua*, marched by just in front of my feet. They gave the impression of going somewhere for a purpose. I watched them with more than casual interest. If they wanted my tree stump I would let them have it. They sting like burning hell. And there were thousands of them, maybe tens of thousands. Happily they went about their business, whatever it was, and which did not involve my stump. One of the big brown *peya* jaybirds began to scream vulgarities from a *varaprieta* tree on the edge of the woods; I stared into the shadows at the edge of the forest wall, for sometimes a deer walking in the woods sets the *peyas* off. But I saw nothing; perhaps the jay was just practicing. When I looked back down, the ants had gone by.

It was getting dark. The shadow of the tall jungle on my left had stretched across me as the sun dipped—now it stretched to the eastern edge of the world. I raised the rifle slowly, checked the sights; the front blade still showed clear in the rear notch. I was all right for a little while.

It turned darker. I wanted to smoke, but then jeered at myself for being stupid, for if a deer was to come out of the woods this was the time. No smoking. A mosquito found a place where the sweat had washed the repellent from the back of my neck. I let him bite. Straining my eyes, I was aware that the darkness was increasing.

The deer appeared between two bushes at the jungle's edge, a shadow amidst shadows. He stood, neck stretched high, turning his head from side to side, ears forward as he sniffed the breeze and stared through the twilight gloom. I did not lift the rifle. This was no time for the slightest movement. So long as I sat very still he could not distinguish me. He moved forward a few steps, froze to rigidity as he searched out dangers of the great open space by looking, smelling, hearing. A yearling, chunky fat, spike horns glimmering in the dim light. Then he snorted—"whistled" as some call the noisy exhalation that is the deer's warning signal—exploded into a series of jumps, fantastic play-jumps high into the air like a bucking horse but with head erect, not down between his forefeet.

Spinning in midair, he lifted his tail and bristled his rump so that the patch of white hair flashed, then wheeled and sprinted farther out into the clearing. Rearing suddenly on his hind legs he lashed out with his forefeet, ducked his head to hook right and left with his horns, shadowboxing, as he dropped to all fours again. Neck arched, he turned to face the woods, giving me a chance to raise the rifle. It had to be a standing shot; no one could lead an animal that one moment jumped high in the air and the next sprinted like a quarter horse. The last glimmer of light from the west showed the ivory bead of the front sight. I centered on the middle of the neck for a clean kill, and squeezed the trigger so that metal slid smoothly over metal freeing the spring that would force metal against explosive to drive the lethal pellet. There was a dull click. With my taut senses I heard or felt a tiny rattle, a tonality within the sound of metal on metal that I read "broken firing pin." But I refused to believe.

The little deer heard the click too, but took it as something to play with. Bounding high in the air to land in the same spot, sprinting a few steps, he stopped directly in front of me, stared at the source of the interesting sound, and kicked his hind feet into the air. I worried the bolt back with as little noise as possible. The cartridge did not eject, and I had to fumble it out manually. It was too dark to see if the base had been dented by the firing pin, which would have meant a defective cartridge, as I wanted to believe. My fingers found another round in my shirt pocket, slid it into the chamber, eased the bolt shut. Meanwhile the little buck cavorted and kicked until, turning, he faced me from the forest's edge, a black shadow amid almost-black shadows. I leveled the rifle. I could not see the sights.

The flashlight was positioned in a notch of the tree trunk I sat on, so there was no need to search for it. I simply lowered my left hand to pick it up and steady it along the forearm of the rifle, thumb on the switch. The yellow cone of light burst through the dark. The little buck flinched, then froze staring into the beam, his almond-shaped eyes gleaming bright yellow. Sights black against the light, front blade cradled in the rear sight's notch, centered on his throat, finger pressing the trigger—and the same flat metallic click. A wave of black rage surged up, burning in my head, pulsing in my ears. I was about to hurl the rifle spinning flat, so if it did not hit the deer it would shatter on the tree trunks—but somehow controlled myself. I switched off the light.

Released from the light's magic spell, the deer snorted and ran bucking in front of me. As my eyes readjusted to the dark I saw him kick his heels high, rear up to shadowbox, race out of sight to the end of the hill. The metallic clicks and the beam of light had been only playthings to pretend to be frightened at, or to pretend to fight. Then he scampered back in front of me and paused, staring, waiting for more of the fascinating clicks. He pretended he heard one, leapt into the air, sprinted a short distance, stopped, his white tail and rump making a patch in the dark. Then, as though a whistle had been blown to signal the end of the game, he walked quietly away to merge into the black darkness of the jungle. Lighting a cigarette, I stood up and began assembling my belongings: repellent, spare cartridges, the book on the Ancient Hunters. I walked down to the trail, down the hill, and over the ridge to the *nanche* tree to my horse. At least I had actually seen how deer play in the clearings.

As I unsaddled at the edge of the porch I reported my failure.

"*Ai, papi*," Maria wailed, "why didn't you take the shotgun or the pistol, instead of that miserable rifle?"

"*Caramba*, I've told you, the rifle is the proper weapon. A deer could just as well have come out on the bench a hundred yards or more below. The shotgun won't hold to that distance; I can kill a deer at forty or fifty yards with the pistol, but I can't hit one at a hundred."

"I was so hoping you'd bring home some venison. Well, maybe tomorrow. How do you want your supper eggs?"

I couldn't tolerate eggs. Temper began to well up in me; I choked it back—I, not she, had lost the deer. "Just coffee, *mamacita*. Maybe a toasted *tortilla*."

THE DEER'S HABIT of coming out to frisk about the pastures at night intrigued me. Deer are forest animals. They do not slip out under the cover of night to graze, for, although they may nibble a few tender new shoots of grass and weeds, they are really browsing animals whose main diet is weeds, vines, and bushes in the woods, and even fruits, but not grass. Deer feed more like goats than cows. So why do they come out into the pastures? Could this be a new behavior pattern developed in the few decades that clearings have been made? What did they do when there were no clearings? One day, quite by chance, I found out.

It was far behind the Jó pasture, beyond our farm. Last year two of Don Margarito's sons cleared a big tract there and planted maize, and since then they have been planting pasture grasses. Before then it was all virgin jungle, without an ax mark to be seen for several miles west to Arroyo Bravo and south for a vast stretch all the way up the slopes of the mountains.

Feliciano had suggested that the woods flanking the pasture might be a good source for posts for a corral I wanted to build. One might imagine that finding fence and corral posts in the great forests would be no problem. But it is. First, one wants certain species only, tough durable hardwoods. And they must be of a certain size. A tree two or three feet in diameter, of dense heavy wood, is useless for posts unless one has a sawmill to cut it into pieces of manageable size. Consequently one looks for stands of timber where there are many hardwoods among the second growth, straight young trees five to ten inches through.

Leaving my horse tied in the shade, I hacked my way through a belt of bushes, dense because they got sun from the pasture side. Beyond this barrier travel was easy, for the undergrowth was sparse for the most part. The serene quiet of the jungle, its cathedral-like tranquillity, was soothing and pleasant, so pleasant that I kept going, on and on, far past practical distance for cutting and carrying out posts. I was playing hookey; there were more useful things to be done than puttering around in the forest. I rationalized that since I had never been back in this particular area, I should find out what sort of country it was.

Not much game let itself be seen—a pair of tinamou scuttled noisily through the dead leaves, then took flight with a great whirring of wings (I looked in vain for a nest at the bases of nearby trees—Maria wanted a clutch of the bright blue eggs to set under a hen). Some time later a faint chirping, almost but not quite birdlike, made me peer through a rift in the lower canopy. High up in the treetops a troop of spider monkeys marched in orderly fashion along a thick liana between two tree crowns and disappeared into the foliage. But animals were all about, as patches of soft damp earth along rivulets and swampy places attested: squirrels, mice, rabbits, and straggly-toed opossums had left their tracks as had larger creatures, like deer and peccary. Twice I saw the three-toed track of a tapir, some days old, and once a set of fresh jaguar prints. Most of the roster of the local fauna was imprinted in the ground.

Then I found the answer to my queries about the deer. Ahead of me between the tree trunks gleamed an expanse of bright orange-red subsoil clays. As I came to it, I found a low mound, a foot or so high, forming an irregular ellipse nearly twenty feet long by a dozen wide. It was a huge nest of leafcutter ants, the busy little creatures that nip leaves into ragged bits half an inch across (they will quickly strip a large tree of its leaves) then march back to their nest by thousands along their neatly cleaned roads, each worker ant with his bit of leaf clutched vertically between his pincers, so that it looks like a tiny green sail. The ants let no plant grow on the mound of clay they excavate from deep in the ground. The sprawling clay mounds make permanent clearings in the forest. This one, bigger than most, was covered with deer tracks made the night before or early that morning—tracks of a single animal who had raced around and around the patch of red clay, criss-crossed back and forth, his hooves printing wide V's where he had driven hard to leap high and all four bunched close together where he landed as he jumped and kicked and cavorted gaily in the tiny open space in the jungle.

DEER STRAY OUT into the open by day, but irregularly and sporadically. Their appearance cannot be predicted by time of day or weather or season. My friends working in the fields and pastures, and I riding the pastures daily, may not see the sun shine on a deer in three months. Then several deer will be seen on a single day, or one or two may appear every day for a week or two. But such erratic behavior does not make it worthwhile to dedicate daytime to hunting, especially when the chances are much better of encountering the animals by night.

Local people cope with this problem by taking their rifles and shotguns to work, for what I call hunting by happenstance. Once in a while a deer or peccary crosses the trail in front of a man on his way to or from a daily chore; sometimes one walks out into the clearing where he is working. In the field or pasture the weapon is hung in the shade of the tree or bush where the ubiquitous *morral* of *pozole* is slung. Days follow days when the gun might as well have been left at home. Sooner or later, though, a deer appears. The farmer turns hunter, picking up his weapon to begin a long stalk. Most men discard hats and shirts in the belief that a mop of black hair and a bronze back is less likely to alert the deer than a yellow palm-fiber hat and a blue work shirt.

The luckiest people I know for chance encounters with game are Chepe Joloche and Don Alberto for different reasons. Chepe is just plain lucky. Two or three people may walk along a trail ten or fifteen minutes or half an hour apart and encounter nothing. Then Chepe comes straggling along, and a deer or a peccary walks out into the trail to stand there looking at him. I resent Chepe's luck, because he is a poor hunter—he cripples more game than he kills outright, and he seldom tracks the cripples down. Don Alberto makes the most of his luck because he works at his hunting the way he works at clearing his fields and planting his crops. When he cripples an ani-

mal he trails it, all day long if need be, not because he is
sentimental about letting a wounded animal suffer but
simply because he has invested a cartridge, which makes
the creature rightfully his.

One afternoon I was on my way home after a long day
looking for a newborn calf. The cow had calved in the
upper Amate pasture. Although her udder was swollen
with milk, she would not go near the calf while I was
in sight. When I found her infant by chance, she became
obstreperous—I don't know where those old cows pump
all that adrenalin from—and set about determinedly to
drive me away. She came in hooking right and left with
those big wide horns and my pony, usually alert, was sluggish, so I had to draw blood with my spurs to keep from
getting knocked down. So it was necessary to rope the cow
to tie her to a tree to be able to take care of the nice little
red calf with the long droopy zebu ears and the little zebu
hump on his withers. These things take time. Consequently I was two or three hours late for my appointments.
Chepe and my *compadre* Candelario had sent word that
they wanted to see me. My *compadre* had finished a weeding contract and wanted to be paid. Chepe wanted to
borrow a saw and plane.

As I jogged homeward over the ridges, Don Alberto
arrived at the house. He had been drinking. His *morral*
clinked glassily as he walked. He and Chepe are not
congenial; Chepe decided to wait no longer, so he set
off down the trail toward the Arroyo del Carmen. Two
hundred yards or so from the house a deer was eating
tololoche berries dangling from a long strand of vine from
an *apompo* tree, at the edge of the swale not twenty yards
from the path. Chepe slipped his shotgun from his shoulder, and fired. The deer fell, then jumped up and ran into
the tall weeds and bushes at the bottom of the swale.

I was crossing the last ridge, the open cleared one behind the house, just across the same swale Chepe's deer had gone into. From the end of the weed patch toward me the swale is planted to Pará grass, which grows knee-high, and the low ridges on either side are in open pasture—visibility is without hindrance. From the ridge I saw a tiny figure—Chepe running into the tall weeds in the swale.

It so happened that the three milch cows were in that little pasture, and one of them had a red calf—a deer-red calf. I spurred down the hill across the soggy hollow to the gate below the house to find out what was going on. There I found my *compadre* and Don Alberto.

"Who's shooting here in the house pasture?" I shouted, with no greetings. "I saw somebody that looked like Chepe."

"It must have been Chepe."

"He left the house a few minutes ago," my *compadre* put in.

"Let's go see what he killed." I was worried about the calf.

We found Chepe looking for tracks in the open swale, south of the weeds, in the Pará grass. "I just killed a deer, a big buck, a real whopper," he called as we came up. "He was right near where you are, eating at that *tololoche* vine. He's lying in here dead somewhere."

"Sure it wasn't the red calf?" That was being pretty crude, but I wanted to find out.

"Calf? I said it was a deer, and a big one!" Chepe's voice throbbed with righteous indignation.

"Are you sure you hit him?" Candelario asked.

"Am I sure! Right back of the elbow. There's a big splash of blood where he fell, right near you. He couldn't have gone far."

It was true—there was a conspicuous red smear amid crushed small weeds and grass.

"He went right up the middle of the swale, through the Pará," added Chepe. "I'm working out his trail—he must be here close."

Alberto continued the interrogation. "Did you hit him good?"

"I told you, right through the heart. Sometimes they run a short way, but they can't run far when they're shot like that."

If the deer had run out into the open as Chepe said, I should have seen him from the ridge, a red deer running over low grass in the afternoon sun. I had looked down the hollow as soon as I heard the shot.

"Are you sure he didn't cross into the thicket behind the swale. Don Chepe?"

"No, he came this way. Here are his tracks in the mud." To my *compadre* and Alberto I said, "If the deer had run up the swale I'd surely have seen him. Chepe must be following some tracks made last night—they come out here a lot at night—I'm just waiting till the moon wanes to kill one. Let's look back in the brush."

They were conspicuously uninterested. Chepe had not asked us to help him; it would be meddling in his affairs.

"Come on," I pleaded. "Chepe did hit the deer—all that blood—and he's going to lose it, looking in the wrong direction. I tell you if the deer had run out into the open where Chepe says I would have seen him from the ridge. I'm going to have a look."

Chepe had trampled out most of the trail down in the weeds, but there was a smear of blood on a *tanai* leaf that indicated the wounded animal had run on a course that could have taken him where Chepe was searching. My idea was that the deer had cut the ankle-deep water in the weed patch. There were myriad little trails where deer had pushed through the soft dense growth. I tried the first, which seemed to lead toward the high ground behind the swale. There was no sign of fresh travel. I returned to try the next one. There, on a bare spot on the damp clay of the bank above the waterline, was a splay-toed track—gleaming fresh—where a deer had passed running hard. It was smaller than I had expected—Chepe had said it was a big buck—but it was new, just made. I looked back. Candelario and Alberto were poking about in the weeds with an obvious lack of enthusiasm.

"*Compadre!* Don Alberto!" I shouted. "Here's where he went! Come help me track him!"

They walked toward me, dully.

"Where's Chepe?"

"Tracking, way up the hollow, close to the fence."

"Here's where the deer went. Look at his track!"

"Mm-hm." Not much interest. My *compadre* didn't want to become involved with Chepe's deer, and Don Alberto was high. Not much help from them, I decided.

They looked about. The leaf-littered high ground was dry and hard, made tracking difficult. Candi moved dry leaves gently with the tip of his machete, looking for some mark on the ground beneath.

Suddenly, a couple of yards from the print on the bank, he called, "Here's blood!" His voice turned crisp. Alberto and I leaned over to see: there was a droplet of blood, the tiniest dot of crimson, on a dead leaf.

"*Caramba*, Don Pablo was right!" Alberto whispered. "Here's where he went!"

The two transformed as by magic. They became alert, eager, Alberto quite sober. They were hunting.

We searched but found no more blood spots. "Why so little blood?" I asked.

"Sometimes they don't bleed much, with buckshot," Alberto muttered. "Rifle bullets sometimes come out the other side—that's when they leave the most blood sign."

They took over. I consider myself a good tracker, but I couldn't have followed that trail. I tagged behind, leaving the task to the experts.

I said the ground was hard and dry, littered with dead leaves. Strands of vines—the cat-clawed *chapapul* and its ilk—laced the small trees and bushed into a seemingly impenetrable mass. I marveled as I always do that an animal as large as a deer could slip swift and silent through such a snarl.

Candi and Alberto walked abreast, on either side of the deer's trail, crouching slightly, snipping through the vines with wrist-action slashes of their machetes. They took great care not to trample out the faint track; sometimes they turned back to check where the quarry momentarily confused them by zigzagging around a tree or other obstacle. They moved fast, just touching the sign with their machete tips: a crushed dry leaf, a faint streak on the ground beneath another, the bruised stalk of a stepped-on plant. The finder pointed with his machete, the other grunted affirmation. They were not talking much but were saving their breath and energy for the rapid slash-slash-slash that opened the way through the tangle. The steel blades rang softly, clingg! clingg! In the thicket the trapped air was sticky hot. Once Alberto checked a swing in midair to point—a red deer hair caught on a thorn. When they pointed out the signs I could see and read them, but I would have missed most of them in fighting my way through the tangle.

They paused. Candi gestured with his machete. "Gutshot, looks like. But he can still run."

Alberto interpreted for me, flat-voiced, "He's hurting; he lay down and rolled here."

Squatting to look closely, I saw a deer hair, then another and another, then a pattern of them over and among the crinkled and crushed leaves.

He went on. And on. Clingg! clingg! clingg! sang the steel blades. A turned dry leaf. A trampled plant. A faint streak on the hard ground.

"He's getting weak," murmured Alberto, "fell here." He pointed to two blurs side by side, where dead leaves had been jostled.

"Went to his knees," whispered my *compadre*.

"Fell clear down, maybe?" I pointed triumphantly to a deer hair on the ground to the right.

"No. Leaves aren't mashed down there. He scraped it loose on that bush—there's another hair caught in the bark."

Daylight, never strong in the thickets, was weakening. If we didn't find the deer soon we would lose him. The hunters crouched lower, but moved a little more slowly.

We came on a long slant to the edge of the *arroyo*. There the banks are a dozen feet apart, six feet vertical on either side. The deer had cut back sharply downstream.

"He's hurt bad—afraid to jump across. We'll find him soon."

On through the dense bush. Then my *compadre* stopped short, held up a warning hand. "There she is! Shoot quick, she wants to get up!"

He had left his gun at the house. Alberto's slung .22 slithered off his shoulder, leveled as the wounded animal tried to get her front feet under her to rise, swung her head sideways to the disturbance we were making. A sharp clean crack! and her travail was over.

My matches were sweat-soaked in the pocket of my dripping shirt, but we found one that would light. Don Alberto let long streams of smoke trickle from his nostrils.

" 'A big buck! A whopper,' says Don Chepe. 'Shot

through the heart,' he says. What a hunter, that Chepe Joloche!"

It was a small gut-shot doe.

DON ALBERTO's hunting luck he makes himself, by working at it. When not in his fields he is usually running peccary with his pack of yapping dogs back in the rugged steep ridges. That is hard enough work for anyone; the couple of times I've gone with him I've discovered that the horseback habit, while it may be good exercise in some respects, does little to keep one's cross-country racing muscles in shape.

Peccary can be hunted in the thickets and jungle with dogs because at intervals they stop to turn on their pursuers. A peccary at bay, his tailless rump protected between the buttress roots of a big tree, is formidable—woe betide the reckless dog that comes too close. Those long curved tusks slash like a machete. But the repeated defensive stands make it possible for the hunter, running, hacking a slit through the vines and undergrowth, scrambling uphill and down, to catch up to his quarry. Don Alberto delights in such lung-bursting, leg-aching races through the woods.

Here there are three species of peccary: a small reddish one, generally considered the most ill-tempered and aggressive; a grizzled gray variety, twenty to thirty pounds big, much like the collared peccary of the arid country of northern Mexico and the American Southwest but without the white collar called *jabalí* or *puerco de monte*, "jungle pig." The third is the *marín*, darker and half again as big as the *jabalí*, with a distinctive white patch on either jowl.

These animals, old-timers relate, used to roam the jungles in great droves, by the hundreds, they say, each species separately of course, although some people claim that the droves of *marín*, the white-jowled breed, were led by a "guide" of the small red kind. While small bands usually scatter and flee when attacked by dogs, turning only occasionally to fight off their pursuers, the large herds are said to have been more aggressive. There are tales of dog packs being encircled, then torn to shreds, and of human hunters suddenly finding themselves the hunted and having to spend uncomfortable hours in the branches of trees. Large droves are no longer to be found in the Xucuapan, though they still occur in the wildernesses high up the mountain slopes.

Late in May six years ago a great drove of *marín*, two hundred some, came down from the mountains. There had been not a drop of rain, and the country was parched dry. Fields of maize planted too early in the month were sallow yellow. The river was low, for a rarity unpleasantly warm; the larger *arroyos* were shrunken, the smaller ones dried up altogether. High on the mountain slopes to the south the thousands of tiny trickles and springs must have gone dry. The rivulets they merged to form dried too—the streamlets that normally bounced gaily down the gullies in chains of small clear cold pools turned to dry streaks on the rocks and pockets of dusty gravels. The herd of big peccary must have begun to work down the slopes, sniffing the stream beds for dampness, farther and farther downhill, guided perhaps in part by instinct, in part sensing increasing moisture in the lower courses of the streamlets. Other thirsty droves may have found water in the upper courses of the rivers. But this drove, thirsty in the stifling hot shade of the rocky slopes, somehow missed the upper watering places and came down into the foothill country. Here the animals found water, not abundant, but enough. But they were far from their *querencia*, their normal range where they had lived, where they knew their way—knew the feeding grounds, the watering places, the sheltered spots in stormy weather—where they had felt at home. So they kept moving, northward, the direction in which they had begun their search, bewildered, ill at ease, lost.

That afternoon Don Eulalio was looking over his recently planted *milpa* on the Arroyo Mojarrero. The stream was dry, but the little alluvial pocket he had cleared collected seepage from the flanking ridges and so retained moisture better than other tracts. His foot-high maize plants, Eulalio decided, looked maltreated but should pull through if the rains began soon. As he walked about chopping the scattered weeds with his machete and straightening up an occasional infant cornplant that was canted over, the first dark forms drifted into the clearing. Then there were more and more of them. The peccary did not come in a solid phalanx, but scattered in twos and threes, a few yards apart, yet suddenly they seemed to fill the field. The animals paid not the least attention to the farmer as he first sidled then ran to his gun hung from a little tree. Strangely, or so it seemed to Eulalio, the animals did little harm to the maize plants as they streamed across the field, walking, trotting, stopping to snuffle the ground or look about, then running a few steps in an erratically moving flood.

In the small leather pouch beside Don Eulalio's weapon were two .22 long-rifle cartridges and there was another in the chamber. He shot three of the big white-jowled animals: the first in the neck, a clean kill, the second through the heart, so that the peccary sprinted to the edge of the clearing before falling. It was so easy that the hunter became careless—he shot the third badly, and the wounded beast ran into the woods bucking and squealing. At each shot some animals panicked, others paid no heed but continued across the planted ground. The last of the herd swarmed by; as suddenly as they had appeared the *marín* crossed and vanished. Don Eulalio stood clutching his empty rifle, staring over the small sunbright clearing ringed by forest now empty but for the yellowed foot-high maize plants, trampled here and there, and the flat dark bulks of the two animals he had killed.

The trail of the wounded peccary could not be distinguished, or had been obliterated by its mates. There was no blood spoor. The hunter turned back from a short distance into the woods to recover his *morral* and to cut an armload of brush and weeds at the edge of the clearing to cover each of his kills—buzzards, ugly drab-black carrion birds, would soon find them otherwise. Then he returned to follow the herd's trail through the forest—a clear enough track: two hundred animals, even in an open, loose formation, cannot move through the woods without leaving abundant sign. Eulalio walked and trotted, slowing only for undergrowth and vine tangles—there his machete slashed a way through for him.

The drove traveled unswervingly a little west of north. If not diverted, Eulalio estimated, the *marín* would come out on the riverbank somewhere near old Don Ramón's place, five or six miles away at the big bend in the river. Where the animals crossed the path to my *compadre* Candelario's house, Eulalio turned left, broke into a run. Candelario is his hunting partner as well as his brother-in-law. And Don Candi had recently acquired a .22 rifle, so he would have ammunition.

He arrived sweaty and breathless. "*Marín!*—Big herd! —Hundreds of them—so many—it scared me!"

"Where, *cuñado?*"

"They came out—in my *milpa*—I killed two—hit another—no more cartridges." He could not seem to get the breath back into his heaving chest. "They crossed the trail—by the big *marota* tree—headed straight—toward Don Ramón's house."

Feliciano was there. "Maybe we could catch up with them in the Amate pasture—they'll have to cross it somewhere."

"In the open," Candelario completed the thought. "That would be good. How many cartridges do you want, *cuñado*?"

"Lend me five."

The three set out at a trot on a narrow shortcut to the pasture. They came out on the crest of a ridge overlooking the expanse of tall grass, so dazzling green in the late afternoon sun that they squinted their shade-adapted eyes. No sound, no motion disturbed the stretch of green—the pasture seemed empty of life. A little yellow-breasted bird dove from a tall dead tree at an insect, gulped it in midair. All three started, then grinned at each other shamefacedly, as he screamed his triumphant war cry, "pisto-que-e-e!"

"Look!" Feliciano whispered, pointing far down the *arroyo*. "Something is moving the grass!"

"I can see it! Down below the *apompo*!"

"They're trying to find a place to cross the *arroyo*," said Candelario.

"There's a swampy place a little farther on that they'll have trouble crossing," said Feliciano. "We can corner them there." They ran down the slope of the ridge through the clumps of waist-high grass, toward the *apompo* tree at the *arroyo*'s edge.

It was not as easy as they had expected, they told me later, shooting the animals in the high grass. Peccary ran by in front of them, behind them—they could hear the beasts but could not see them. When one sprinted across open spaces amid the grass, they could not hit it—they do not know how to lead a moving target. What saved the day for the hunters was that the *marín* did not, would not scatter. Cutoff animals insisted on coming back to rejoin the main herd—the lost bewildered creatures were trying to stay together. On strange ground, far from their range, the only solace the beasts had was the togetherness of the herd.

Don Eulalio, after wasting three shots, finally killed a peccary in a little open space in the grass. He stopped shooting, though he had a cartridge left; he had three kills to carry home to butcher. My *compadre* killed two, and Feliciano one. The leaders of the drove finally found a way across the swampy tract, and the herd moved on.

The herd of *marín* continued its futile march, now northwesterly. Early next morning Don Domingo sat on his porch, fifteen miles by trail farther along, sipping black coffee. Suddenly his hogs came running, squealing with fright, from a thicket a couple of hundred yards to the south. "Jaguar!" he thought, and ran into the house for a gun and shells. He glanced down the shotgun barrel before shoving in the load. Black. No light. There was a mud-dauber nest in the muzzle. By the time he poked it out with a cleaning rod, loaded, and ran outside, the *marín* were trotting and galloping across his *patio* in a great stream. Standing at his front door he shot six with his 16-gauge single-shot.

"I could have used up the whole box of shells," he said later, grinning broadly. "But I figured six would feed me and my help and all my close neighbors."

"There must have been two hundred of them," he went on. "I'd never seen anything like it. My *tata* used to tell me that there were lots of such herds in the old days here, but I'd never seen one before."

The herd swung away from the river, through thickets,

pastures, and forests, and came out on the main trail, *camino real* ("royal highway"), as it is called in a fossil Spanish phrase, leading to El Ixtal. The animals turned to follow the open path.

Elderly Don Epifanio Cruz was hiking up the trail, bent over under a load of maize, when, peering ahead the way one has to carrying a heavy load with a tumpline, he saw the peccary coming toward him. Many were massed in the open trail, others were shadows slipping through the woods on either side. They came at a steady trot; if they saw him they gave no sign, but continued as though they would trample him down. He slipped the tumpline from his forehead to drop the sack of corn, scrambled up into the safety of a small tree. He dropped his shotgun when he dropped the sack of corn.

"I felt bad, Don Pablito," he told me later on, "seeing all that good meat go by, and my gun laying on the ground. They ripped the sack to pieces—slashed it with their tusks as they ran over it—scattered the corn but didn't eat any. I figured from that they were from away back on the mountain, had never seen corn before. They ripped up my hat too—it had fallen off in the *camino*. But that didn't matter—it was old and worn out. It was funny: I was sad about having dropped my gun, I was mad at seeing the critters tear up the sack—*jijole*, it cost me six pesos—but I felt good at seeing a big herd of *marín* again. That's the way they used to travel—in big herds—in this country when I was a boy—" and he went off into a long tale of youthful memories.

By trail it is scarcely a dozen miles from Don Epifanio's tree to El Ixtal. The drove of peccary, however, did not appear in Don Panuncio's pastures till late next afternoon. The animals must have stopped to feed and rest, perhaps wandered aimlessly about the forests, until they came back on their north-northwesterly course. Josefino, looking for a stray cow, encountered them. He stared wide-eyed, then spun his pony about to race back to the house. His mount was sweat-lathered when Josefino swung off to run into the store, where Don Panuncio presided as usual.

"Don Panuncio! *Jabalí* by the hundreds, out in the pasture by Arroyo Verde! Big black ones!"

"Big black ones! Do they have any white markings?"

"Yes, on the cheeks."

"They must be *marín*. Didn't you ever see a *marín*, Josefino?"

"Not until now, if that's what they are. There are lots of them!"

There were a number of men in the store, fifteen or so, purchasing, visiting, having a drink.

"Come on, everyone," Don Panuncio shouted. "It's been years since there was a big herd of *marín* in here. Let's go get some."

"But Don Panuncio," someone said, "I need a kilo of sugar, and a liter of kerosene, and a—"

"*A la chingada*, that can wait—the *marín* won't. Let's get going—I'm closing up here. But first, who needs a gun or ammunition?"

It was the following evening that I stopped by, on my way home from town with a canoe load of provisions.

"You missed out, Pablito, *por Dios*. You should have been here with us. They say the herd passed near your house a couple of days earlier, but it was better here in the short-grass pastures."

"What herd, Don Panuncio?"

"A herd of *marín*, the big kind of peccary. And a big herd too, such as I haven't seen here in the Ixtal for twenty years."

"Where would a drove of animals like that come from?"

"They must have come down from the Sierra. Josefino

saw them out in the pasture along the edge of the river,
and came to let me know. We worked them over—the
seventeen, no, eighteen *cabrones* of us. Mostly on horseback, but a few on foot. When we got to Arroyo Verde
I made them wait for the foot people, so we could spread
out to make a long line, really long, all alongside the drove,
which was sort of milling around close to the riverbank."

"There were lots of them, really?"

"Were there! I calculated at least two hundred, big
and little. We opened fire. The *marín* ran back and forth
along the riverbank—I think they were afraid of the river,
and were trying to stay together. Then all of a sudden
they broke, scattered in every direction. Some jumped into
the river, some ran right between us. But we had our
share."

"How many did you get?"

"I killed five with the Belge autoloading—decided that
was plenty for me and my friends. The others killed one,
two, up to three apiece. Benito got three. We killed thirty-
eight all told."

"Thirty-eight! What a slaughter! No wonder *marín* are
scarce!"

"It was a slaughter—but there may never be another
chance like that. Besides, most of the herd was left."

But that was the end of the drove of *marín*. No one
ever saw it again, at least as a unit. Some of my neighbors believe the animals reassembled and returned through
the deep forests to the Sierra. More likely the final disaster broke the herd up permanently, the animals scattering through the jungles of the foothill country in twos
and threes and fours.

LATE IN THE DRY SEASON the rising sun burns
through the thin mists early. Pairs of *chachalacas*, olive-

brown birds with long droopy tails, plump and meaty for all their roadrunner silhouettes, climb to the tips of trees in the thickets, or fly to the top of the jungle canopy, to greet the sun's warmth. The female shrills—or so my friends and neighbors translate her call—*"Me quiero casar! Me quiero casar!"* ("I want to get married!") The male booms a bass disapproval of such uneconomic frivolity: *"No hay cacao! No hay cacao!"* ("There isn't any cacao"—that is, money.) A distant pair answers, then another and another until the early morning is raucous with their marital argument. People listen to them and grin—*"Oiga las chachalacas* (Listen to the *chachalacas*) asking for a sunny day—it will be a nice bright day today." Wives often ask wistfully, *"Viejo,* couldn't you shoot a brace of them? They taste so good stewed up with rice."

Bird shooting is a very minor form of hunting locally. The meatiness of the quarry ordinarily is computed closely against the cost of ammunition. *Chachalacas* suffer more since .22s have become popular in the last four or five years; a bird weighing but half a kilogram feathers and all was not regarded as paying for a shotgun shell. My neighbors shake their heads in mild disapproval as I blast 12-gauge shells at doves, though for the most part they are tolerant of my strange habits.

Parrots are an exception to the rule of cost evaluation. Local people shoot them, large, medium-sized, and small, as often as they can with a vindictiveness that takes no account of ammunition prices. "I eat every parrot I can kill, *compadre,*" said my *compadre* Santiago. "They're clean feeders, after all, and always fat." He glowered. "Fat on my green corn, on my oranges, on my cacao, the *cabrones!*"

It is amazing how much damage a flock of parrots can do with their powerful sharp beaks, ripping into the ears of green corn, one after another, nibbling only a few grains from each ear, each bird leaving dozens of ravaged husks for the benefit of ants and other insects. Parrots can strip a heavily laden orange tree in no time. They eat the seeds, not the pulp, and the ground beneath the tree is soon littered with pecked and damaged fruits torn from the branches—dozens for every one the birds actually clean of its seeds. Even the hard woody hulls of cacao fruits are inadequate defense against those beaks. The birds tear through them to get at the acid-sweet lavender pulp that surrounds the seeds. Once the hole is made, insects finish the destruction. So far as I have been able to observe, the parrots do not actually eat avocados at all, but a flock occasionally settles on a tree to nip through the stems of the fruit, dropping it to the ground. The farmers' bitterness toward the birds has reason. In addition, there is the fact that parrot, stewed or fried, is far tastier than chicken.

There are of course some birds large enough to be considered worth hunting: the turkey-size curassow, its slightly smaller relative called *cholina* (with a bare turkey-like head, white breast spattered with black dots), the larger species of tinamou. But these are jungle birds, shot more often on chance encounters than deliberately hunted. Only in the breeding season in March, when male curassow and *cholina* call incessantly, do hunters search for them in the great forests.

In the season of the *nortes*, when the rain-swollen river and streams flood vast expanses of flatlands down below El Ixtal, great flocks of migrant teal, both cinnamon and bluewing, are common, and so are smaller flocks of native ducks. *Pishishi* is the local name of one of the natives— "pi-shi-shi-shi!" the birds call in a high thin pitch as they fly, somewhat as Canada geese gabble. These are strange little birds—smallish in body, russet-brown with huge wings that unfold in flight to show black feathers and white speculae, and with very long yellow legs. The other native is black all over, except for a large white speculum on either wing. Both the natives have a discouraging habit of roosting in trees at times—more than once have I noted a flight apparently settling on a pond, made a long careful stalk, to be unnerved at the last crucial moment by the ducks flapping out of the trees overhead.

Here where we live, in the hillier country where flooded areas are abundant but smaller than down on the flat coastal plain, the flights of ducks are smaller as well. But there are still enough to make hunting worthwhile. Local hunters stalk skillfully to get within range, then ground-sluice the birds on the water—holding just a trifle low on the nearest one so that the shot ricochets and spreads among the flock at a low angle. Three or four *pishishi* or black ducks, or eight or a dozen teal, is a good payoff even for a close-fisted man.

DON RUFINO, Don Natividad (he was not yet my *compadre*), and I crawled on our bellies through the grass and weeds out a long point. A raft of teal rested on a flood-formed pond—ducks seem to like such temporary ponds because of the many floating seeds from drowned plants. Before we were within range a sentinel saw us, flew up shouting his warning, and the whole flight lifted. We stood up, muddy and disgusted. Then a straggler got up with a flurry of wings, cutting across close to us. Still a newcomer on the river, I felt a compulsion to show off—stepping in front of Don Rufino I swung across the teal, knocked him tumbling out of the air with spraddling wings. It was a simple crossing shot, from right to left, but I thought it would be impressive to men who, as I already knew, do not know how to wing-shoot. I waited for some words of approval, admiration, or enthusiasm. There were none. My companions stood silent, a little glum. Finally Don Rufino waded out nearly waist-deep to recover the bird. Returning, he dangled it by the feet, thoughtfully. It did look pretty small.

"Don Pablo," he said in his quiet way, "how much do those cartridges cost you?"

"Why, about a peso and a half, buying them by the box."

He jiggled the dead teal. "A peso fifty centavos. That's a big price for such a little bit of meat—just not good business." He became the wise old hunter counseling the novice. "If you haven't hunted much"—I gritted my teeth—"you should learn to think of such things. If the flock hadn't spooked, you could have got six or eight or maybe ten on the water with that same cartridge."

This is probably why I have put up with Juanito for so long: he thinks wing shooting is fun to watch, never seems to worry about its leading me into bankruptcy.

In defense of ground sluicing it must be noted that with a single-shot gun, such as most men have, one shot is all you can expect to get all day. The ducks have a thousand— or thousands—of other ponds to go to, but there are not thousands of hunters as in duck season along a Stateside flyway to keep moving the birds around, eventually sending some back to you. Days may go by before any ducks alight on that pond again. So if you need a bag of ducks sufficient to feed a large family, the sensible thing is to get all you can with that one shot.

ELDERLY NEIGHBORS RELATE that in their youth not only were there fewer people on the Xucuapan, but fewer of them had firearms. Consequently the hunting of small game, especially kinds that can be taken in ways other than by shooting, was of more importance, dietwise, than it is now.

There are two animals that go to earth in relatively shallow dens when pursued by dogs—the giant gopher, brown with a row of white spots on its sides, tailless, called *tepescuinte*, and the armadillo. A large brush rabbit, bigger than a cottontail, and another rodent called *serete*, rabbitlike but with short round ears and short stiff black hair, also go to ground, but often their burrows are longer and more difficult to dig out.

Occasionally, on a Sunday, several neighbors assemble with their dogs for this sort of hunting. They go into the jungle whooping and shouting at the yapping dogs, singing, telling yarns as they walk along—the more noise the better, to stir up animals in hiding so the dogs can run them into their burrows. It is as much a social occasion as a hunt.

A kaleidoscope of scrawny yellow and red and black and white dogs barking shrilly at the mouth of a den, snarling and snapping at each other for the privilege of sniffing in it. Slapping them away with the flat of his machete, Don Noë probes to find the direction of the den with a length of supple vine. "Curves off to the right," he mutters. A deep rumbling growl like that of a big dog sounds from the depths.

"*Tepescuinte*. Hear him?"

Antonio and Don Estéban are cutting short lengths of stick to plug the mouth of the den.

"Does an armadillo make any kind of noise?" I ask.

"No. That's how you know what you've got in the den."

"How about a civet cat?"

They guffaw. "That *cabrón* animal you smell right away!"

They begin to dig down through the tough red clay

with their machetes, aiming at intersecting the burrow, jabbing the blades vertically, prying, scooping out the loose dirt by hand. They are happily excited, while to me it seems rather dull. Finally Don Noë breaks through, about two feet down. They take turns enlarging his tunnel. After a bit they have opened a large vertical pit. The trapped animal suddenly surges up into it—Antonio's machete flashes through its skull. We take turns hefting it, admiring it. Half a mile away some of the dogs begin to bell. Those that have stayed near the burrow race off toward the sound.

"They've got another one!" Don Estéban shouts. "Let's go!"

All three whoop to encourage the dogs. We set out noisily through the forest.

PERHAPS the most popular small-game animal of all, abundant and easy to take, is the iguana. A recent dramatic work seems to have made Americans iguana-conscious, though whether that work or other sources have contributed to the store of misinformation about the creatures I do not know.

A friend from the States, en route to the ruins of Yucatan, had written the date of his arrival in Minatitlán. He would stop over for a visit, he wrote. Over a cold beer after some exchange of news, he said he wanted to buy some copal—black copal, the good kind. A Tehuana I know in the market stocks it, so we went to see her. Outside the market we passed several country people, most of them from the nearby Nahaut-speaking villages, selling iguanas, each with a dozen or so of the big ugly lizards hobbled by crossing their forelegs over their backs, breaking and knotting pairs of fingers together. The creatures glared defiance out of their round reptilian eyes.

"Look at all the iguanas," I remarked. "This time of the year they're fat, the females are full of eggs, so they are quite in demand."

"Oh yes," he replied, unslinging his camera. "Interesting. Taste just like chicken, don't they?"

"What makes you think so?"

"Why, everybody knows that!"

"I don't, and I've eaten the things. They're insipid, tasteless, and awfully tough."

Zoologists, so I have been told, classify iguanas into a number of distinct species. Locally the term "iguana" is reserved for the green kind—bright banana-leaf green while young, darkening when mature to black with a greenish cast, with alternating dark green and black rings about the tail. Another, larger species is called *garrabo*. It has a shaggier endowment of pseudo-spines along the back, and has gray and orange marking. In the central portion of Veracruz state there is a black and red form called *tilcampo*. All are equally sought, and equally edible—or inedible, according to your palate.

Like other reptiles iguanas have lightning-fast reactions, scant intelligence. As a noisy outboard pushes a canoe along, iguanas sunning themselves on the branches of spreading *amate* trees high overhead escape by diving, or rather dropping, forty, fifty, sixty feet into the river. They are at home in the water and can swim considerable distances under the surface. But in May, when the river is low and wide gravel bars are exposed, they use the same tactic to land bellybuster on the bare gravels with appallingly loud "plops" as often as in the water. One would imagine that such a blow would scramble their insides, but though they lie stunned a few moments, they get up to scuttle into the river, apparently unharmed.

The favorite habitat of iguanas and *garrabos* is the

bamboo thicket at the river's edge, but any tangle of dense brush near moist or swampy places suits them too. A hunter sometimes can stalk an iguana dozing in the sun on a bamboo branch to slash it with his machete, or if it flees into the open he can often overtake it as it blunders about in the grass. A favorite, and effective, technique is that of lassoing the creatures with a slip noose on the end of a long light pole.

In the dry season, the females burrow into soft sandy banks to lay their clutches of twenty to thirty eggs. Laying is a long slow process. The den is begun ahead of time; finally the female enters, kicks back soft moist sand to plug up the entryway, so that despite her attempt at concealment the place is conspicuously marked. The iguana hunter, if he may be so called, paddles along the river's edge looking for small circular patches of fresh moist sand. When he sees one, he goes ashore, scoops out the sand by hand, pulls his victim out by the tail. Sometimes two or even three iguanas are found in a single den, to be dragged out one by one. The unlaid eggs are considered a delicacy. They are long slim ellipses, hard-shelled, and they cook hard, quite different from the leathery-shelled turtle eggs, which do not congeal no matter how long they are boiled.

An iguana is prepared by singeing it over the coals till the outer layers of skin peel and can be scraped off, leaving a thin smooth black layer of lower epidermis. Then it is dressed, the eggs, if any, are recovered, and the carcass is cut into chunks to be boiled in salt water. Local country cookery is a far cry from the elaborately prepared, imaginatively seasoned cuisine of highland Mexico. After lengthy boiling, meat and eggs are dipped out and served. The meat is white, hard to the point of toughness, and, as I told John, completely insipid.

Once I found out the reason for singeing rather than skinning iguanas.

Maria wailed, "What in the world am I going to give the help to eat?" (There were four lads working for me getting subsistence at the house.) "There are hardly any eggs—the hens are on strike—all molting. You don't catch any fish."

"You know I broke the tip of my spinning rod. I just can't seem to set a hook with one of these homemade fishpoles—I just waste my time."

"Well, I don't know what to cook."

"*Caramba*, give them what we eat—rice, beans, *tortillas*, some rousing good hot chile sauce."

"But that's all I've been giving them for days and days! They don't say anything, but they're getting tired of it."

Little Rosamaria broke in. "*Mamá*, why don't you cook them an iguana?"

"There's a great big one," her brother chimed in, "suns himself about noon on a sandbank across the river. We see him every day."

"I'll shoot it for you if you'll cook it up," I offered. "The boys will like it."

Maria hesitated. "I'll tell you the truth—"

"High time, too, after all these years."

She made a face at me. "I'll tell you the truth, I just don't like to singe them. The rest I don't mind, but the singeing business gives me the willies."

"That's no problem. I'll skin it for you."

"We'll help you, *Papi*," the youngsters chorused.

After issuing the usual warning to the kids about sitting very still in the bottom of the canoe, I paddled upstream to the place they said the iguana sunned. There it was, sound asleep. I shot it through the head—no feat at six or seven yards. By good luck it hung up on a small bush instead of rolling into the water. We took it home, to the shade of the *guásima* tree, to skin it.

As I set to work I discovered that an iguana's fat forms a layer between hide and flesh. It is the yellow of drawn butter, the consistency of a lightweight crankcase oil. It dribbled away as we removed the hide.

Dubiously I took the dressed carcass to Maria, while the youngsters nailed the hide to the front wall. "This might turn out to be a little tougher than usual," I told her. "We lost nearly all the fat."

It was tough, very tough. I did not sample it; I knew all about it simply by watching the lads' jaw muscles bulge and strain as they munched at it.

I have eaten iguana a couple of times when the cook went completely wild. After boiling, she sautéed the thing up in a sauce of tomatoes, onions, a little chile and garlic, olives, capers, and Heaven knows how many spices and herbs. Iguana prepared thus is worth eating, but what the hell, an old stirrup leather done up with all those trimmings probably would be tasty.

IN OLD, settled areas of southeastern Mexico, where the jaguar has long since been exterminated or driven away, there is a voluminous folklore about the big spotted cats—voluminous but not varied, consisting of tales of people's hairsbreadth escapes from being killed and devoured by the ferocious beasts. Where a few jaguars still roam, however, as here in the Xucuapan, men who know them firsthand tell no yarns of jaguars attacking human beings, nor do they fear them. My neighbors are not fond of the animals—far from it—they pursue and kill them whenever they can, for the big felines are avidly fond of domestic pork, wreak havoc with droves of pigs that wander in the forest, and sometimes, though less often, kill small calves. But the creatures do not attack man.

When now-elderly Don Chon, freshly mustered out of Carranza's forces, moved to the Xucuapan, the beasts abounded, naturally enough, for their normal prey, deer and peccary as well as lesser animals, were abundant.

"It was rough in those days, Don Pablito," the old man told me one evening. "People had difficulties in raising hogs, and even poultry. The living houses had sidewalls of thin little poles, or maybe a flimsy screen of palm fronds on the north and east sides. But the hog house always looked like a military stronghold, made of big logs. Some men laid the log walls with the timbers horizontal, but mostly they set them upright, in deep holes like corral posts, close together like a palisade. If they didn't build a substantial hog house the jaguars would rip it apart in the night to get at the pigs. When the pigs were out feeding in the daytime, the spotted rascals would kill them. Not many people had cattle in those days, but those who did had to keep the small calves penned up in the *patio* if they hoped to raise them."

"Sounds as though it must have been a tough place to go into the livestock business, Don Chon. What did you do?"

"Well, I had my 30-30 that I'd brought back from the war, and my *compadre* Miguel Alor had his, too—you know that he was in my company for most of the war. Then we rode to Acayucan, to see my *padrino* Don Faustino Castillo. He had a big ranch there, still had lots of cattle, even after the Revolution. And he had always had a pack of big savage dogs. He gave me six, two dogs and four bitches, good strong young dogs. They'd never hunted jaguar, but they were natural hunters, and brave —it didn't take my *compadre* Miguel and me long to teach them to run jaguar. So we began to hunt. Whenever a neighbor came to tell us he'd lost a hog or a calf we'd go find the trail—jaguars often come back to a kill, you know.

The dogs would set out, barking, and we'd run after them until they treed old 'spotted shirt.' We had jaguar hides all over the place—used them to dry cacao on, the way people use cowhides and mats nowadays."

"Couldn't you sell them in town?"

"Two or three pesos was all a hide would bring in those days, sometimes not that. Later on, when my *compadre* Panuncio moved in, he found out where to send them to get a better price. He brought some good dogs too. We used to hunt together, often."

"Were there mountain lion in here too?"

"A few. They weren't as bad at killing hogs and calves as the jaguar, but we used to kill them too. We used to eat them—the meat is white like pork. Jaguar meat is too rank, too strong to eat. Anyhow, we thinned out the jaguars around here."

"Killed them all out, did you?"

"No, we couldn't, because they kept coming down from the back country. It wasn't till years later, when my *compadre* Roberto—El Güero—moved in there, and later my *compadre* Amaranto, that the cats began to get scarce. They hunted them back upriver. *Compadre* Güero was thin as a fishing pole in those days—didn't have that big belly then. Few men could run through the woods after the dogs the way he could. There always will be a few here, I suppose, drifting down from the Sierra, until the slopes of the big mountains are settled—if they ever are."

"Do the jaguar ever fight back, Don Chon? Do they ever attack a man? I've heard a lot of stories like that, down below." I gestured downriver, toward town.

"Those are just town people's stories—they don't know what they're talking about. I never knew a jaguar to attack. They killed some of our dogs, but never charged us. Not even wounded ones. I don't know why. They're not really afraid of a man, the way other animals are, but somehow they just don't want to tackle him."

Only once, here in the Xucuapan, have I heard a story about a jaguar attacking a man. That story is not true. It was Don Panchito Magaña who told it to me. Don Panchito is a recent arrival, from Jalisco, who lives across the river down toward the railroad. He is a nice little person, but like a lot of Jaliscienses, has a fondness for big talk and the tall tale.

I had too many hogs, so I decided to cut the herd down. The fat gelts were no problem of course—they could be loaded into a canoe and sold in town. But there were several sows I wanted to get rid of—they were good brood sows, but lean; town buyers wouldn't want them. So I funneled into the grapevine the information that I was selling some good sows cheap. Don Panchito came to buy one; we agreed on a big white sow, at a reasonable price. It was late afternoon. He stayed overnight and next morning, not very early, I set him and his purchase across the river in the canoe. He had the ends of a length of rope tied to the sow's legs, to drive her along. That is a good way to handle hogs—if they try to run, or go the wrong way, one simply yanks their legs out from under them. The white sow gave him a lot of trouble at first, but he finally got her headed down the trail.

Near noon, she lay down in the shade and refused to move. He sat waiting until the heat of the day had passed, then got her up to continue the long slow journey. Near dusk, down close to Arroyo Robalo—a very short day's travel—she quit again. When a pig tires and quits, one either carries it—she was too big for that—or waits for it to rest and recover its strength. Don Panchito tied her close to the trail, then he walked back to Don Uvaldo's house, half a mile away, where he was invited to spend the night.

Early next morning he could not at first find the sow. Then he saw her hind legs projecting from under a patch of dense low bushes, as though she had crawled under them for shelter or to hide. He seized the legs to drag her out. He could not move her—something seemed to be holding her fast. He heaved mightily—she came loose so suddenly that he nearly fell backward. He tugged again. This time she came clear of the bushes, and he saw that she was dead—the whole back of her neck and part of the shoulders were eaten away, the torn flesh still dripping blood. Then, he says, he heard a roar. Across the low bushes the jaguar that had been feeding on her reared up on its hind legs and sprang at him. Don Panchito drew his pistol, fired, hit the attacking beast, which fell into the brush, then jumped up and fled. Don Panchito went back in search of Don Uvaldo, who has some good dogs and a rifle, and together they pursued the wounded jaguar and killed it.

Now some of this is true and some is not. It is true that the jaguar killed the sow and was eating her. It is also true that Don Panchito wounded the beast with his pistol. But the animal did not attack him, did not spring at him, even though he was taking its meal away from it. That part is a lie.

In proof, I happen to know that Don Panchito carries his pistol, not in his waistband, but in the *morral* slung over his shoulder, mixed in with a good many other odds and ends he carries about. No one could possibly extract a weapon from such a container while an attacking animal was in midair, springing at him. In addition, that little 32-20 would not stop a charging animal the size of a jaguar, much less knock one down in mid-leap. Finally, Don Uvaldo told me later that the beast was wounded, but in the side, back toward the flank. It had been standing sideways to him when Don Panchito fired.

All in all, this incident seems to be the best proof of all that jaguars are not aggressive toward man—this one certainly had provocation: hungry, it was rudely deprived of its meal, then it was badly shot, but not in a way to render it helpless. It was obviously a gentle animal, well-disposed toward man. I never mentioned my deductions to Don Panchito. As I said, he is a nice person—it is just that those people from Jalisco have the habit of talking big and tall.

One trait of the jaguar on which all knowledgeable hunters agree is that the animal, if not aggressive toward man, is not afraid of him, and has as well an enormous streak of curiosity. My *compadre* Candelario has killed two while jacklighting. Both, he says, came walking toward the light, not charging but walking calmly, blinking and peering at the strange phenomenon with obvious interest.

"I like that," Candelario grins. "When they walk up to within twenty feet of you there's no reason to miss the shot."

Another expression of this curiosity is the big cat's custom of following a man for a mile or two along a jungle trail, staying a hundred or two hundred yards behind most of the time, sometimes closing to peer at the man-thing around a jog in the path, never coming out in plain view. The tracks of jaguar playing this game have been seen many times by later travelers, and on a few occasions the second traveler has managed to overtake the beast to watch him following and spying on a neighbor.

There is a well-known story about one of the early settlers in the region, one Don Procopio Alvarez, and a jaguar. I never knew Don Procopio. He had gone on to his reward before I ever saw the Xucuapan, but all his kinsmen and friends insist the tale is true.

It seems that a *compadre* of Don Procopio's had taken

a couple of packhorse-loads of cacao to town to sell. Among the provisions he brought back was one of the old-fashioned sixteen-liter wicker-bound jugs of *aguardiente*—he brought it on his own back, not trusting the precious liquid to a packhorse. He then invited a group of cronies to a small gathering in honor of one of his favorite saints.

Don Procopio lived some miles away, but with alacrity he hiked down the narrow winding path through the giant forest in late afternoon.

The *jícara* dipper of *aguardiente* began to make the rounds to the accompaniment of congenial conversation. It was pleasant, but the night was still young when Don Procopio found he had drunk too much. He decided to go home. His friends tried to dissuade him—true enough, they said, there was a piece of a moon, but under the jungle's double roof no light would penetrate. In those days flashlights were considered city folk's useless luxuries (the technique of jacklighting had not yet been introduced into the region); there was not even a spare coal-oil dip mounted in a wind-shielding metal box. But Don Procopio insisted he knew the trail as he knew the palm of his own hand, so with drunken obstinacy he set out into the night. The exercise, unhappily, did not sober him. Finally he came to a small bright open space. A huge termite-riddled tree had crashed to the ground some time before, smashing the younger growth about it and tearing a great hole from the upper canopy where its crown had been, a space through which moonlight flooded. Don Procopio lay down, or fell down, and drifted off into drunken slumber.

A jaguar came down the trail, traveling in a direction opposite to that of our protagonist. The beast stopped short on seeing the recumbent figure in the patch of moonlight. Then, silently as only cats can move, he began to circle the strange object, staring, sniffing, listening to the rhythmic snores. Gradually he shortened his circles, until he stood close to his fascinating find. He stretched his neck to inspect more closely, lifted one of his big forepaws to rest it gently on Don Procopio's chest as he sniffed at the face—who knows, perhaps to learn what brand of liquor would put a man-thing to sleep in mid-jungle.

Later Don Procopio used to relate that he sensed the presence of an animal through the alcoholic mists of his sleep. He thought it was a dog and was trying to wake up enough to shoo it away, when he felt the pressure on his chest. He opened his eyes to see in the moonlight the great bristling snuffling muzzle of the jaguar inches from his own nose.

Don Procopio squeezed his eyelids together to shut out the horrid sight, opened his mouth to scream in terror and anguish. It must have been a phenomenal scream, a wild blast of ear-bursting sound that shook the branches in the treetops high above.

Perhaps the cat was nervous. When the man-thing which had been so tranquil, quiet but for that interesting buzzing snore, suddenly emitted such a shocking noise, the jaguar's interest vanished. He leaped backward, turning in midair as cats can do, and scampered up the trail in the direction from which he had come—that is, toward Don Procopio's house. That terrified person, wide awake and sober, had no desire even to seem to pursue the jaguar; he turned down the trail, running at his best speed toward his *compadre*'s house, where he arrived in a very short time, pallid, breathless, and trembling.

They poured a few drinks down him to pull him together, until finally he could gasp out the account of his awful experience.

As you would expect of a group of intelligent people, not one of them believed him for a moment. Though they did not openly challenge his strange tale, the most kindly appraisal was that it all had been but a drunken dream.

But the yarn reminded the men of other incidents of the jungle, and as the *jícara* of raw white liquor made the rounds they related other encounters with beasts—with jaguars, with fer-de-lance, with great droves of the nasty-tempered little red peccary, with stud tapir in rut, which some woodsmen insist is the most dangerous animal of all. And there were recounted adventures with other creatures of the forests, unfortunately less well known to zoologists: the *chanecas*, ugly little dwarfs who can assume the form of a beautiful nude woman to lure the unwary traveler from the path, there to pounce and devour him. They told of the *salvaje*, also anthropophagous, a great burly figure resembling a man in form, naked but covered with long shaggy gray hair—perhaps a kinsman of the abominable snowman of a far-distant realm. The *salvaje*'s feet are turned backward to confuse pursuers— vengeance-seeking relatives of his victims—for it is known that he is mortal and could be slain by resolute armed men. But the feat has never been accomplished, for no one can unravel the confused trail he leaves. Voices lowered cautiously to report on the vicious *naugales*, human witches who assume animal form to wreak their depredations and who can be slain only with a silver bullet scored with a Cross. The *jícara* was passed around and around and the yarns were spun until the sun's disc shattered the darkness at the edge of the world east of the jungle.

Don Procopio had all but recovered from his fright, but he insisted he would not go home alone—at length four or five of his cronies agreed to see him along the way. Scoffers at his tale all, when they reached the scene

they found their judgment wrong—the story was writ
clear in the soft damp ground for all to read. There were
Don Procopio's footprints, weaving from side to side of
the path as he went, he thought, homeward. There was
the opening in the forest where the tree had fallen, there
was the clear imprint of his body where he had lain down,
or fallen down, there were his belongings scattered about:
his hat, his *guaraches* still in the *morral*, his machete, just
as he had dropped them. The big pad marks of the jaguar
came down the trail, then around in a closing spiral as
the beast cautiously approached the sleeping form. Big
spread-toed motion-smeared prints showed where the cat,
shocked by that appalling scream, had leaped back, and
there were the cat's tracks where, digging his toes into
the ground, he had sprinted up the trail. And there were
Don Procopio's tracks where, springing to his feet, he too
had dug his toes into the ground, running like hell in the
other direction.

Kin and friends of Don Procopio relate that he lived
his reasonably useful, only occasionally alcoholic, existence for many years after. But all agree that he never again
slept off a drunk in the jungle.

10

A Trip to Town

ANDRÉS GOMEZ and Pablo Perez decided to go to town
to outfit themselves with clothes, footgear, ammunition,
and other necessities—or so they told their fathers when
asking for permission to make the trip. Lively, full-blooded
young men, they may have had other intentions that they
did not mention in requesting parental permission (my
tocayo, "namesake," Pablo acquired a rousing good dose
of gonorrhea during the excursion—I know, because he
came to me to be syringed full of penicillin to cure it).
But all this is beside the point. What turned out to be
important was that they neglected to take along certain
documents that Mexican law requires a male citizen to
carry: a card showing record of or exemption from military training and a voter's registration certificate.

They walked to the railroad station one Monday because there was no one there they knew well enough to
entrust with the care of their saddle horses, found someone who would give them lodging overnight so they could
catch the train shortly after daybreak on Tuesday—the
westbound train runs Tuesdays, Thursdays, and Satur-
days. At the next station Antonio Cruz, an age-mate from

downriver near El Ixtal, boarded the train. His plans were similar to theirs—a trio based on friendship and common goals was formed. Like his newfound comrades, Antonio did not carry his documentation. Country people don't make a habit of carrying important papers about— there are too many times when a man is caught and drenched in a sudden thundershower or has to wade or swim some brimming stream or even the river. Important papers are carefully stowed away in the house, in cans with pressure tops or glass jars with screw-on lids.

What the three young bloods did not know was that a vigorous nationwide campaign to search out draft dodgers and other nonconformist citizens was under way. They had not had more than two or three beers and priced denim pants and shirts at more than a couple of stores when Policeman Lázaro Cuevas spotted them.

Don Lázaro was not a local product—he had drifted down from Guanajuato or Zacatecas or some such place up in the highlands. He was heavy-set in build, though not fat, heavy-jowled with a flat, fat-padded face that contrasted strikingly with the lean angular features of local folk. He never was well shaved—the pits and lumps of old acne scars made it difficult to run a razor over his fleshy cheeks. He wore a .380, hammer cocked, resting on the thumb safety, in a low-slung quick-draw holster. Blackjacks are not standard police equipment in any town hereabouts, but he carried one in his left hip pocket—he was ambidextrous. They say he used to like to use it. He was a mean cop. He was also a shakedown artist. I am happy to report that he has since been fired from the Lomas police force—"moralization," as they call it, of the police is a difficult task, but they are working at it everywhere in Mexico.

Don Lázaro knew the customs of townsfolk and country

folk; he could spot a back-countryman as far as he could
see him. When he saw the three young men from the
Xucuapan he knew he had a windfall. He stopped them
in the middle of the winding alley known as Calle Héroes
de la Revolución.

"Let me see your military-service cards."

"Why, uh, I didn't bring mine," mumbled Andrés. "I
have it, but it's at home."

"Oh, so it's at home," Don Lázaro mimicked. "Where's
your home, if you have one?"

"In my father's house on Arroyo Bravo, in the Xucuapan."

"You're supposed to carry the card at all times—if you
really have one—it's a federal offense to be without it.
How about you—you, what's your name?"

"Antonio Cruz."

"Let's see your card."

"I didn't bring it with me."

"Or you don't have one. Jail and a big fine is what
you'll get. You there, what's your name?"

"Pablo Perez."

"Where's your card?"

"It's at home too. I have it, but I left it where it
wouldn't get wet or damaged."

"Shut up! I don't have time to listen to a lot of lies."
He drew his gun. "Get over against that wall, facing it."

Hands against the wall, arms braced, feet together far
to the rear, bodies suspended off balance. Don Lázaro
searched them. No weapons—they knew better than to
carry weapons in town; they had left their machetes at
the railroad station. But they had wallets, with money
in them. He pocketed these, stepped back.

"Stand up now. Walk down the street toward the
Municipal Offices. Slowly. You're going to jail."

They walked quietly. Arrested townspeople shout protests as they are marched along. Country folk don't. They distrust the whole unfamiliar ambient—anyhow, there is no one who might come to their aid. There is no recourse. They march to jail in grim silence. Don Lázaro knew this, so he holstered his pistol. He could draw fast enough if he needed to.

Down the street Juan Pereyra had been drinking dark thick Turkish coffee with Don Ahmed, a Syrian who operates a clothing store. He stepped out into the street, hitching up his gunbelt as the three young men came by followed by the policeman. "*Hola*, Don Lázaro. Been having trouble with these people?"

"They don't have their military-service cards. We have orders to pick up people without 'em."

"Drunk and disorderly too? Carrying weapons?"

"No, just the cards."

"Well, if that's all, why don't you let them go this time. They're all right—I know them. They're from upriver, from the Xucuapan."

"No, I'm taking them in."

"You let them go. I'll vouch for them, if they weren't disorderly."

"They're probably bad actors. That one," pointing at Andrés, "was in the jug a year or so ago—something about cattle rustling."

"I know all about that. It's all settled now. These lads are all right. Let them go. I'm telling you."

"Well, if you say so—"

"He's got my wallet!" Antonio blurted.

"And mine! And mine," said the other two.

"You take their wallets, Lázaro?"

"I was just going to check them at the station to see what identification they have."

"Give them back."

"But, but I have to check through them."

"Give them back, I tell you."

"Look, *Comandante*." The voice harsh, resentful. "You may be the boss of the *Columna*, but you've got nothing to do with the Municipal Police."

Don Juan's hands hung loose at his sides, but his right hand was not far from the ornately decorated butt of his gun. His voice was flat, almost mild. "That may or may not be so. But I'm going to have something to do with you right this *chingado* moment if you don't give those wallets back. And leave these people alone as long as they behave themselves."

Don Lázaro mumbled something, then fumbled the wallets from his lefthand pocket. His hands shook—he dropped Pablo's on the street, showed the other two toward their owners, turned and slouched off.

Andrés was the first to speak. "Thanks, many thanks, Don Juan. We were in big trouble till you came along." The other two chorused their thanks.

"You lads be careful now. Don't drink much. If you get in any trouble that bastard will be laying for you. Keep your noses clean. *Hasta la vista*." He walked away.

"*Caramba*," Andrés said to the others, "I thought Don Juan would sort of have a grudge against me or something, after that other time. But he doesn't."

Pablo summed it up: "He's *buena gente*, that Don Juan."

STIRRUP LEATHERS CREAKED as the riders dismounted in the front yard. loosened cinches, and tied their horses in the shade of the *guásimo* and the old mango tree. Our youngsters ran out to tell Don Juan about their new pet: a baby *tepescuinte* that my *compadre* Santiago had given them. His men straggled to the porch, hung their weapons on the nails high on the posts, then sat or sprawled in the shade.

Maria said, after the exchange of greetings, "Don Juan, I have a big pot of peccary stew on the fire. Or would you rather have steaks? It's fresh meat, just killed this morning. I'm salting it now."

"Doña Maria, I think we're good enough friends so that I can beg off without seeming rude—you'll understand I'm not scorning your invitation. But we've been eating all the way up the trail—*pozole*, coffee, chocolate, chicken stew, venison steaks, fried catfish—"

"You mean that the situation has changed?" I asked.

The hammock creaked under his weight as he sat himself down in it. "You people of the Xucuapan are so exaggerated. You're extremists. At first, except for you," he bowed formally, something of a feat when sitting in a hammock, "and Don Panuncio, and a few others, we would have starved on these patrols—the rest of the people wouldn't even give us a *jícara* of water to drink. Now they smother us with food—and you know how it is, one can't refuse or they think you're deprecating their hospitality. We'll probably die of indigestion this trip."

"Of course you haven't the faintest notion as to why the change."

"I have no idea." He made his eyes large and round and innocent, but a spark of laughter glittered in them.

"You wouldn't possibly know that those lads Andrés and my *tocayo* Pablo and Antonio have many relations and friends along the river, and that we of the Xucuapan are a pretty clannish outfit. You are now one of us."

"Well, that's all right. The Xucuapan is a good place, except it's so damn far back in the woods."

"If you can't stand food, how about a drink? I have a

bottle of pretty fair rum stashed away for this occasion—
aguardiente for your troops."

"Rum would be fine—maybe it'll settle my stomach.
Don't give my boys too much *aguardiente*—just a small
drink while they rest."

11

To Live by the River

THE RIVER is a remarkable phenomenon, not just as a feature of the natural landscape but in the way it affects —regulates is the more precise term—the lives of men who live along its banks. I of course am more conscious of this riverine power than are my neighbors, for things that they, having lived all their lives at the river's edge, take for granted as the normal way of life are to me novel and striking. I had never lived in intimacy with and in bondage to a river before.

This intimate relationship derives of course from the rusticity, the frontier pattern, of our living conditions. Many a modern American city is built beside a river, but except for the limited few of its inhabitants who work or sport on the water only rarely are the people aware of the great stream rolling past their streets, though its water may come from their taps, though much of their merchandise may be brought or carried away by barges that ply it, though they may cross it often on high wide bridges. Only when their river surges in uncontrollable rage, threatening disaster, do all the city dwellers become conscious of its presence.

One of the first things that a newcomer to a riverine way of frontier life learns, something that those born on the river have known since they first became aware of the world about them, is that a river is never a constant in any of its multiple qualities. Mariners say that the face of the sea is never the same twice. With equal justice can this be said of the river. It is always changing, from day to day, from hour to hour, moment to moment. Rising in freshets and floods, lowering in dry weather, its level fluctuates continuously; its current speeds or slows as it floods or shrinks. High waters are cold with the chill of mountain rains, while at low stages the sun warms the slow-flowing current in the long pools. Its form changes too. In floods great tranquil eddies disappear as the rising waters roil deeply, submerging the obstacles that form pools and eddies, and the current tugs at the bamboo thickets, bushes, and grasses along the banks. At low stages rocky ledges, gravel bars, and huge black water-polished snags of tree trunks appear in the bed, making the reduced curent meander from side to side in its course. Turbulent water is ever gnawing at the banks that confine it, undermining, washing out great masses of earth and gravels and even blocks of stone, to use the materials to build new shoals downstream.

Color of the water varies with the angle of sunlight, with the brightness or cloudiness of the day, with the rise and fall of the water, turning opaque when flooding, murky when lowering, crystalline when low. A local thunderstorm on the mountain slopes to the southeast, where the headwaters form, tints the river a grayish brown. A cloudburst to the southwest, where the Arroyo Mazate and Arroyo de la Ceiba rise, paints the water orange-red from the clay ridges these streams sluice down. A regional storm blends these hues to one or another tone of warm cinnamon brown.

At low level the current makes little sound that can be distinguished from our house, twenty-five feet above and forty feet back from the river, though close at hand low gurgles and a soft hum of the current is heard. I wake in the night without at first realizing why. Then through the soft hiss of rain on the roof-thatch and the rattle of the drops on the corrugated-iron porch roof I hear the mumbling growl of racing, rolling, swirling floodwater. As I sit up, Maria reaches over to nudge me.

"Oh, you're awake," she says. "The river's rising."

"Yes. I hear it. I'm going down to check the mooring lines of the canoes."

Down below the region we call the Xucuapan, well below the confluence of our two rivers in the low flat country where the river is wide and deep, and where to rise a foot it must flood albeit shallowly thousands of acres of low plain and swamp, its endless changes are more subtle. Here in the foothills, the water pours through a narrow ravine between steep banks fifteen to thirty feet high, so its variations are more violent: a heavy drenching rain in the Sierra raises the water level a booming dozen feet or so in a few hours. When the floodcrest passes, the river level drops almost as rapidly as it rose, while far downriver the plains and swamps may remain flooded for days or even weeks. But everywhere along its course, upriver and down, the river ceaselessly changes, pulsingly rises and falls, running swift or slow, cold with mountain rain or warm with sun, gurgling softly or chattering over gravel bars when low, rumbling as it swells with flood pressure, hissing and booming as high water rips through the vegetation along the banks.

We who live along the river and its tributaries are inextricably linked to it, dependent on it, subject to its beneficent and malevolent caprices. The river system provides the life fluid for us and our animals, cleanses and refreshes us after a hard day's labor. It is our main line of communication—our principal highway to the outside world. When it floods heavily it interdicts all but lengthy, roundabout, and often difficult land routes—we must travel the river at such times or not travel at all. So imbued are we with the thought of water travel that we interpret all geographical movements by waterflow: whether by canoe or trail we say we go "downriver" or "upriver," not north or south. When we leave the river we go *adentro*, "inland"; contrariwise *salimos*, "we come out" to the river from inland. Extreme or unseasonable floods, expression of the river's malicious whim, damage our fields and pastures and would drown our livestock if we did not hurry to drive the animals to the safety of the ridges. Magnanimously the river feeds us well from the great store of water creatures that it nurtures. Sometimes the river kills us; rare is the year that passes without drownings.

To an inhabitant of the riverbank, water travel is inevitable and essential and a canoe is as much a necessity to his way of life as is a sound roof over his head. Often a man's best lands may be strips of fertile alluvium flanking the river. He goes to and from work by canoe, poling and paddling with long driving strokes that send him gliding over the water faster than one can walk along an open trail. At harvest time a short portage from field or orchard to canoe is frequently more efficient, even with the extra handling of burdens in loading and unloading the canoe, than a long pack over bad trails, man-back or with pack animals. All local produce except cattle are easiest taken to market by water. Mounted men who must cross the river go out of their way to borrow a canoe to cross their saddles and other gear, and themselves as well —the horses are led out to swimming depth and across

by one man in the canoe while another paddles. The sad-
dlery is thus saved from damaging frequent immersion
and the saddle cloths are kept dry—cold wet cloths are
thought to hurt horses' backs.

Canoes are hewn one-piece from solid logs, preferably
of mahogany because the wood is so durable in the water
and because it is smooth grained and easy to work. But
soft fragrant *cedro*, well painted and tarred, makes a light,
buoyant vessel, if a little shorter-lived than mahogany.
Good sound trees of desirable size, close to the river or a
major stream so the finished vessel can be floated out
easily, have become very scarce. As a substitute some
canoe makers favor the tough, incredibly cross-grained
macayo, though it is difficult to work and tremendously
heavy until it has had a long dry season to dry out. Others
recommend the pale hardwood *macuile*. One listens to the
canoe maker with respect, and usually accepts his dictum
as to what tree bole will or will not serve. Canoe makers
are specialists, experts. Most men buy their canoes, for
few can make one properly.

Canoe making perhaps is better termed an art than a
craft. The expert, his log cut to proper length on the
ground, bark and soft sapwood removed, finds the longi-
tudinal center of his piece by measurement: he cuts a
string or liana to the diameter of each end of the log,
doubles the measuring string evenly, measures it again to
find his center, marks it with a cord or a length of smooth
tough vine. This is one of his few fixed measures. The
complex curving tapers at bow and stern, varying from
the strong curves at gunwale level to those that fade gradually into the straightness of the centerline of the hull,
he shapes by eye, roughing out the work with his ax,
planing it to finished smoothness with an adze. Since each
canoe is carved from a tree of different size, there can

be no standard measures for these curves, or predesigned patterns. Yet the final shapes are most important: too bluff a bow taper will make the craft sluggish in the water, heavy to make move along; an extremely long slender taper at the bow reduces carrying capacity of the craft. Lateral asymmetry will make the bow fall off to one or the other side, a nuisance and an added strain on the paddler on a long trip. The even taper of the stern is for streamlining, to give maneuverability and easier advance— a blunt or flat stern is considered to create a "drag" in the water.

Finally the bottom of the hull is adzed off smooth and flat, for stability. The piece is turned over with wedges and levers, and the inside hollowed out according to the shape defined by the finished exterior. Gunwales are curved gently upward at bow and stern—the curvature once more determined by eye, not by measurement, except for the standards of the canoe maker's memory. One more set of measures is made. Thickness of the bottom is controlled by drilling several holes through, along the centerline; a stick or withe is marked for the hole that shows the estimated proper thickness, and the wood of the floor around the other holes is planed down with the adze until the floor is leveled to the desired point. Last of all, the testing holes are plugged with snugly fitted dowels, driven up hard.

Sizes of finished canoes vary considerably, according to the needs of the maker's client, from tiny slim slivers that barely keep two persons afloat to big hulls of two tons burden. Typical proportions are long and slim, for length-to-breadth ratios average somewhere near ten to one. My big canoe is of fairly typical proportions. It must have been a few inches more than twenty-six feet long before a foot or so of projecting stern was sawed off to mount the transom for the outboard; it is thirty-two inches maximum width, just behind the break of the taper at the bow. Like all these canoes, mine was made with the butt of the log for the bow so that the natural taper of the tree trunk makes it a bit narrower astern. The weighted bow steers steadier, pivots evenly on a turn.

These craft lend themselves well to the use of outboard motors, which have become popular in the last ten years for freighting loads. One can get to town with a load of hogs or cacao in a day—eight to ten hours from our house— and home again in a day and a half with a load of provisions, sugar, salt for the kitchen and for the cattle, rolls of barbed wire, lime for leaching the maize, and the like, when paddlers took three working days—thirty to thirty-six hours—for the downriver run and five to six days bucking current on their return. Simply by sawing off part of the tapered stern, without disrupting the underwater streamlining, a transom can be fitted for the motor. The length of the canoe and its weighted bow make it easy to load so as to keep an even trim; the motor's downdrag at the stern does not make the bow rear out of the water but rather, on level keel, the craft slides along nicely.

Among their many uses, the canoes serve for harvesting the foods the river offers, fish, turtles, and crustaceans. Fishing is little commercialized but, like hunting, is a spare-time activity that contributes a store of proteins to the starchy basic diet of maize, rice, and beans. And like hunting, fishing has a special attraction of diversion—of sport—of a change from the long dull routine of labor in fields and pastures. Personal preferences come into play: some men hunt more, others do more fishing, but most men do a good deal of both. The river contains flavorsome species, both abundant and easy to take if one knows how.

Mojarra is a word thought of as the name for a fish, but actually it is used to mean "panfish," for it includes three species in the river: *mojarra azul*, in form, coloration, and fin pattern so like the bluegill that I am sure it is the same, or at least a very close relative; the *sanpedreño*, with a pronounced fleshy lump projecting forward over its head, white in the water, turning a pale lavender as it dries in the air; and the *tenwaiyaka*, which looks much like a white crappie. There are also catfish— several small species (or perhaps genera—I do not begin to understand the complex taxonomy of these fishes), scarcely worth taking, whose main mission in life is stealing bait, and a large kind called *jolote*, which runs from five to fifteen pounds and some still larger. My friends and neighbors distinguish between two kinds of *jolote*, a white and a black, and point out a series of differences that I cannot for the life of me discern. There are minor color differences (both "white" and "black" are relative terms); the two are probably color phases of the same fish.

Panfish are caught most often on hooks baited with big green grasshoppers or tiny white shrimp. The fisherman ties a fifteen-meter length of line (formerly heavy hardtwist cotton cordage but for the last few years nylon monofilament, forty- or fifty-pound test)—tremendous line for fish that run from one to two pounds—to the butt of his rod, then to the tip, which leaves him twelve meters or so for fishing. The rod, a long, slim, and very straight seedling of a jungle tree called *castarica*, which dries tough and flexible, is used to throw the baited hook into the shallows at the foot of the banks, where the fish feed, with a cast like that of a fly fisherman, jerking the hook from the water, lashing back then forward to drop the hook in the desired spot. Ordinarily one man casts from the bow while his companion paddles the canoe slowly, keeping it the proper casting distance from the bank. With the short heavy line and heavy hook, the handling is no great feat, but accuracy of the casts is notable. Brush and snags abound in the shallows along the banks. One must drop the hook neatly into whatever small open space occurs. A snagged hook is simply yanked loose—snags are the reason such heavy gear is used—but when one frees his line by tugging and hauling he catches no fish at the spot.

I say the casting is not much of a feat although I cannot do it. The *castarica* rods are weighty, their action is so heavy and slow that my timing, learned with flyrods, is completely off. With sufficient practice the handling could be learned, of course, but it scarcely seems worthwhile— except when I lose hook after hook and yards of thread-line to the bamboo and the snags.

While casting with the heavy rods may be a skill, science is cast aside when a bluegill slams onto the hook— brute force takes over to horse the fish out of the water and into the canoe.

Bluegills, lumpheads (for want of a more correct name), and to some extent the species resembling white crappie feed on vegetal matter as well as on insects and shrimp. When the river level reaches the dangling tips of the sprawling grass called *camalote* that spreads along the riverbank in places where the bamboo has not been able to take over, panfish, schools of them, tug busily at the leaves, tearing off and eating bits of grass. The yellow, cherry-size fruits of the *tomatillo* tree, which have an unpleasant soapishly sweet taste, fall into the water by the hundreds from trees leaning out over the bank and are gobbled by the *mojarras*. (I have caught a few fish using *tomatillo* fruits for bait, but their pulp is so soft that it is difficult to make them stay on a hook.) The *guatope* trees that line the riverbank in places shed their spidery white flowers, whose long tubular bases are nectar-filled like those of honeysuckle. As the blossoms float gently through the air to the water surface, schools of panfish churn the water to gulp them down. *Mojarra* also eat maize. This is why Doña Chabela laboriously lugs buckets of cooked maize down the steep bank to wash off the lime and hulls of the grains, rather than doing it at the more accessible well. A few grains inevitably spill in the washing, or she spills them on purpose, so that the fish will become accustomed to coming to the shallows to feed on maize in late morning. When she has a school so well prebaited that they no longer pay any attention to her presence, she takes a short stiff pole with four feet of nylon line, baits her hook with a grain of maize—the hominy-like grains are easy to set on a hook—and yanks out panfish. If she catches one, she eats it herself; if two or three, she fries the surplus for the kids; five or six and she invites us all.

Here in the foothills where the current is usually brisk and the water temperature cool or even chilly except for brief periods late in the dry season, the flesh of catfish is firm and crisp and sweet, quite unlike the mushy muddy-flavored meat of the catfish from the lower reaches of the river, where the tepid, lethargic waters are charged with the pestilential drainage of vast swamps. Hence catfish are much sought here—the big ones, the *jolote*, of course. A throwline baited with almost anything—bits of shiners and minnows ticked with a machete as they dozed in the shallows, chicken guts, a scrap of cartilaginous venison, a dead chick—gets results. Doña Serafina, Don Rufino's wife, bakes golf-ball-size pellets of *masa*, *tortilla* dough, alongside the fire so they turn sticky inside, leathery outside, and stay on a hook well. Don Rufino hooks some big catfish with them—I nag at Maria to get the recipe, but there is some trick to the baking or roasting that Doña Serafina is chary about revealing. The best catfishing technique of all is the setline: a rope between two stakes in the riverbed, at just the right part of an eddy's swirl, with eight or ten baited hooks on short leaders. My contribution to local fishing has been the introduction of swivels, the kind you put on your leader for trolling—fewer catfish kink the leader to get away. Properly tended through the night—the fishermen sit on the bank nearby, swapping stories, going out to take in the fish as they hear them splash and fight, then rebaiting the hooks—a setline can supply several households with fish.

Catfish steaks, deep-fried, are most edible. Better still are catfish *tamales*—the only kind of *tamales* without cornmeal. The fish is cut into small chunks, doused with a sauce of tomato, chopped onion, salt, and a touch of chile if you like, wrapped in a thick layer of *acuyo* leaves, then in an impermeable layer of *toh* leaves. *Acuyo*—they call it *momo* in Tabasco—is a weed in fields and pastures, with large roundish pulpy leaves that have a faintly minty flavor plus a hint of sweet anise. The outer wrapping of *toh* leaves retains the moisture, so the contents of the package steams with all its flavor inside. Result: the best catfish you ever ate.

When the setline has worked as it should, and there are more catfish than can be consumed in a day, some of the quarry is fileted, then cut into long spiral strips, half an inch thick by a little more wide, salted, and draped over the rack of small poles that is to be found slung in the smoke above the kitchen fire in every well-ordered household. Smoke does something interesting to catfish. The result may not be compared with smoked Alaska king salmon, but it keeps well and is tasty too.

There is a big *tomatillo* tree that grows just over the edge of the bank in front of the house, just downstream from our canoe landing. I have learned to tie the canoes up short when its fruit ripens so that the tree does not shed the messy yellow pellets into them, for it leans out over the river and dumps most of its crop into the water. The first time I saw it in production I learned that panfish feed on its fruits, gulping them down as they plunk into the river. I tried using them as bait, but did not catch any fish; the fruits would not stay on the hook. One day I heard a heavier splashing than small panfish make. Peering over the bank I saw a school of larger fish, somewhere near a hundred, all about the same size—about twenty inches to two feet long.

"Manuel!" I shouted. He was setting posts in the corral. "Manuel! Come look! What kind of fish are these?"

He came at a run, looked. *"Macabil,"* he said, without enthusiasm.

"Are they good to eat?"

"Well, some people eat them. They have lots of bones."

Some *tomatillo* fruits were falling on the land side of the tree. The first few would not stay on the hook when I cast. Finally one, less ripe and firmer, kept its place—it scarcely hit the water when the butt of my rod kicked as a sizable fish struck hard, then ran as the hook set. I became very busy. The braking device of the spinning reel was set as tight as was safe with the four-pound test line—the fish stripped off line at will, I retrieved when and as I could. Sunlight glinted on the spray as a big silver fish leaped full length into the air, thrashing about to throw the hook. He looked and pulled like a six- or seven-pound fish. I played him even more cautiously, worrying about that four-pound test monofilament (actually he weighed four and a half pounds). Charging downstream he stripped line from the reel, turned to race up-current while I cranked frantically, until he again took it from the brake. Twice more he came out of the water to walk on his tail. He was just the kind of fish one uses sporting tackle for, a gamy scrapper. Recalling steelhead I had hooked—some that I landed and some that went away with lengths of broken line—I turned the disc to ease a few ounces of tension off the brake. Gradually he tired, and I could work him closer and closer. Then it was necessary to go down the steep bank to land him. I almost lost him when my feet slipped and I went down the last couple feet on the seat of my pants—by luck I managed to raise the rod as I slid to keep the line taut.

I scrambled back up the riverbank, clutching him firmly, forefinger and thumb in his eyesockets. When I reached in his mouth to work the hook loose he bit my finger till blood came. He had a set of knifelike teeth across the front of his mouth. I found a twig to force the hook free. Happily I took him to the kitchens, to be greeted with Maria's "Are you going to eat *that?*"

I burned with resentment. Here I had caught a fine fish, a big silvery fish, a fighting fish, on a thin strand of line after a long tussle. To have my prize scorned.

"Of course I am!"

"That's a *macabil*. They have lots of bones."

"All fish do—that's why they're classed as vertebrates."

"But these are tiny nasty little bones—spines, we call them."

"I've eaten fish before. I'm going to weigh it, then you scale and gut it and fry it up nice and brown."

Usually I clean my catch, but locally that is woman's work. Men do the heavy work, the difficult things: felling the jungle, roping wild cattle, catching fish; women the simple routine chores: collecting small firewood, milking tame cows, gutting fish. As a rule we divide the labor a bit differently in our house, but she had to be put in her place.

I didn't eat it. I couldn't. The flesh was shot through with tiny, wiry, tough bones. Some had barbs, just like fish-hook barbs, on their tips. There were double ones, like V's, with barbs on their tips—a man could choke to death if he got one of those caught in his throat.

That is frontier life—learning about one's environment as one goes along. I now know I can catch *macabil* whenever I want—sometimes when I do not even want to. They will take a hook in the shallows, or in deep water where panfish do not feed. They will hit a small spinner or silver spoon. They are fun to take on light tackle, for they are all fighters—they even put up a considerable battle on the massive tackle my neighbors use. When, for all my strategy, other fish won't bite and *macabil* is all I take home, Maria does them as most of our neighbors do: in a fish stew, flavorsome because the flesh gives good taste to the broth. We eat the soup and the vegetables, leaving the meat to the cats, who have better techniques for handling hundreds of small barbed bones.

ALMOST EVERY MAN owns a harpoon or two—a barbed steel blade welded to a conical socket to which a wooden shaft is fitted. Town blacksmiths make the implements to order, heavy or light, as one prefers. The harpoons serve not only for panfish, but for predators such as *robalo*, which we call "snook," garfish, and a small but well-flavored striped fish with a wide toothy mouth called *guavina*, none of which will take the still baits used by local fishermen (I get them on plugs and spoons, but no one else fishes with such gear). When long afternoon shadows wipe the sun glare from the clear water, men go harpooning; they watch for fish in shallows, then hurl their weapons with a sidearm motion that gives a low flat trajectory. Sometimes near dusk great swarms of Mayflies dance just above the water. Catfish surface to gulp down the insects, and fall easy prey to the harpooner.

The most effective harpooning is done at night, by flashlight. When the water is low and clear, panfish and other small species seek shallow nooks at the foot of the riverbank, sometimes sheltered by weeds and trailing branches, sometimes open—it is clearly the shallows they seek, not cover. Local people maintain the fish "are cooling off," for the dew-laden night air is often cooler than the water; more likely it is the time when the large predators are acitve—fish too large to maneuver well in scanty water. The harpooner with a flashlight stands in the bow of the canoe, and his companion in the stern paddles slowly and very quietly—the least thump of the paddle against the canoe frightens fish away—steering the craft just a few feet out from the bank. Panfish usually lie quiet for a few moments, canting over sideways to keep their backs to the beam of light. One must thrust the harpoon rapidly and accurately before the fish dart away. If the fisherman lacks a harpoon (for they do get lost occasionally), a machete, swung in a slashing or stabbing motion, depending on the position of the fish, can be used effectively. But a harpoon is better, especially when the quarry is partly hidden by weeds or brush. As the canoe glides silently, the fishermen watch for snook, catfish, and garfish often encountered cruising near the surface just outside the shallows.

A few hours of harpoon fishing usually produces a bountiful catch, and a mixed one as well—samples of almost everything that inhabits the river, even turtles, and once in a long while an alligator, like my *compadre* Nato a few years ago. He drove the harpoon deep into a six-foot 'gator floating quietly on the surface, realizing with dismay as he did so that the retrieving line was old and worn, and in any case had not been intended to hold such a powerful quarry. By luck his brother Lino had brought his shotgun and managed to blast a load of buckshot into the side of the struggling animal's head, just behind and below the eye, before the line broke or the 'gator tipped their small unstable canoe. Exotic strays from saltwater are encountered now and then. Don Rosendo has the bill of a small sawfish nailed to the front wall of his house for friends to admire. He says the strange fish looked so formidable he was almost afraid to harpoon it—he had not known such creatures existed. One of Don Amaranto's sons harpooned but lost an otter that surfaced in the flashlight's beam one night not long ago. The struggling animal bit through the retrieving line. But even without such unusual encounters, night harpooning is a productive technique if the eye is sharp and the hand is quick.

The big "white" river turtles are a pleasure of local gourmets. For the life of me I don't see why: most of the edible parts consist of rubbery skin with a thick layer of gelatinous fat; the meat is white, dry, and flavorless. Much better to my palate is the red meat of the small *hicotea*, "painted turtle," but there is no arguing with tastes. The big white turtle yields many times more meat and fat, and the *hicotea*, though it loves to sun itself on logs and snags projecting above water, is wary and difficult to take.

When freshets are receding, the water still murky, white turtles often feed on submerged vegetation in the shallows. Turtle hunters paddle along the edges of the river to harpoon the creatures under the bow of the canoe. When water is clear, the spearman waits at a pool or eddy where he expects to find a turtle feeding. The creature surfaces to breathe, finally—a dark shadow that turns to brown amid the gray shadows of the clear water. It floats a minute or so, its nose just out of water, its armored back awash, not much of a target at best. The hunter whips his harpoon in a long flat throw; steel sounds as it drives through the thick shell—or thumps as the point ignominiously glances off the curved target.

IN THE SUMMER thundershowers lash the jungles and clearings with rain and whip them with lightning blasts while thunderdrums of the ancient rain gods boom overhead. At times the storms center on the mountain slopes where the river is born—the clear waters turn muddy-opaque, swell to the edges of the banks. River dwellers scan the roiling currents: the freshets of June, July, and August bring the runs of giant shrimp, *mayacaste*, down from the creeks and streamlets. Trails are sticky and foul, gullies turn to mudholes, stream crossings are swimming-deep. But the cattle are safe on the ridges, and canoes skim lightly over the river's crest. We take to the water to reap its harvest.

The *mayacaste* run downstream—just the reverse of salmon in northern climes—running from the headwaters of the streams in the foothills to spawn in the brackish mangrove-bordered waters of the estuary near the sea. Running by the thousands, tens, hundreds of thousands, even thousands of thousands, for the attrition is high. Nature is harsh with the giant shrimp as she is with other creatures subject to the high production–high attrition system. Vast numbers of adults are required so that there may be enough survivors of the run—thousands on thousands of females each with several thousand eggs, hundreds on hundreds of males to fertilize the eggs at the spawning grounds, for the newly hatched sprat will be preyed on by many foes as they migrate upstream to the headwaters of the river, to its tributary streams, to the shallow rivulets where they grow to maturity. In form the *mayacaste* are like the marine shrimp that you peel and eat on Fisherman's Wharf, but bigger—the females are six or seven inches long, nose to tail (if a shrimp can be said to have a "nose"); the males are thicker, meatier, and two to three inches longer. The tiny sprat are gobbled down by minnows and other small predators. As survivors outgrow the mouths of these enemies they become victims to others: panfish, for example—the shrimp never outgrow the vast mouths of snook and catfish. They elude such foes by hiding in crevices in the rocks, in the hollow joints of broken bamboo stems, or by migrating to the shallow upper reaches of small streams that large attackers cannot enter. In the shallows the decimated crustaceans are beset by new foes—birds, cranes, herons, bitterns, and egrets—I have seen grackles, who are not waterbirds at all, kill adult shrimp in very shallow water. Raccoons and coatis hunt them too. But despite the tremendous losses there remain many many adult shrimp to begin the downstream journey when the summer rains flood the stream.

The shrimp are quick and agile, darting this way or that in lightning evasive action. Man could not capture them except by using a great close-meshed net like the seines used in salt-water fishery, but even such a net could not be managed in the violent flood currents. The *mayacaste* can be taken in abundance because of their propensity for hitch-hiking. With their many legs they clutch twigs, branches, even the flotsam the river carries downstream to the sea.

Man is the only lazy animal, the only creature who

works hard at devising new ways to avoid expenditure of physical energy. The giant shrimp do not hitch-hike to save effort, but to hide from their foes: the voracious cat-fish and snook, the sharp-toothed *macabil* as well, and a great brown fish hawk, perhaps an osprey, who snatches them at the surface. Far downstream wrasse and other hungry salt-water species temporarily leave the salt sea to feast on the fluvial delicacy. So, grasping the bits of wood that spin and race downstream in the current, mo-tionless so to seem like lumps on the bits of flotsam, the giant shrimp drift seaward. Thus they elude their river enemies, but put themselves within reach of another preda-tor: man.

"THIS IS A BIG freshet," Maria says ."The river is booming. The *mayacaste* will surely run."

"Mm-hm," I reply, as I look for a plastic bag for my cigarettes and matches. A slow steady rain is falling; what began yesterday as scattered heavy thundershowers has turned into a general storm.

"Aren't you going to see if they're running?"

"Not now. I'm going to the Playas pasture. The calf of that gray cow the kids call La Burra is tied in a low place that could go underwater if this rain keeps up and the river keeps rising."

"Last time they ran you were in town, and we didn't get a taste—the only people on the river who didn't eat shrimp."

"I'll be back in a couple of hours."

"If Don Rufino and Don Guillermo show up, what shall I tell them?"

"If they show up it's a sure sign the *mayacaste* will run. Those two must be able to smell the shrimp from way back in the woods. Tell them to take the canoe and start fishing. They know where the paddles are. Tell them I won't be long."

The Tabasco saddle is slung from a beam in the store-room. Made for such weather, for swimming flooded streams—a naked frame of tropical cedar and hardwood fork from which rigging and stirrups are slung—it is easier to dry out than my rawhide-cased, leather-covered Texas saddle. The Arroyo del Carmen will be swimming-deep.

Don Rufino, Don Guillermo, and Feliciano are sitting on the porch sipping coffee when I return. They had been out on the river; the long-handled paddles are leaning against the porch roof.

"*Buenos días, señores.* Nothing happening yet?"

"*Buenos días,* Don Pablo," they chorus.

Then Rufino says, "They're passing, but all swimming free. There's hardly any trash—twigs and branches and things—going by for them to ride on."

"Well, maybe after a bit there'll be some."

"There should be," puts in Don Guillo. "The river's rising fast."

As the river rises it picks up flotsam from along the banks left by previous freshets. By early afternoon the water has risen almost two feet more. Bits of branches, sections of dead bamboo stems, even small logs begin to dot the surface.

"Let's go look," Rufino says.

We each take a paddle and go down to the canoe. It is no longer a long way down the bank—the river is lapping close to the foot of the *tomatillo* tree. In the canoe are a couple of big bowl-shaped wicker baskets, two feet across at the rim, and a five-gallon can. Guillo goes to the stern to steer, Feliciano and I go to the midsection, Rufino to the bow. We swing out into the rushing current, driving the paddles deep and hard. Seventy or eighty yards upstream from the landing is a stretch where the flow is slowed a trifle by the half-submerged trees on either bank, and the floating bits of wood are concentrated in mid-channel. We drive the canoe up to the place. I lay down my paddle to pick up a basket. The others stroke steadily, just hard enough to keep the canoe stationary in the rushing stream.

"There's one!" Rufino shouts above the rumble and roar of the current. "On the piece of bamboo!"

To the right is a pencil-thick joint of parched yellow bamboo stem, less than a foot long, bouncing amid the rolling water. Underneath hangs the yellow and brown bulk of a shrimp, upside down, tip of the curled-up tail projecting into the air. Expertly the paddlers steer the canoe to the right so that the bit of bamboo and its pas-senger will pass about a foot away, just clearing the turbulence at the bow. I crouch, knees braced against the side of the canoe, basket held in both hands, dip and scoop inward as they have taught me, dump the shrimp and his vehicle into the canoe. The water pours out through the open weave of the basket as it lifts. Feliciano stops, snatches up the shrimp, and tosses it into the five-gallon can, which is too narrow and tall for it to flip out of—the shrimp nips his hand with its pincers, drawing blood. Feliciano swears, slams the shrimp into the can harder than necessary. Guillo, behind me, chuckles.

"Another!" Rufino calls, pointing to the left with his paddle. They steer left, letting the canoe drop back a little. Just as I reach with the basket, a swirl of current swings the chunk of wood the *mayacaste* hangs from be-yond my reach and on past the canoe. The paddlers turn about to paddle downstream, stern foremost, in pursuit. They lay the canoe close alongside the piece of wood with the shrimp, I scoop it up, toss it into the can and the wood over the side. It takes but a moment to do, but we are a hundred yards down from our station. I exchange the basket for a paddle to help drive the canoe back up.

Taking turns with the basket, we continue. So does the rain. A heavy rumble of thunder comes from the south over the mountains. Sopping wet as we are, we grin knowingly at each other. As long as the rain keeps on, the river will continue to rise and the shrimp continue to run. When the flood crest passes, the creatures disappear—finding shelter along the riverbanks to await the next freshet.

The can, containing fifty shrimp or thereabouts, is nearly full. We take it to the house. Soon Maria sends the youngsters, making a portable tent of my poncho between the two of them, to call us to dinner, a dinner of *mayacaste* in their rich broth, boiled with herbs and savors in just barely enough water. We wolf it down, grateful for the heat of the steaming broth, for we are chilled from the long soaking.

"We've eaten—the kids, Doña Chabela, and I," Maria tells me. "That's the last of that first canful."

"You mean the whole can is gone?"

"That's right. Chabela ate nineteen—I counted."

"It's not polite to count, but interesting to know. I sometimes wonder what happens to all the food in the kitchen."

"Well, no matter. You can catch more. Don Rufino and Don Guillo can't very well complain—after all, she's Rufino's mother and Guillo's aunt."

After nightfall, the *mayacaste* climb on top of their stick rafts instead of hanging underneath as they do in daylight. Their avoidance of light stands them in good stead, for should they emerge above water in daytime their many avian foes would make short work of them. In the dark, when aquatic predators are most active, they cluster on the drifting sticks and twigs—two, three, four, half a dozen on a bit of branch that barely stays awash with their weight. They can be detected far away: in the flashlight's beam their eyes reflect ruby pinpoints of light. One piece of branch about four feet long by an inch or so through has fourteen passengers. Rufino, basketing, shouts; we cease paddling to let the canoe drift downstream abreast of the stick, while he grasps the upper end gently, rolling it slowly as he scrapes the basket beneath it. Two of the crustaceans leap free—he catches an even dozen. The five-gallon cans fill rapidly. We take them to the kitchen, sip some coffee, smoke, return to the canoe. The eleventh can is half full when suddenly there are few shrimp. The flood is cresting. On the eastern horizon, for the river is high enough now so that we can see over its banks, a faint paleness, forerunner of dawn, tints the sky.

"The run's about over. Let's go in." My shoulders and back ache from swinging the long heavy paddle. In the kitchen the table is piled high with boiled shrimp, a big pot of shrimp in their broth is bubbling on the fire, there are shrimp broiled on the coals, delicious with a pinch of salt and a few drops of lime juice. I find a bottle of *aguardiente*, and we have a round of stiff drinks. Then I change to dry clothes and we gorge ourselves. Feliciano counts out the mountain of boiled shrimp into four equal piles so that he and Don Rufino and Don Guillo can each take their share, while I stretch out in the hammock. I can just mumble a sleepy reply when they make their farewells, saying they'll return next time the shrimp run.

FAR DOWN the river, near town, scarcely an hour or two from the market place in a light canoe, live several professional fishermen. Their palm-thatched huts sit on the natural levees of the river, at that point deep, wide, and slow; a few yards behind them, whichever bank of the river they live on, are vast stretches of swamp. Before dawn and in late afternoon their womenfolk set out smudge pans—large sherds of broken pottery vessels, worn-out enamelware skillets, and pot lids—filled with glowing coals, bits of rotten wood, and nuts of the *coyol* palm, which smolder to make a thick greasy smoke to disperse the clouds of mosquitoes. When the men paddle their canoes to town to sell their catch they bring home a five-gallon can or two of drinking water—down there the river is bitter and salty from the sea tides when low, thick with chocolate-colored silt and mud in time of floods, and, low water or high, has a faint stink of rotting vegetation from the swamps that flank it and drain into it. They tolerate the miserable environment because the fisheries are amazingly rich, and they have a market close at hand.

I know most of those people—one, Don Consuelo, especially well—so I know that they have a whole kit of fishing techniques unused by us upriver. Panfish they take in quantity with circular throwing nets, the same type of long conical net with a retrieving line at the apex that one sees far across the Pacific Ocean: in Hawaii, in Malaya, in the Philippines. Don Consuelo has tried time and again to teach me to handle the net. It looks so easy, so effortless when he tosses it out to land elegantly round over a shallows where the panfish are feeding on a bait of coarse-ground maize. But there is a trick to it that I cannot seem to master. Don Consuelo, however, visiting his netting places—small baited squares in the shallows cleared of driftwood and brush and grass so that the net hauls in clean without snagging—gently tosses his net over many fish every day.

At certain seasons he uses basketry fish traps with inverted conical mouths. At other times he can use these traps for live storage, to keep his catch until he wants to go to town.

Another professional secret is his method of taking big white turtles on hook and line. In his *patio* he has a thrifty planting of bananas of a tiny, very sweet variety called *siete-en-boca*, "seven to a mouthful." He places ripe stalks of this fruit in favorable spots to prebait the turtles. Then he fishes, with a thin 3/0 hook, point filed needle-sharp, embedded in a piece of the little banana. He does not use a pole. The medium-weight nylon line between his finger-tips, he waits quietly. Turtles do not hit a bait like game-fish, or even like panfish, but munch it slowly and cau-tiously. When he feels the faint signals that the animal is feeding he sets the hook hard, for a turtle's mouth is tough and bony. The creature is hooked, and to boat. Townsfolk pay a good price for the hard-shelled reptiles. No one up where we live knows how to do this. But Don Consuelo and his neighbors down in mosquito country are professionals.

THE GENTLE ART of fishing is many things to many men. It may be, to those such as Don Consuelo, a pro-fession. To others like me and my near neighbors, it may be a pleasant way to augment, in spare time, the protein content of the daily diet. Fishing may be a healthful out-door sport for ribbon clerks and presidents. But to Don Bernando it was a vice.

When he came hiking up the trail that day, leaning against the tumpline supporting a bulky load on his back, I knew who he was. I had met him down at El Ixtal, where he worked for Don Panuncio. He had no land of his own, unlike most of us on the river, but Don Panuncio "lent" him tracts to sow to corn, and in return Bernando planted them with grass after harvesting his crop.

His wife, Maria del Carmen, one of Doña Chabela's daughters—thus Don Rufino's sister—carried a smaller pack, also with a tumpline. Their two small daughters, looking at a distance like animated blue and pink morning-glory blossoms in their flare-skirted little dresses, trudged behind.

The little family set their loads down on the porch—at close range it turned out that each little girl also carried a bundle—greeted us, and went in to visit Doña Chabela. Thus we learned that they had come to visit Don Rufino.

Don Bernando is an exceptional man. Were one unkind, one might describe his appearance as a caricature of the regional type of country *mestizo*, more Indian than Spanish genetically. Where most men are slim, with slimness that conceals a wiry muscularity, Bernando is outright skinny. He is a bit above average height, or so I believe, for I have never seen him stand up straight—he slouches at the shoulders, droops at the waist, sags at the knees. He has the wide cheekbones and long aquiline nose, projecting mouth parts, thin lips and narrow angular chin typical of the southern Gulf Coast people. But his leanness and his hollow cheeks make his cheekbones seem even wider, his nose seem longer, his jaw lanker.

Even his name is a bit odd. In the course of my travels south of the Rio Grande I have met a number of Bernardos, and even more Fernandos, but never before had I heard the two names combined into one.

Three or four days after Bernando's arrival, Don Rufino came to borrow a canoe. He and his brother-in-law, he said, wanted to catch a few panfish. I still had a small canoe, very light and convenient for fishing (later, leaky and battered, it came to its end as a salt trough for the cattle). In this the pair embarked, to return after what seemed a brief time with a handsome string of panfish. This came to be a daily or every-other-day occurrence. Obviously a master fisherman was about. Don Rufino is competent, but he never made catches like that by himself.

Don Bernando occasionally came alone to borrow the canoe. Sometimes he brought a harpoon instead of the *castarica* fishing pole, taking back two or three big turtles instead of panfish.

Every time he, or he and Rufino, stopped by the house to say thank you for the loan of the canoe, Maria and the youngsters stared wistfully at the catch; I stared with bitter envy. The fish were biting and I had no time to go fishing. Candelario and I, just the two of us, were building a great long fence that was to keep the cattle out of the *milpa* when planting time came, and the chore progressed slowly.

There was a moon waxing big; it would be a fortnight before night-lighting would be effective, for panfish see the canoe's shadow far away by moonlight.

"*Papi*," said Rosamaria, "Don Bernando took home a beautiful string of panfish today."

"Must have been twenty, at least," her brother added. "All big and fat."

"It's been so long since we had a good meal of *mojarras*," Maria said. "Of course I know you're busy."

Doña Chabela rattled the pots and pans around on the *fogón*, the raised clay-filled box where the kitchen fire burns, grumbling and mumbling loudly as she does. ". . . nothing but beans and rice . . ." (slam! crash!) ". . . stuffing themselves on good fat panfish . . ." (rattle! bam!) ". . . for all Bernando's a lazy *hijo de su puta madre* . . ." (crunch! slam!)

[193]

"Doña Chabela," I bellowed, "I've told you before, don't use that kind of language in front of the kids!" She gave the cooking wares one final slam, then began to cry because of my rudeness. The children, who love her despite her growling, began to comfort her.

Maria glared at me. "Sounded as though she cracked the last good bean-cooking *olla* shoving it around. If she did, there won't even be beans to eat around this house."

Defeated, I rode back to the fencing job. The ground was dry and hard, but I could still dig a dozen post holes before dark.

Next morning I waited for Bernando. Happily he arrived early to ask if he might borrow the canoe.

"There it is, if you need it. Help yourself. But from now on the canoe earns a share of the catch when you use it to go fishing," I answered, meanly.

He smiled gently. "But of course, Don Pablito. When I return we'll divide the catch." Something about his manner hinted that he had been expecting this, perhaps even wondering why I had not imposed the condition sooner.

On my return late that afternoon the odor of fried fish pervaded the house.

"Don Bernando left them for the canoe's share. Eight: six big ones and two medium-size ones."

"How many did he catch?"

"Twenty-three. He counted them in front of me. Eight for us, eight for Rufino, seven for him."

"For Don Rufino? I didn't see him this morning."

"No, he didn't go fishing. But Don Bernando borrowed his fishing pole."

"Borrowed his fishing pole? With a forest of *castarica* not ten minutes' walk from where he lives? Why that racketeering, chiseling *hijo de—*"

Maria silenced me by pantomime, clapping one hand over her mouth and gesturing with the other toward the kitchen where Doña Chabela was listening. "It was all right," she said. "Eight was plenty for us. Besides, he said to tell you he wants a pasture-weeding contract."

"He does! How wonderful!" Labor was scarce. Tiny weed seedlings in my pastures were turning into lush verdant bushes that devoured soil nutrients the grass needed, and would soon shade out the grass as well.

"Yes. I told him that you'd probably have something for him if he showed up early tomorrow before you leave for the new fence line." Don Bernando agreed to chop out the weeds on a large tract in the Playas pasture for a reasonable sum. He set his own pace. One day he would work like a wild man, and till late in the afternoon; next day he would quit early to come borrow the canoe for an afternoon of fishing. Soon he worked hard one day and not at all the next. This of course was not my concern. The whole point of the contract system—the reason it appeals to my neighbors—is that the contractor sets his own pace, works long or short hours as he pleases. As long as he gets the chore done, it doesn't matter how he does it. Thus he feels independent, controlling his own working time— Bernando has a large measure of the pioneer's urge for independence. I liked it because it meant independence for me, too—I did not have to stand around overseeing the chore—I could get that thrice-damned fence built. The canoe was earning its share of flavorsome panfish, too. It seemed an excellent arrangement.

Presently it became necessary to go to town, to bring home some provisions, and a little cash too—cash to pay to my *compadre* and to Don Bernando for their labor, and to others I hoped to recruit. The logical thing to do was to take a load of hogs in to sell; there were eight fat ones.

Here where there are no good roads, where the river winds
and turns, making long distances out of short ones so that
transport is slow and costly, it simply does not pay to take
a ton of maize to town to sell. But hogs and poultry repre-
sent ways to concentrate bulky grains—they are in effect
neat and efficient ways to package large quantities of corn.
A ton of hogs (my eight fell short of a ton but I'm using
round numbers) represents several tons of maize but can
be taken to market in a single trip, instead of several. This
is efficiency. This resolution of the transport problem is not
unique: Iowa farmers devised it long ago.

So I hinted broadly, and Don Rufino and Don Bernando
stayed one late afternoon on return from their fishing to
cut poles to make a cage for the pigs in the big canoe and
to attach the small canoe alongside *en falco*, "as a stabil-
izer," somewhat like the outrigger of the deepsea canoes
of the ancient Hawaiians. Then, amid an ear-shattering din
of squeals, we loaded the fat hogs so that I could set out
at dawn next morning. Coming home, I could tow the
small canoe or load it aboard the big one.

The chore done, my two helpers gave me their verbal
lists of purchases of things they needed. Dutifully, I jotted
the items down.

Don Rufino and some other neighbors do this often,
when they know I am about to make a trip to town. When
I bring their order they pay me for it, occasionally in cash
but more often in labor. Don Rufino's shopping lists are
usually modest, like those of my *compadre* Candelario. But
Don Bernando's was lengthy: provisions such as sugar,
salt, lime to leach the maize, cooking oil, soap, a handmill
for grinding the corn, a new machete with a couple of
triangular files to sharpen it, dress goods, thread, zippers,
and buttons. I was in a trap. As I wrote the items I could
estimate that their total cost would likely be more than the

agreed price of the contract he was working on. I didn't know Bernando well enough to have any notion whether he was punctilious about paying his debts. On the other hand, refusing such a request is not good personnel relations. A refusal is interpreted as being just what it is: an expression of distrust. Here where the labor market is a seller's market, a workman feeling himself insulted is likely to offer his services elsewhere, and I was shorthanded. A trifle unhappily, I resolved to take the gamble.

On the way home from town, the shadows were long as I approached El Ixtal, so I steered the canoe into the mouth of the creek. The river was low; there were too many snags and gravel bars for night travel. Don Panuncio's hospitality can be counted on, so I often stay overnight. In return, now and again there is some errand I can run for him in town.

We relaxed and chatted awhile. He poured another drink and then said, "I hear Don Bernando is working for you now."

"Does Bernando owe you some money?" I asked, alarmed. I had no desire to get caught in the crossfire between Don Panuncio and one of his debtors.

He looked down his nose, the way he does—you can never tell whether he is enjoying a private joke or planning a trap for the unwary. "No, he doesn't. That's what I wanted to tell you. Bernando is on the level. When he needs money for provisions and things, you can lend it to him without worrying. He'll pay it back. Of course he may pay it back mostly in fish and turtles—"

I felt a vast relief, remembering Bernando's unfinished contract and the large order of goods I was bringing him in the canoe. I didn't quite understand the business about the "fish and turtles," but that couldn't be serious.

I began to find out when I got home. There was a huge

river turtle on its back in the middle of the kitchen floor. It couldn't go away because it couldn't turn over.

"How did you catch that thing?" I asked Maria.

"I didn't. Don Bernando brought it, just today."

"Was it pay for the canoe?"

"No, he brought a few *mojarra* for the canoe—he said he didn't catch many today. The turtle he sold me for ten pesos."

"Did you pay him?"

"No, he said to tell you to put it on the bill."

That's the way it went from then on.

Bernando worked just enough to keep me interested in him. He always had a contract going, slow but sure. And he went fishing. If he was spearing turtles, he'd take the time—not much for him—to catch a few panfish with which to pay "the canoe's share," then sell Maria a turtle. When he knew that *mojarra* fishing was good, he'd spear a small turtle, present it very formally "for the canoe," then offer a string of luscious panfish for sale.

He didn't live a marginal existence. He himself went around in patch-on-patch dungarees and work shirts, but they were always shining clean. Maria del Carmen was a good housewife, and she used quantities of soap from one month's end to the next. She and the two little girls put on new or almost-new dresses every time they came to visit Grandma Chabela and my Maria.

I began to observe Bernando with interest, not only because of his fishing skill, from which I hoped to learn, but because he was obviously a unique character—I collect characters the way some people collect ivory elephants (not physically of course but neatly inventoried in my memory, which makes it an inexpensive hobby). When he worked, he worked hard, but his heart was not in it. It was when he came to the river's edge that he came aglow with enthusiasm. I watched him many many times.

He would walk out to the edge of the riverbank and stand staring at the flowing water. Then he would swing his long nose from side to side savoring the breeze. Next he tilted his head back to look at the sky, the cloud formations if there were any, and finally return his gaze to the river.

I would say, "How does it look today, Don Bernando?"

He might reply, "It's not good for panfishing today. I think I'll see if I can spear a turtle."

On a number of occasions I tested his pronouncement—fished assiduously, trying all the baits I could find, and never got a nibble.

Another time he might say, "This is a good day for *mojarra*, but not on grasshoppers. This is a day to catch them with shrimp."

I would go along the edge with my spinning outfit and a bottle full of nice juicy green grasshoppers, wearing my arm out casting—and nothing. Then I would take the other canoe, find a few shrimp in broken joints of bamboo in the water, the way he taught me, put one on a hook, and whambo! a big fat bluegill.

I tried to get him to explain how he knew all this. He couldn't put what he saw into words, somehow. He would try, but he couldn't clarify it—I really don't believe he was concealing his knowledge from me.

"You can tell by the sky," he would say. "The shade of blue, the way the clouds move if there are clouds, or the lightness or darkness of the overcast."

I would stare at the sky—clear, or with scattered clouds, or solid overcast, without seeing anything to indicate to me whether fish would bite on grasshoppers or on shrimp.

"You can tell by the water, the way it runs," he would say.

I'd look at the water—it was running downhill, the way that water has run since the beginning of time, fast or slow depending on the flood stage of the river. I couldn't get a clue.

I want to explain this clearly, which is difficult because I don't understand it myself—if I did, I'd be as good a fisherman as Bernando. But there was something he saw in weather factors: amount of light, wind, air temperature; and in the water: level of the river, speed of current, clarity of the water, and so on that he was able to put together in a sort of equation that either added up or did not add up to the sum, "Fish will bite." Patently the factors could vary and still combine to form the proper total, just as 5 + 5, 7 + 3, and 4 + 1 + 2 + 3 all equal 10. He went fishing on bright days, on overcast days, on windy days, and caught fish. On other days that seemed the same to me—bright, overcast, or windy—he knew the equation did not add up right, so he stayed home strumming his *jarana* or went to chop weeds in my pastures.

I have wondered at times whether it could be possible that he had just a touch of that sixth sense that many animals have, that is, the sensitivity to abrupt changes in barometric pressure that affect animals' behavior before a storm, making even staid old farm beasts run and jump and frisk and play.

Of course, to this weather knowledge or weather sense that told him when the fish would bite, what baits they would take best, and where the turtles were feeding—in deep pools or shallow ones—he added a great deal of skill in handling his hook and line and his harpoon. When I say "a great deal of skill," I mean something special, here where most men deserve expert ratings at handling these implements. Most of the local fishermen cast their baited hooks with a remarkable accuracy into the little openings in the weeds and fallen brush that line the riverbanks. But the heavy hook with its chunky grasshopper or shrimp bait—

the white shrimp are fairly big—makes quite a weight. Most fishermen let it land with a resounding plop. Bernando had a way of checking his hook with a back flick of his wrist to make it hit the water almost as lightly as a fly— he could lay it inches in front of the nose of a bluegill without frightening the fish away. That, with the heavy, slow-action *castarica* poles, takes some very neat timing. And takes many fish.

Feliciano went turtle spearing with him twice, as I recall. Now Feliciano has quite a high regard for his own talents with a spear that makes him tend to deprecate the skill of others: "He missed a handsome big one right out there in front of him; I would have got it." But he came back quite chastened from his outings with the master Bernando.

"That Don Bernando," he gulped, "that Don Bernando is really something. Long throws, cross-throws where the turtle was out in the current and moving fast—he never missed a one. I believe he doesn't know how to miss— couldn't miss if he tried."

I watched him spear a few myself. Riding along the river's edge, on several occasions, I saw him waiting for the turtle at the lower end of an eddy. He would have the canoe crosswise, its nose against the bank, so neatly balanced against the swirl of the eddy that by lounging easily against the long-handled paddle jabbed into the river bottom he held the craft firmly in place. His right arm he held cocked, balancing the spear point upward, the base of the shaft against the gunwale of the canoe, so its weight did not tire him. I would rein up, hook a leg over the saddle-horn, and watch. He knew the turtle was there, and that it would have to surface—in ten minutes, or forty, or an hour— I never clocked one, but sometimes they take a long time between breaths. Meanwhile Bernando would wait, slouching relaxedly against the paddle, spear in hand.

When the turtle rose to take air, a brown bulk in the clear grayish-white or grayish dark of the water, Bernando would balance his spear rapidly and throw with the flat, slightly sidearm motion of a big league pitcher slinging his fast one. But Bernando's big splay-toed feet were not striding through a pitcher's box. They were planted athwartships of a wobbly canoe.

The spear always made an abrupt hollow sound, plock! as it smashed through the shell. The stricken turtle would dive, tugging the floating spear shaft about by the retrieving line. Bernando would paddle over leisurely, pick up shaft and line, and haul in his prize. But I remember him best in the waiting posture, slouched against the paddle, spear poised, holding the canoe in balance against the current effortlessly.

Bernando had other strings to his bow: the strings on his *jarana*. He was, I came to learn, widely famed along the river as a musician. Whenever a *fiesta* was given anywhere nearby he was recruited to play. The *jarana* is always built for six strings, but in the Xucuapan it is strung with only four. It is essentially an instrument of accompaniment, defining the rhythm—few players do more than strum a few chords, "*tum, tidi-dum, tidi-dum*," while the singer carries the melody of the sound. Bernando, however, could play the melody on his *jarana*. He could coax some real music out of a guitar, too, if there happened to be one around. He could play any popular tune that he had heard once or twice on someone's radio, as well as the *sones* of the *huapango*.

Consequently, whenever there was a *fiesta* given anywhere nearby, there he was sure to be, his nimble fingers on the strings of his *jarana* from dark till dawn. At such affairs, the musicians at times are paid a few pesos, at times not, but invariably they are kept well lubricated with *aguardiente*. Sometimes hosts are niggardly with drinks to their guests, not for thrift but in an effort to avoid fights and bloodshed that so often accompany the *fandangos*, but tradition requires that the *músicos* be adequately supplied. This was to Bernando's liking. He had a chronic thirst that only quantities of the raw white liquor could quench.

So from early in the soft tropical night, from the time the strings began to throb out their rhythm to the singers' falsetto *son jarocho* and the dancers began to drum their heels on the dancing platform, there Bernando would be, a shock of lank black hair dangling over his sometimes bleary eyes, his fingers rippling over the strings of his *jarana* until daybreak. When the new day came, he could not of course go to work. He went home with a supply of the hair of the dog to cure his hangover. And the weeds grew in my pasture.

Bernando's visit to his brother-in-law Rufino lasted nearly two years. He did some work during that period, caught and sold me many fish and turtles, played many and many a tune, and drank enough liquor to float my big canoe. One day, of a sudden, he came to tell me he was leaving and wanted to square up accounts. When we totaled up the items on the credit side of his ledger, that is, the contracts completed and the fish and turtles turned in over the preceding few months, since we had last squared accounts, they came to just seven pesos less than the amount I had advanced him in cash and in goods he had ordered from town. He paid me in cash, somewhat to my surprise—I had expected panfish.

Then he asked to borrow a canoe, to move his family and belongings downriver to a point near the railroad. He had some relatives down there, he said, who would bring the canoe back. He was going to town to live.

A few days after he departed downriver with all his possessions and family in the small canoe, a couple of youngsters came poling the canoe upstream. They said their Uncle Bernando had sent them to return the craft and paddles. I offered to pay them, but they said no thanks, Uncle Bernando had paid them and had told them not to take any payment from me.

When Bernando got to Lomas Bonitas he managed to find work for a time. He was lucky. There are more unskilled workers than jobs there. Then things became difficult, and Bernando did what many another country boy has done in town: he fouled up. He drank too much. He became acquainted with the local jail. I saw him and a couple of others pulling weeds in the Plaza de Armas under custody of an armed policeman. The cop wouldn't let me talk to him. I went to the police office to see what I could find out. Nothing serious, the officer in charge told me, just dead drunk in the middle of the street. They were going to turn him loose that afternoon, so there was no point to trying to pay his fine.

"Why don't you take him back upriver with you, Don Pablo? Take him back where he belongs. We're getting tired of lugging him in off the streets," the policeman pleaded as I was leaving.

A couple of trips later I encountered Bernando in better circumstances. He was peddling his merchandise—two long slim poles with forks at their tips, the kind women prop their clotheslines with. These poles are of softwoods because women like them to be lightweight—by the same token they snap easily. A frantic housewife, her fresh wash about to drag on the ground because of a broken clothesline pole, will readily pay up to five pesos for a new one. Bernando hiked two or three miles to an *acagual* where he cut and peeled a few nice straight poles with the proper

kind of forks, carried them back, and went about selling
them. It was easy work, said he, and well paid—he made
ten, twelve, or fifteen pesos a day. Good wages. He looked
seedy. He was skinnier than ever. His clothes were patched
and repatched, and not very clean, not like they used to be
back up the river. It seemed probable that most of those
"good wages" were going for *aguardiente*, not for soap.
There are some mean little dives that sell bootleg *aguardiente* where a man and a couple of his cronies can get blind,
falling-down drunk for ten or twelve pesos.

Some time afterward, on another trip, I met both Bernando and Maria del Carmen in the street. He looked about
as he had when I saw him selling poles. She was thin, and
also unkempt—she who had always been so neat. Her hair
was uncombed, and she wore an old patched dress that
also had been affected by the soap shortage. She wore in
addition the unmistakable mark of a fading black eye.
Formerly, Bernando did not beat her.

We chatted in the street, they inquiring about their
people up in the Xucuapan, I giving them all the news I
knew. As we were parting I remarked, as casually as I
could, "I'm going home tomorrow. I don't have much of
a load this trip—if you people happened to be going upriver I could give you a lift."

They understood just what I meant—if they weren't
managing, I would take them home. But they laughed.

"No thanks, Don Pablito," Bernando said. "We're not
going back yet."

"We're accustomed to town life, now," chimed in Maria
del Carmen. "We don't want to go back to the jungles."

That was the last I saw of them.

It has occurred to me since to wonder why, when the
going got rugged in town, Don Bernando did not fall back
on his fishing talent. Fresh fish sell at a premium price in

town. My friend Don Consuelo, the professional fisherman who tries to teach me to handle a throwing net, lives well by local standards. He may live in a mosquito-plagued hole, but his wife and the ten kids are well fed and well dressed, he is paying for a correspondence course in radio repair for his oldest son, buying an outboard motor on installments, and, on the side, supports a couple of saloon-keepers. I can think of only two possibilities: either Don Bernando's weather magic and fishing techniques didn't work down on the big river in the low country or he was temperamental about his art, like an artist who would rather starve than draw ladies' shoes and underwear for the ads.

A lot of water rolled down the river after that occasion before it occurred to me that it had been a long time since I'd seen Bernando. My trips to town vary from a month to a month and a half apart; I had not encountered Bernando every trip, so it was only after a long series of trips—nearly a year—that the thought struck me that maybe he was no longer there. His kin upriver received no news. Then by chance a cattle buyer I know happened to mention Bernando, whom he had known at El Ixtal. I probed after the lead, and Don Miguel laughed, saying it was the strangest transformation he'd ever seen. When he told me, I thought he had Bernando confused with someone else, for it didn't sound like the Bernando I knew. But Don Miguel at last convinced me.

He told me he had encountered Bernando away back up on the headwaters of another river, in a place called Cerro Nanchital, where there is a big highway construction project to provide access to an area where *Petroleos Mexicanos* is planning to open up a new field. Bernando, so the story went, has been working there for some time—not only that, but he is working his head off—hasn't missed a

day's work in months and never misses a chance to make
a bit of overtime. Maria del Carmen and the little girls—
I didn't get it quite clear if there are three or four of them
now—go about clean and neat in new dresses, just the
way they used to. Maria takes in some laundry, which on a
construction job back in the wilderness is a highly lucra-
tive business, so that they are really racking in the pesos.
And what was more astounding, Bernando has given away
his fishing tackle, sold his *jarana*, and wouldn't take a drink
even if it was for free.

From the standpoint of the national economy of Mexico,
this drastic transformation can only be counted as a net
gain. But from the point of view of the picturesque, it
seems a little *triste*.

SOME TIME has gone by since I first began to put
together the story of the Xucuapan. The foregoing tale
about Don Bernando I wrote a while ago. I am trying to
keep this account factual, but at the same time it seems to
me quite unfair that I should have to rewrite long sections
of it because of human frailty not my own. Hence I shall
bring the yarn up to date by means of this epilogue.

It so happens that not long ago when I was in town, I
saw a familiar figure ambling down the street, and who
would it be but Don Bernando. He was carrying two five-
gallon tins of garbage. I knew what he was doing, because
I have numerous friends among the Tehuanas and others
who have stands in the marketplace. When the owner of a
fruit-and-vegetable stand accumulates a quantity of over-
ripe and damaged fruits, trimmings from travel-worn cab-
bages and lettuces, and miscellaneous trash, he pays someone fifty centavos to carry two cansful to the river to dump
them. If the carrier is alert and the garbage is juicy, sometimes a hog buyer can be talked into paying another fifty

centavos for the garbage to slop his pigs. That makes a peso. But still and all it is not one of the better employments tht urban life can offer.

I hailed Bernando. He set down his burdens, we exchanged salutations, and had a long visit in the middle of the street. He was anxious for news about his people on the river, so I told him all the news and gossip I knew, the good with the bad. Bernando's cousin, the father of the youngsters who had brought the canoe back, had moved way up the other river—he had fought with Don Gregorio Linares, wounding him seriously but not fatally with a machete, paid a heavy fine, then moved away to avoid possibilities of vengeance. Maria del Carmen's side of the family were all well, except that Don Rufino's newest baby had died. And so on.

Then came Bernando's turn. I told him I'd heard he was getting along pretty well on the highway project, and he said that had been so. But the job was coming to an end; he worried about it, and began drinking again. Came to work drunk one day, squabbled with the foreman, drew his machete. They disarmed him before anything serious occurred, but he was fired and went to jail to boot. They sent him back to the jail in Las Lomas, bound hand and foot with half-inch rope (the foreman was a miserable type, with no *cojones*, who avenged himself not like a man but through the impersonal machinery of the law). When released from jail Bernando went on a real drunk—he smiled proudly and with a touch of wistfulness at the memory—blew all his savings, and that was that. He was back in Las Lomas, broke as when he left it. Maria del Carmen and the little girls had come down from Nanchital, of course. Something would turn up soon.

There was an awkward pause. I didn't quite know what to say, aside from trite phrases as "What a tough break" and "Life is like that" and such. His big splay-toed foot rested on the edge of one of the cans of garbage, his elbow propped on the raised knee, he cupped his chin in his hand in a pensive attitude. Down the street was the garbage dump, at the edge of the river. Beyond, the sluggish, roily waters, littered with trash, flowed past. He swung his long nose from side to side, savoring the breeze (which just then smelled mostly of stale garbage), tilted his head back to gaze at the heavens, then looked at the water of the river once more and said, "Don Pablito, on a day like this back upriver, with a few grasshoppers a man could catch a real nice string of panfish."

I believe he is coming back to the Xucuapan soon.

12

Pound of Flesh

ONE OF Chepe Joloche's specialties is journalism—journalism of the lemon-yellow shade. He travels up and down the river and over along the Arroyo Bravo disseminating the latest gossip. Unfortunately he has not found out how to make this function pay. All he gets out of it is an occasional free drink or meal or a *jícara* of *pozole*, and some sort of ego gratification—apparently enough to make him give plenty of time to this activity; the fact is, he has a flair for dramatizing his news. With another background he might be writing a syndicated Hollywood column.

I had come in from a long morning in the pastures to gulp down a quart or so of *pozole*. Barely toasted cacao beans had been ground up with the maize to give the *pozole* a delicately bitter tang and coat it with a rich veneer of buttery cacao oil. Those of us who work on horseback cannot carry the *morral* with its *jícara* and ball of ground leached maize unless we are going to work where the *morral* can be hung up in a sheltered place— the first run in the open pastures after a calf that needs doctoring, and the *jícara* is reduced to splinters from slamming against the pommel of the saddle.

So I had come in to quench my thirst. I was sitting on the porch gulping the cool, faintly bitter drink when Chepe came striding up the trail, *morral* slung over one shoulder. He had been on a trip—had left his shotgun at home lest he encounter Pereyra.

"*Buenos días*, Don Pablo."

"*Buenos días*, Don Chepe. How goes it with you?"

"Well enough. Lots of work to do—no matter how hard he tries a man just can't seem to get caught up." (Precious little *work* he does!) "And with you?"

"Toughing it out. Having a hard time finding people to weed the pastures."

We both knew I wasn't offering him a job, but perhaps he would spread the news. He fielded it too neatly for my liking: "Everyone is pretty busy this time of the year. And it's hard work when the pastures have as many weeds as yours do."

I saw I would get no free advertising from him. Then we discussed the *milpas* and the state of the weather. I don't recall if we thought it was raining too much or not enough, but eventually we agreed that there was something wrong with the weather—it was out of kilter that year, and it would be a miracle if anyone made a crop. (The harvest turned out bounteous, as usual.)

Such preludes to conversation are normal procedure with many of my neighbors, not just with Chepe. Long ago I stopped trying to hurry people to the point. I simply wait, and in their own time they get there. I drank the last of the *pozole*, munched some of the *shish*, the "settlings," and set the *jícara* down without inviting him to a dipperful.

"Have you killed any deer lately?" he asked casually. He was coming to the point of his visit at last.

"Not since that one." I motioned to the red hide nailed

to the front wall of the house. "We still have a few strips of jerky left."

"Your nephew Benito killed a really big one night before last, a tremendous deer, twice as big as that one."

"That's nice. I'm glad to hear my nephew had good luck." I disregarded Chepe's technique of deprecation—the hide on the wall came from a very ordinary medium-size deer, and I had no intention of becoming involved in an argument about it.

"He nearly died because of it."

"How could that be?"

"Don Domingo was going to shoot him." Chepe's eyes glittered as he watched for my reaction, knowing as he did that both men were my friends.

"Oh?" I feigned complete disinterest. "How do you know that?"

"I was there. Night caught me coming back from El Ixtal"—I noted the detail; if it should be important I could find out from Don Panuncio if Chepe had really been there, and why—"so I asked Don Domingo for *posada*. Before dawn Don Benito and Don Felipe killed this big deer, this *tronco de venado*. Don Felipe held the light, and Don Benito shot him in the head with his .22."

"Mm-hm." A listener punctuates a long story with short comments or grunts to show that he is paying attention.

"They dressed it out and quartered it in Don Domingo's back pasture, where they shot it. They wanted some money, so they brought it in to sell to Don Domingo. He is feeding eight or nine workers from down by the railroad."

"Don Felipe went there too?"

"No, he waited by the big mango tree at the fork of the trail. I found out afterward that he had been with Benito—Benito didn't mention him. Felipe doesn't speak to Don Domingo."

"So I've heard."

"Don Benito came to the house alone—we were having coffee. It was just getting light. He brought the whole deer; it just about covered that skinny little bald-faced sorrel horse—he came on foot, leading the horse. I guess it couldn't carry him and the deer both."

"You just don't know that horse, or you wouldn't say that."

"Well, anyhow he came leading it. Then he tried to sell the meat to Don Domingo. Don Domingo wouldn't buy the whole deer, or even a half. Finally he bought a quarter, at three pesos a kilo. They weighed the hind quarter—it weighed ten and a half kilos—"

"Ten and a half kilos! It couldn't! There aren't any deer that big in these woods!"

"They had cut the quarter with all the loin on it, not the way you do it. And it was a big deer—about as big as any I ever saw."

"What then?"

"Then they started to argue about the money. Don Benito wanted the thirty-one fifty in cash. Don Domingo said, 'No, I'll put it down in your favor on your bill.' Benito owes a big bill for provisions. But he said, 'No, I have to have the cash. The contract I'm doing for you goes to pay the bill.' "

"He's doing a contract for Don Domingo? I didn't know that."

"Yes, a big pasture-weeding job. Twenty hectares, they say. Don Felipe and Felipe's kid brother are helping him. So they kept on arguing—both of them got pretty mad. Don Domingo wouldn't give him the cash, or even part of it. That Doña Dolores, the woman he has for a cook, was already cutting the quarter up."

Chepe paused for effect, or to see if I was listening. I said "Mm-hm" again.

"They were yelling pretty loud. Then Benito says,

'*Bueno*, if you are so hunger-ridden and too miserly to pay a few pesos for good meat, you probably need it worse than I do—I'll give you the whole *chingado* deer. May you get fat on it,' he says, and he took that short cut-down machete he packs, like a dagger, cut the ropes on the saddle horn and cantle, dumped the other three quarters of the deer in the dirt right in front of Don Domingo, and got on the skinny pony and rode away. Don Domingo stood there a moment. He got pale, then he got red in the face. Then he ran into the house for a gun."

I tried to sound bored. "He didn't find it, I suppose."

"He grabbed a shotgun but couldn't find the cartridges. Then he picked up the .38 automatic, the one with the fancy butt plates that he usually carries, but when he got out to the door Don Benito was out of sight around the bend in the trail."

It sounded bad. I didn't want to say anything that Chepe could use to embellish the tale on subsequent re-citals, to make it worse. I shrugged. "They'll get over it. They're hot-tempered men, but too smart to make big trouble over a small matter." I doubted that I was sounding very convincing. Chepe started a reply, but a diversionary ploy occurred to me.

"Three pesos a kilo for the venison wasn't very high, at that. *Carajo!* I paid you four pesos per kilo for the last piece of deer meat you sold me, and you tried to charge me five."

Chepe realized his slip. "Well, it's worth five, but Don Benito was in a squeeze, they say. I hear he needed the money to buy medicine."

"Medicine?"

"That's what I heard. One of his wives is pretty sick. The younger one."

13

The Ax and the Jungle

SAVANTS WHO study the history of Mexico before the arrival of Don Hernán Cortés make much of the importance to the Ancient People of the cult of the Maize God, the benevolent Maize God with his cohorts of capricious Rain Gods and alternately complacent and cruel Earth Goddesses. Other gods were worshipped too in those long-past times—gods more spectacular and bloodier—but the deities of agriculture received an especial adoration.

Throughout Mexico, Christianity has long since replaced weird belief in the betasseled God of Maize, in the jaguar-fanged Rain Gods and snake-entwined Goddesses of the propitious Earth. Nevertheless something remains: a ritualistic awe, a devout attitude toward maize cultivation, for maize is the staff of life. So is wheat in more northerly climes, but though Kansan and Nebraskan wheat farmers of my acquaintance plan their cultivation cycle with care and handle the crop with greater efficiency than my present friends and neighbors handle their corn planting, I have never observed among the wheat growers the slightest trace of that aura of mysticism associated with the planting of maize here on the Xucuapan and as well over most of

Mexico. Preparation of the *milpa*, the "corn field," its sowing, cultivation, and harvesting are the most important
activities of the year even to persons whose principal income comes from cattle raising or from cultivation of the
cacao, from whose russet seeds your breakfast chocolate is
made, or from planting the plump white grains of coffee
or the long slim pods of the vanilla orchid.

Over most of southern Mexico maize culture is still
carried on by a technique that was near forty centuries old
when Cortés made landfall on the coast of New Spain. The
forest is felled, allowed to dry, and then burned, and the
precious seed corn is dropped into holes stabbed into the
ground with the long tapered point of a hardwood planting
stick. True enough, there were, and are, a few places
where at Spanish insistence fields were made that could
be plowed by oxen—nowadays, occasionally by tractors—
by grubbing out the stumps, in the same laborious way that
our early American pioneers made their fields. But over
most of the region the old chop-and-burn system prevails
to this day.

Once the primeval jungle has been felled and a crop
planted and harvested, the land is left to fallow for several
years according to a millennia-old system. This is not because of soil exhaustion, as some scholars (nonfarmers,
they) have speculated. It is because of weeds. Many of the
charred stumps have deep roots that, unaffected by the
burning and laden with stores of moisture and nutrients,
push up exuberant growths of shoots. The tubers of the
great lianas and roots and dormant seeds of the shade-
inhibited underbrush of the big jungle all react to the new
abundance of sunlight by sending up thousands of thousands of sprouts. Wind-carried and bird-carried weed seeds
that earlier could not penetrate the gigantic rain jungle,
or if they did could not sprout, then prosper in its shade,

bursting forth in wild profusion. The result is a dense tangle of vegetation; such a welter of shoots and vines and sprouts cover the ground within a year after clearing that no primitive farming implements can control them. Nor can modern ones—the stumps and snags and charred remnants of forest giants prevent the use of plows and animal- or machine-drawn cultivators. But by the time this horrid snarl of weeds and brush and vines has appeared, the first crop of maize has matured and been harvested.

After a couple of years a growth of small trees begins to take over, shading out the tangles of weeds and vines. Four or five years of fallowing produces a dense stand of young trees, four to six inches or so at the butt, ten to fifteen feet tall, mostly softwoods easily cut down, and a few small shrubs and vines. This second-growth bush is called the *acagual*. Four- or five-year-old *acagual* is easy for the modern farmer to handle, and was easy as well for his primitive ancestors: the heavily shaded bushes and vines are still abundant enough to provide tinder for a hot blaze, but no longer form a hopeless tangle, and the young softwood trees are easy to cut, and as well dry out rapidly, so the tract burns clean. The modern farmer with his machete filed sharp—there is usually little ax work in an *acagual*—clears a hectare, which is 2.4 acres, in six to eight days of hard, sweat-dripping labor, while the same expanse of virgin jungle would take him fifteen or twenty days to fell. For the ancients, who had no steel cutting blades, more days of hard labor surely were necessary, but the man/days ratio between *acagual* and virgin jungle must have been about the same.

Thus, once the great initial effort of felling the jungle had been made, a stable population could live comfortably by cultivating the *acaguales* and rotating them in four- or five-year cycles. A fallowed *acagual*, hectare for hectare, actually produces more foodstuffs than a tract of freshly cleared jungle, for, as a result of the repeated clearing and burning and the destructive action of sun and rain and insects on the remnants of forest giants, all the field, not just part of it, can be sowed.

Several of us were sitting about on a rainy afternoon late one January. At that time of the year all the talk is about plans for clearing land, for "making a *milpa*." Someone asked my *compadre* Antonio if he intended to clear big jungle that year. Antonio, long, lean, with walrus mustachios—as we say here, "may Heaven forgive me for speaking like this about my *compadre* but the fact is that" he has more interest in sipping *aguardiente* or riffling through a deck of cards than in laboring with ax and machete from sun to sun.

"Not I," he said. "I don't bother with the big forest any more. I have my good *acaguales*." Not only his words, but his self-satisfied tone made clear that he felt sure that he had it made—he sounded precisely like that person at the club who refers with feigned casualness to his portfolio of blue-chip stocks.

The *acagual* system of farming—clearing, planting, fallowing—never exhausts the soil. Apparently the weeds and vines and bushes, and then the rapid-growing softwood trees that shade and kill them, have nutrient requirements different from those of maize. Their deeper roots bring up and convert to usable plant foods minerals that maize roots cannot reach—the *acagual* growth returns these substances to the soil as it completes its cycle and dies, or when it is cut down and burned to mineral-rich ash. So the soil, by fallowing, is contantly refreshed. In the old settled areas of Southern Mexico, Indian towns listed in sixteenth-century Spanish censuses exist today and their inhabitants still clear and plant and fallow the same lands their ancestors farmed when Spain was a Moorish colony. The length of the fallowing period varies according to soils and climate—in semi-arid northern Yucatan ten to twelve years of fallow are necessary rather than the four or five of our well-watered, fertile Xucuapan.

A stable population with an unchanging economy can farm the same lands for centuries. Here, we attack the receding virgin forests, year after year, for two reasons. One is, of course, the importance of cattle raising. Many new clearings are planted to corn, then to pasture grasses— a perennial crop—thus never enter the *acagual* fallowing cycle. Herds increase. New pastures must be made. Each year we cut down more hectares of ancient forest to provide feed for the increase of our herds. The other factor is population expansion. Anyone who doubts the demographic explosion in this part of the world should come here for a visit. Most people in their thirties have eight or nine offspring—if they don't it's because they have ten or a dozen. And there are the special cases like my *compadre* Santiago, with twenty-one. The birth rate was always high, but mortality rates, especially infant mortality, were ghastly high. In the last few decades, new medicines— antimalarials, antihelminthics, sulfonamides, and more recently penicillins and the new antibiotics—have reduced the death rate miraculously. So there are many young men who need land—they go back into the jungle to start their clearings, build a house for the bride, cut down more forest. And year by year the primeval forest recedes to the steely cling! of the machete and the deeper ring of the ax.

When it is late winter in temperate climes and crocuses bloom to signal approaching spring, here it is the beginning of the long dry season, when my pioneer neighbors go into the woods to chop out underbrush, lianas, and saplings in the tract of jungle they plan to convert to a maize field. This is pleasant work. The big forest, freed of the clutter of small plants, shrubs, dangling and looping vines, assumes a parklike appearance and gentle breezes waft through where never a breath of moving air was felt before.

As the farmer progresses with his preliminary clearing, he studies the big trees to see which way they lean and how the lianas lash their crowns to adjacent trees. He must be a practical botanist, capable of distinguishing from far below the species of the vines that criss-cross the treetops: some species, thick as a man's arm up in the higher canopy, may dry to a flimsy dust when cut at the roots; other species dry instead to a wiry tensility capable of swinging the several tons of a falling tree to one side or the other before breaking under the strain. So the farmer observes carefully as he works, planning how to fell the big timber. The season for putting the ax to the open forest is late February or early March. Some trees can be cut from the ground, but those whose buttress roots flare wide are best cut high.

The farmer rigs a scaffolding of hardwood poles selected from the clash of his preliminary clearing lashed together with the strands of tough vines. Taking off his shoes or *guaraches*, he climbs onto his platform—it looks makeshift and flimsy but is really well made—curls his toes over the edges to swing his long-handled ax—a meter, 39.3 inches, is the standard measure for an ax handle. He chops just as he does when standing with his feet braced against the ground, swinging waist-high, power-loaded strokes. He does not undercut and overcut like a northern logger, but drives his falling cut deep to the center of the trunk on the side toward which the lean of the trunk, the imbalance of the lopsided crown, and the lashed vines will make the tree drop. The back cut he sets at the same level, his ax biting in until the weight of the unbalanced tree rends the remaining fibers so they creak and screech in protest. Danger! The farmer tosses his ax to one side, jumps or scrambles down from his scaffolding to run to safety. An unseen tough liana in the top or a flaw in the heartwood can twist the falling tree so the butt kicks—thrusts back violently off the stump. The defeated giant topples, slowly at first, then gathering speed until it smashes against the ground in a crash of splintering branches. The farmer shrills a war whoop of victory.

The purpose of all this effort—of the sweat that saturates faded, patched work shirts or glistens on smooth muscled torsos of those who strip to swing their axes—is to destroy the jungle's canopies, to bring sunlight to the tender green maize plants that will be sown there. Although a surprising amount of sunlight filters through the interwoven mass of vegetation above one's head, it is far too little to trigger the photosynthetic processes that make the corn plants grow. So the mighty forest must fall, the big spreading limbs of the crowns shattering and splitting as their own weight drives them down. There on the ground the hot sun slakes them, so that they dry out and can be burned.

Farmers plan their work so as to have the timber flat on the ground by the latter part of March. This leaves the remainder of that month, the hot suns of April, and the scorching days of early May for drying the trunks and shattered limbs and slash so they can be burned.

This method of making fields is not unique to the Xucuapan. It is a standard practice over most of southern Mexico and in many other tropical areas the world around. Geographers, anthropologists, and other scholars write voluminously about this way of converting jungle to farmland, calling it by such names as the "slash and burn" system, implying that it is a haphazard hit-or-miss sort of operation. It is no such thing. It is an agricultural technique keyed to a very tight schedule, and one planned with care and foresight—such foresight as is possible when one depends on the vagaries of the weather and the perils of long-range prediction. Trying to outguess the weather is the farmer's nightmare in all places of our planet.

If the farmer waits too long, or the summer rains begin unseasonably early, the thick layer of *broza*, "tinder," the dead leaves and twigs and splinters of shattered branches that carry the fire from log to log, will become soggy wet, completely fireproof. If one cannot burn off the clearing one cannot plant: all the season's work has gone to waste, and there will be no harvest. It happens sometimes.

The tropical farmer cannot protect himself by beginning to clear very early in the year. Should he do so, the drenching *nortes* of January sluice away the *broza* on the slopes; on level ground they keep it so wet and dank that it rots, dwindling away before burning time. Even if he begins a little early, and thanks to his cunning has the luck to lose but little *broza* to the *nortes*, and then burns his clearing off well in advance of normal time, he still cannot make a crop. He still must wait for the rains to dampen and soften the dried hard ground to plant his kernels of maize, which need much moisture to sprout. Even if they sprout they would wither and die under the scorching May sun if the rains came late. And when the ground is burned off and bare, baked dry though it is, there are weeds that can burst through it—vines like *cundeamor* ("smotherlove," its name derived from its profusion and dense growth habit), *pata de cabra* ("goat's foot"), and many others. By the time of the first rains, the new field would be choked with weeds.

So as time for burning draws near, we farmers anxiously watch the weather, visit our clearings to decide whether or not the debris is dry enough, study the skies. The month of May is the time great thunderheads pile up in the east from midday on, distant lightning flickering across between them. Some of us—many of us, in fact—burn off our clearings a bit early, so as to plant immediately before the rains. Others, and I am of this persuasion, burn late, at the last possible moment, then plant after the rains begin. Folks say, nay, insist, that on May 15, the feast day of San Ysidro Labrador, patron of farmers, rain is sure. Actually we know weather is not so punctual—it may rain a week earlier or two weeks later. Farmers watch the weather, fretting, fidgeting. Columns of black smoke billow up on the horizon as the time gets close, and other neighbors have set fire to their clearings. Daily the thunderheads pile up higher and higher. We know that one day one of them will suddenly dissolve into an enormous black overcast with flashes of lightning and roars of thunder, then loose a torrential downpour—a cloudburst—the first of the series that turns into general rainstorms.

Some men, pretending an icy calm, wait until the proper time, setting fire to their clearings just before the first heavy rain. Others lose their nerve, burn too soon—even before the slash has dried properly, so that it burns poorly and leaves a tangle of scorched trunks and branches that make planting difficult. And there is often someone who waits too long. So we wait, watching as the booming thunderheads pile up. We are racked with anxiety, hoping to see some sign indicating whether it will rain soon or not, gambling on the cloud masses. The boldest gamblers, from Monte Carlo to Vegas, who wager their fortunes on the turn of a card, the roll of the dice, the bounce of the ball in the roulette wheel, are pikers compared to the average farmer who bets his livelihood against a cloud.

They tell a wry little story here, about a mythical *ranch-*

ería whose inhabitants agreed that to avoid all this emo-
tional tension they would designate one day on which all
members of the community would set fire to their clearings.
No longer would they have to go through the agony of
watching the pillar of black smoke from a neighbor's
clearing while deciding whether to burn or not to burn.
All went well for several seasons, until one year one of the
farmers for some reason did not make a *milpa*. On the
appointed day, about noon when the sun was high and
hot and had slaked off the traces of morning dew, everyone
but this one man set out to their clearings to burn off the
tangle of dry felled trees and brush. The loner stood
watching. In front of him, to right, to left, behind him,
billows of black smoke rose heavenward. Everyone but he
was burning off the felled jungle. In his mind's eye he
could see the yellow flames roaring through the tangle of
dried slash and logs, devouring the dried wood to leave the
fields clean for planting. His nerves exploded. Frantically
he ran into the kitchen, seized a brand from the cooking
fire, and set his house ablaze!

This little tale perhaps is not really funny. It probably
has not much point—unless you have stood, staring at the
cloudy sky and watching the black smoke from your
neighbors' fires billow upward, while you wondered
whether to burn off your clearing or to wait till another
day.

ARMCHAIR CONSERVATIONISTS love to deplore what
they call the wasteful aspects of this method of agriculture,
pointing to the destruction of valuable timber in the burning, the destruction of green manures that the leafy vegetation would have provided, the heat damage to the humic
materials all too scant in tropical soils. This is arrant
nonsense. I do not mean to imply that I am opposed to

the principles of conservation. I am not—I myself am a conservationist of deepest dye. But I want my conservationism to be practicable. Mexico, a country with a fast-growing population, has a far greater acreage of rock-faced mountains and arid deserts than it has of fertile land. Good land must be planted. But no useful crops can grow in the shade of the virgin jungle—even "shade crops" like coffee and cacao cannot prosper until the forest canopies are thinned or, better yet, eliminated and low-growing, controllable shade trees are planted. So the jungle must be felled.

That much valuable lumber is destroyed in the burning is untrue. These are mixed forests, with both deciduous and evergreen (not conifers, but trees that do not shed their broad leaves) forms of many species. Valuable woods, such as mahogany and *cedro*, "Spanish cedar," are scarce. They were cut out long ago. While there are young trees useful for fencing and the like (which many of us cut over before felling a tract of forest), most of the wood is useless, consisting of huge softwoods or very heavy, brittle hardwoods—trash from a lumber standpoint. The loss of green manures is problematical. Much of the mineral content of the leaves, trunks, and branches, converted into ash, is restored to the soil.

The problem is how to dispose of the debris: the enormous trunks, huge chunks of shattered boughs, branches, twigs, long segments of thick vines, and the rest. To farm a piece of ground the farmer must be able to get at the soil. He cannot in fresh-felled jungle. A tract of freshly cleared jungle is a horrible mess—no other words can describe it. Huge trees—a foot, two feet, three and four and even five feet through, piled across each other like jackstraws—broken boughs as thick as a man's waist, smaller branches, lengths of vines, all forming a mat from one to six feet thick over the surface of the ground. How can any farmer plant and cultivate a field like that? You can't walk across a freshly felled tract of jungle. You climb over, crawl under, squeeze through. Now and then you can walk the slick-barked bole of a tree that fell in the direction you want to travel, but you do it at risk of limb if not of life. A tract of freshly felled jungle is, to repeat, an awful mess. An impossible, unfarmable mess. The only practical way to get at the fertile soil underneath is to loose the ravening fire on it—to let the flame-yellow fangs rend it, gulp the dried-out wood down their yellow and red and blue flame throats. The fire, sucking in ground-level air as its heat drives the pillar of smoke upward, rumbles, crackles and growls as it devours its prey. Coals glow through the night despite the cool damp night air that smothers the last flickering flames. Next day's sun dawns on a patch of white, light gray, and dark gray ash, on black-charred stumps amid the green and brown of the surrounding forest.

The *acagual*, "second growth bush," the product of the clear-and-fallow system, burns off cleaner than newly felled virgin jungle. If too long a time elapses between felling and burning, the weedseed-saturated soil bursts into a green mantle of vines and small growth, wet and cool, that will throttle the flame. A badly burned *acagual* is just as miserable to try to sow to maize, and to weed and harvest, as a badly burned tract of forest: the charred trunks and meshed branches are much smaller but much more numerous and dense. So the tropical former plans his work carefully. He may fell a tract of big forest and, while that begins to dry, another tract of *acagual*. But both are timed to be ready to burn—the big gamble—just before the rains. When does it rain? "On the day of San Ysidro Labrador it must rain," my neighbors aver. But San Ysidro perhaps has little regard for those who pay him homage only when they have dried forest on the ground and who do not mention his name the rest of the year.

Last year the first rain—a roaring gully-washer—fell on May 27. The year before, the first rain was on May 12—a tremendous cloudburst that made the river swell to its banks. (That one almost did me in—I had twelve hectares of forest on the ground and seven of *acagual*, a sizable investment for a small operator—but happily eight days of hot dry weather followed the cloudburst, so on the eighteenth I set the clearings afire. On steep slopes where the surface runoff sluiced away, the *broza* burned badly. In a few hollows, rainwater retained at or near ground level dampened the flames; there, tangles of tough scorched branches remained and promptly grew into patches of vines and weeds that nothing larger or less agile than a rabbit could get through. But most of the fields could be planted.)

It is after the burning that one may, with luck, attain as through a peephole another glimpse into the personality structure of pioneers. The topic has been the subject of much unenlightened discussion. One theory, spawned in the dime novels of our great-grandfathers' boyhoods, perpetuated in bastardly heritage by Zane Grey out of Hollywood, is that pioneers are bold, gallant heroes. (The villains in such fairy tales are Indians or half-breeds or Mexican bandits or Mormons.) This is of course quite silly. There are and always have been both bold and craven pioneers, gallant and mean ones. Another theory popularized by some not very good historians a few decades back is that frontiers are peopled by misfits who cannot cope with the requirements of stable society and therefore escape to the looser ambience of the frontier. This is not true either.

But there are, I am convinced, certain personality traits that distinguish the pioneer from his contemporaries in the old, settled lands. One of these is a creative instinct, for it is a creative work to convert wilderness into the domain of man. It is as creative as painting a picture or writing a symphony, for all it is done with machete and ax in work-roughened hands. Perhaps a closer comparison to the process of wresting gentle fields and pasture from the savage, primeval forest would be with the old-fashioned sculptors, who with mallet and chisel battered raw rough blocks of stone into forms of subtle beauty.

My friends and neighbors of the Xucuapan are little given to mawkish sentimentality. They may dandle the newest baby, but rarely caress the others, or their spouses, physically or verbally. But on more than one occasion I have watched while one of them stood gazing at a new clearing that burned off well, and heard him say with a sigh, "How beautiful! How lovely!"

A stranger hearing him (and as I did when I first knew this place but did not yet understand it) would say, "My God! Is he out of his mind? What is beautiful about that scorched clearing, that raw ugly gash in the landscape, that expanse of dead white-and-gray ashes and carbonized black snags and stumps?"

Later, as you know him better, you realize that the pioneer looks at but does not see the hideous black-gray-white patch but rather sees what will be there: the serene blue-green of a tall, thriving cornfield, its generous leaves rippling softly in the breeze, the tasseled ears thickening and ripening under the warm sun. Like the painter who sees on his empty canvas all the forms and colors and movement he will put there from his palette, and the sculptor who sees in the raw stone the exquisite form he will release with mallet and chisel and drill.

The Mormon pioneers of barren Deseret verbalized this creative drive when they said, "It is also blessèd to make

a blade of grass grow where none has grown before." Or
did they say, ". . . to make two blades grow where but one
grew before"? No matter. The essential meaning is the
same. And it is the essence of pioneering.

THE LONG TAPERED point of the heavy hardwood
planting stick is jabbed into the ground, with both hands
if planting before the first rain when the ground is dry
and hard, one-handed after the rains begin. Stabbed hard,
so that when withdrawn it leaves a slim tapered hole four
inches deep and an inch and a half in diameter at the top—
narrow enough and deep enough so the raccoons and
coatis cannot reach the seed with their long clever fingers,
nor can the iridescent black grackles and their smaller
blackbird cousins called *huachines* reach the seed with
their slim beaks. The planter's left hand draws five kernels
of maize from the pouch slung at his waist—five, not more
or less—and tosses them neatly into the hole. Rarely, a
grain falls short, or over; it is pushed into the hole with
the tip of the planting stick or picked up by hand and
dropped in. Charcoal-blackened *guarache*-clad feet, ash-
and charcoal-smeared denim-clad legs take two short steps
forward, about a meter, the point of the planting stick is
thrust hard again into the belly of Mother Earth, and five
more seed grains are dropped into the raw wound. Two
more steps forward, and on and on down the long row.
And the next row a meter-length away.

In a long day's labor, after the first rain when the soil
is moist and softened, a man can plant about three kilograms of seed, 6.6 pounds, of the fifteen kilos that is the
rule-of-thumb estimate per hectare. In other words, he
can plant a strip one hundred meters long by twenty wide
in a day, and complete the hectare in five days. Almost
no one does it this way. It is considered good agricultural

practice to sow the field in a single day, or if it is large, two or three or four. So one recruits assistants, paid by the day or *ganado mano*—"trading work," as we used to say when I was a lad. The trails upriver and down are pounded by horses' hooves and human feet as planting time draws near and we trek back and forth recruiting. "*Compadre*, I want to plant on the twentieth of May. Can you come help me? You and my godson?" "Don Fulano, could you give me a hand on the twenty-sixth? I am going to put the seedcorn into the ground that day." No one refuses—except because of a prior commitment. "I already promised Don Mengano I'd help him on the twenty-sixth and twenty-seventh. But you have a big clearing, I can come the twenty-eighth with my four boys, if you haven't finished." No one refuses to help plant the sacred maize.

There are no rituals before or after planting, unlike the ways of the Indian people in the long-settled country down toward the coast. Once, long ago, I visited an elderly friend who lived on a fertile islet amid the swamps of the coastal plain. It was just before planting time, and I found him in a newly burned-off field with his sons and grandsons, marching around in procession, carrying incense burners smoldering with copal gum, and chanting in a tongue I did not understand but knew (since I knew those people well) to be an Aztec dialect. My friend gave me a well-thumbed prayerbook from which to read aloud certain prayers at the north, the west, the south, the east points of the field. We went from his field to those of each of his many sons, blessing each, so that the lands could be sown with maize with the assurance that Tonantzín, the Sainted Virgin, would give a bountiful crop.

Here on the Xucuapan custom demands nothing so ceremonious—a round of drinks for all hands and a meal of

turkey in *mole* sauce when the planting chore is done is
the extent of our ritualism. But nonetheless one senses that
here too there is something sacred about the planting of
the maize.

HERE JUST AS IN IOWA abundant rain and warm sun
make the corn grow. The kernels push soft green leaves
upward from the planting holes, even as the rains wash in
rich light silt. The first leaves grow, stalks form, and soon
there are clumps of corn—some of five plants, some of four,
many of three and two, some single ones—over the field.
The sun, the rain. The leaves darken to a green with a
bluish cast as they grow, stalks thicken and push upward
toward the light. But weeds grow too—sprouts from tough
old root stocks and from seeds, crawling clinging vines
that smother the tender corn plants with their clutching
tendrils. All of this luxuriant, useless growth devours the
sustenance—soil nutrients and moisture—that should go to
the maize plants. The weeds, tough resilient foes of the
gentle maize, must die. The farmer attacks them with his
machete.

The machete is an implement of a wide variety of uses,
almost an all-purpose tool. Descended, as remarked before,
from the mariner's cutlass, it serves well for chopping trail
through dense undergrowth and for hacking down the
brush, vines, and small softwood trees of an *acagual.* It can
serve to skin and gut and quarter a deer or a beef. It is
useful for fishing, and even for trimming one's toenails.
It is excellent for purposes of mayhem and murder. But it
is the most miserable agricultural implement in mankind's
tool kit.

Good agricultural practice requires that a cornfield be
given its first weeding no later than twenty to thirty days
after planting. Otherwise the hungry aggressive weeds

will rob essential plant food from the tender maize. But at that time the weeds are still low, ground-hugging, lying between the countless small hard stubs and stumps of bushes chopped off an inch or two high in clearing—also the fault of the machete: in clearing, one chops high to protect the edge, which would dull rapidly if scraped across the dry hard ground or would be nicked if there are scattered gravels. The stubs and stumps are much more abundant in the fallowed *acagual* clearing than in one made in virgin forest.

To weed at the proper time the farmer must bend almost double at the waist and swing with long flat strokes just at ground level. The stubs and snags catch the blade, wrenching his elbow and shoulder. The farmer's back aches, his elbow and shoulder hurt as he straightens up to resharpen the dented blade with his file. So he lets the weeds grow taller, to more than knee-high, to be able to chop them down with long easy swings a few inches above the ground, above the troublesome stubs and snags. But by that time the weeds have damaged the young maize plants, decreasing their eventual yield in corn by nearly a third. And many of the chopped-off weeds revive, and continue to grow until the maize grows high enough to shade them out. I have tried hoes, but the hoe, meant to cut weeds at the roots, also gets caught by or jounces off the tough stubs of bushes, so is ineffectual too.

Inefficient though the weeding with machete may be, it is still useful, in fact essential if the corn is to produce at all. Once the weeding is accomplished, sunlight, rainfall, and fresh soil make the maize plants grow rapidly. Wide ribbons of dark-green leaves arc and dangle on the tall thick stalks and rustle in the breeze. Shade from the stalks and leaves retards revived and freshly sprouted weeds between the rows; the pernicious plants grow slowly in the shadow of the maize, and as a rule no second weeding is necessary. The stalks thrust skyward—to seven, eight, nine feet tall.

My neighbors define the growth of their maize by terms referring to stages it goes through: the striking of the secondary roots; flowering of the male spike; formation of the male spike; formation of the female flowers that will be the corn ears, and later their tasseling; filling of the ears and plumping of the soft milky kernels until they are ripe green corn, *elote;* drying of the tassels as the grains harden and begin to dry. When the tassels have dried and the husks begin to turn to a yellowish gray, the time has come, the farmer knows, for *doblando* the *milpa,* for "doubling," in the sense of "bending double."

His *garrabato,* a two-foot-long stick with a branch that turns off at right angles to make a sort of hook six or seven inches long, in one hand, machete in the other, the farmer goes to his field. Often he uses an old machete, a *rabón,* "tail," (like "rattail") filed to thin, needle-like blades, lightweight and easily manipulated. He slashes the knee-deep to waist-deep weeds around each clump of maize; if pasture grass has been interplanted between the clumps of corn he chops the weeds closer to the ground, with more care. The *garrabato* he uses to push or pull the weeds apart so the razor-sharp blade can slash them through, then with the hook he drags the cut weeds back out of the way of the next stroke. Then, one at a time, he hooks the stalks of the clump of maize over and ticks them lightly just below the ear of corn with the back of the blade so they fold over but are not cut through or broken off. He lops off the tip of the stalk that was above, now is below the ear.

When the farmer has finished, his field has a queer, truncated look. The clumps of maize, freed of weeds at their bases, are doubled over, the thick plump ears canted downward. Now the rain can do the precious kernels no harm as they dry and harden inside the husks, for the thick layer of husks that envelops the corn from butt to tapered tip drains the water off efficiently. An ear of maize in its normal growing posture on the stalk, that is, with tip upward, will fill with rainwater. Some trickles down the tubelike opening formed by the tips of the husks. Some is drawn in by the wick of dried cornsilk. The grains with the soggy, saturated husks begin to sprout, the water-logged stem rots and breaks off. On the damp ground, leaflets of the sprouting grains force through the rotting husks until they form a dense clump of puny bright grain grass. Soggy sprouted corn even before it falls to the ground is sour with a stink of putrefaction, worthless. Domestic animals may eat a bit of it mixed with good corn, but soon refuse it completely. However, when the corn-stalks are nicked and doubled so that the ears shed water instead of absorbing it, the maize kernels dry crisp and firm.

Animal damage is lessened too. The flocks of parrots—the gaudy-colored small parrots called *guirinas*, the medi-um-sized *cotorras*, the large blue-pated *palencanos*, and yellow-headed *loros reales*, all with sharp hard beaks that rip through the protective husks to nibble the tender grains near the tip—the *peya* jays and the big brown yellow-tailed orioles called *sakwas*, corn destroyers all, have diffi-culty in attacking the upside-down ears. Bird pests peck vainly at the butt ends of the corn, where the husks are thickest, give it up as a bad job, fly away. Raccoons and coatis, who climb an upright corn stalk, riding it to the ground if it bends or breaks, rarely find the ears on the doubled-over plants. Even the field mice cannot find, or cannot gnaw their way into, the doubled corn so easily. Peccaries, stealing into the field at night from the jungles, are not deceived. They smash down the corn plants, straight-standing or doubled over, to devour the maize. A *milpa* ringed by bush and jungle is their delight. Night after night they make their forays. They are obstinately fond of maize—driven off one night they return the next. They are difficult to shoot, for they do not hold to a light as deer do, but turn their heads away and sprint into the blackness.

Three years ago I made a *milpa* that flanked a low area, dense and dank, a semi-swamp, with a tangle of bamboo thickets mixed with larger trees—just the sort of place that peccary like. I'd seen their tracks often, when I tried (in vain) to stalk deer there. From the time my corn-field eared out, the beasts began to attack it. They were, it appeared, a couple of small bands of six or eight individuals—each one of the enormous herds that old-timers tell of soon would have demolished the whole thirty acres. Sleepness night after sleepless night I molested them, but they kept coming back. Even when we were doubling the *milpa*, so that man-scent must have lain thick on the field, they filled themselves with corn nightly. Some nights I took the dogs to run them. One night the big dog Capulín caught and killed a piglet, which screamed as it died—the dog came yelping back out of the dark, a great gash in his shoulder (which next day cost me eight wide-spaced stitches to pull together), the sow in close pursuit. I shot at her but missed—I had to hold high so as not to kill my dog—and at the shot she turned and fled. I missed with the right barrel too. Shooting conditions at night are less than ideal: shadows flitting into shadows across a flashlight's gleam.

On another night I killed a young boar—more by luck than by marksmanship, admittedly. He was fat as a butter-ball, damn him, with all my corn in him—but we ate him, which helped even things up a bit. At harvest time I made a count of clumps of corn mashed down around the edge of the field, of ears ripped open on the ground and devoured: the beasts had eaten nearly three quarters of a ton of maize. To a man working alone as some of my neighbors do, with little or no hired labor, in a field of four or five acres, such a loss would be serious.

Domestic hogs also cause damage. Most people pen up their pigs as the *milpas* begin to ripen—it is considered the proper thing to do, and of course the wide-ranging animals are likely to get into their owner's fields. But some men do not bother, through carelessness or because their maize lofts are barren and they do not have enough feed to keep their animals penned. Locally hogs run almost wild. Most of their sustenance they find for themselves in the pastures and the woods—and in gardens and fields—with only a small ration of grain morning and night to accustom them to returning to their pens. They are fed heavily only when the time comes for fattening for market. A large drove of hungry porkers can wreak havoc with a cornfield, and, like their wild cousins, once they find a field they stubbornly return no matter how many times they are driven off. Their enthusiasm for corn can cause bitter ill feeling between neighbors. Blood has been spilled because of it.

The doubled corn dries quickly as it dangles point down. While it could stay in the field for several months, the usual practice, especially where peccary or neighbors' hogs abound, is to harvest it soon. The farmer picks it, sorts it into "good corn," "damaged ears" (bird-pecked and the like), and *molcate*, "nubbins." Depending on the location of the field and transport, the farmer may stow it in a *troja*, a "storehouse" built in the field, with pole walls and floor and roof of thatch, or, if he can, will bring it home daily with pack horses or by canoe if the field is close to the river. If he builds a *troja*, each day he brings the maize home in a sack—a big ninety-kilogram coffee sack—on his back with a tumpline of soft tough *majagua* bark, trip after trip until it is safely stowed on the *tapanco*, the pole loft under the high gabled roof of his house.

Yields are not all they should be, despite the fertility of the soil. The "good corn," large, plump, undamaged ears, is measured by the *sonte*, an ancient Aztec measure equaling eighty *manos*, "hands," or four hundred ears. The rule of thumb is that a *sonte* yields about fifty kilograms of shelled corn. An average yield hereabouts is twenty *sontes* per hectare, that is, about a ton of shelled corn, plus a couple of hundred kilograms or so of grain from damaged ears and nubbins—it takes many many sackfuls of nubbins to shell out a hundred kilos of corn. My friends and neighbors talk, over a glass of *aguardiente*, about harvests of thirty *sontes* per hectare—a ton and a half, plus nubbins—but that is the liquor talking; their *milpas* never yield such bumper crops. This compares poorly with the fields over in the Tuxtla country, west of here, where plowed fields sowed with improved seed—hybrids developed by Mexican government agronomists—average three tons per hectare. And the agronomists say such fields and plantings should yield four.

Part of the trouble, of course, is due to the unimproved seed we use, part from late weeding, and part from the dense clumps of five stalks springing from the planting holes. The agronomists insist that if a grain drill is not used, planting by hand should be done by sowing two or three grains of seedcorn at half-meter intervals, in rows a meter apart.

These data on how to improve the corn yield are interesting, but impractical. I have been able to get hybrid seed on several occasions for myself and for a couple of my *compadres*. But to turn these lands into plowlands would be difficult, and so expensive as to be impossible. Machinery could not be brought in without construction of a road. The point is that the *acagual*-fallow system is self-perpetuating. To grub out the myriad stumps of small trunks and old, well-rooted bushes of a fallowed tract would probably be almost as costly in man-days of labor as rooting out the giant stumps of fresh felled jungle, hectare for hectare. And after every fallow period it is the same. That is one of the effects of farming with machete and ax.

14

The Red Bull

THE GYR BULL, light-rust-colored, three quarters of a ton of malevolence, fought all the way to the snubbing post against three lassos Don Panuncio, Josefino, and a lad called Bernardino had on him while Jorge hazed. Gyr is one of the zebu breeds; southeastern Mexican cowmen argue endlessly as to whether Gyrs are wilder and meaner than the ill-tempered Indo-Brazilian strain. This was one of Don Panuncio's newest acquisitions—the best of a lot of new bulls.

"I'd hate to tell you what these bulls cost me, Pablito," he had said a few months before as we watched them, just delivered, walk about cautiously in the corral that was strange to them. "You might think I was bragging. But *qué cabrón!* The bulls are half the herd."

I watched the animals move around, slowly, quietly but uneasily, with rippling smoothness more catlike than cattle-like. "*Por Dios*, they're handsome! Beautiful animals, Don Panuncio! Whatever they cost, they're worth it," I murmured. "And the Gyr—what a bull!"

"Best of them all, I think that's the one that I bought the lot of them for."

Now it had been the Gyr that Josefino found in bad shape, with a wound turned into a mass of infection on his long, dangling sheath. Apparently the bull had snagged himself on a barb while hopping over a four-wire fence, and the ugly slash—a partial circumcision—needed attention. And assessment as well: a bull with a badly injured prepuce cannot get an erection, cannot carry on his trade, and so is worthless no matter how handsome an animal he may be. That was why they had driven the beast into the corral along with a bunch of cows, why they were working him to the post with three new lassos.

"We've got the *hijo de la guayava!*" shouted Don Panuncio as they flipped their ropes into the fork of the snubbing post. "Let's all keep an even strain—he can't bust three new ropes! Jorge, *collolèale*"—collar him—"to the post."

"This calf is mine," Jorge yelled back. He dismounted, a fifteen-foot length of inch rope in his hands, enough to give four round turns about the bull's neck and the post and leave enough for the knot. "Just keep the *hijo de su madre* snug against the post and I'll tie him up in no time."

He ran in toward the bull, but on the opposite side of the post. There he flipped the end of the tie rope over the bull's neck and around the post with a litle jerk that made the flying end snap back into his hand. He flipped it again— one round turn. As he tightened to take up his slack, the red bull exploded into action—lunging wildly, trying to hook around the post at his nearest enemy. The tie rope ripped through Jorge's hands, so the single turn went uselessly slack. Bernardino's lasso—either because it had a flaw or because he was holding so tight that his rope took all the force of the animal's jump—broke like cheap string at the *rozadera*. The bull jumped high in the air, dropped with all his weight against the two remaining ropes that bound him.

"Run, Jorge, get away from there!" shrilled Josefino. Jorge ran.

The bull fought the ropes. The nooses choked him as he struggled—he became frantic. A tremendous leap, and his full weight wrenched at the taut lassos—Josefino's broke, the length of elastic new rope whipping back like a recoiling spring.

"Make new nooses!" Don Panuncio roared. He sat his saddle twisted back at the waist to watch the bull's efforts to escape, to ease the tension bit by bit as needed. "Hurry, before the *diablo* gets away!"

Another desperate lunge, then another that burst the strands of the last lasso. Don Panuncio's new rope had been stretched like a guitar string. When it broke under tension, the broken end snapped back like a whiplash across the old man's face—across his eyes. The blow momentarily stunned him; he was still wiping his eyes with the back of his hand when the bull charged.

The cowboys screamed a warning, and the old man spurred his horse. But the horse responded slowly and the bull was upon them, driving his short blunted horns into the horse's rump and sending him sprawling to his knees. As the horse lurched to his feet, the bull circled to hook him under the flank, lifting horse and rider into the air and flipping them in a somersault. Don Panuncio was caught underneath his mount. The bull began to gore the fallen horse, slamming his horns against the animal's rib cage, then backed away a bit to search for the vulnerable belly. He had ripped deep into the abdomen, and the neighing horse's guts were streaming out when Josefino and Jorge fired their pistols. They perforated the bull's heart and lungs. He raised his head to look at the new foe. Jorge, on foot, had run in close. The bull lowered his head, charged him. Bernardino had retied his hondo, whipped a loop at the bull, catching him around the neck, jerked him off stride just in time to keep him from overtaking Jorge. The bull fell clumsily. He tried twice to get up. Then a flush of blood streamed from his nostrils, and he collapsed.

"*Virgen Santísima*, Don Panuncio's dead!" Josefino wailed after they had rolled the dying horse off the old man's body.

"He's not! Look at that vein in his forehead! It's pulsing." Bernardino fumbled a round pocket mirror from his pocket, held it in front of the unconscious man's mouth. "It's steamed up! He's alive!"

"The poncho! We'll carry him to the shade on it."

Jorge ran to the wounded horse for the poncho behind the saddle; the beast had struggled to his feet to stand, anchored by the stream of gut that poured from the wound in his belly.

Josefino took charge. "There's good shade under the *mulato* tree. Bernardino can stay with him, in case he wakes up and wants water or something. Jorge and I will go for help—to carry him in, get a canoe with a motor to take him to town, or whatever Doña Carmen wants."

Shocked men rode or walked to tell their neighbors: the new bull had killed Don Panuncio. Days later came the news that the doctors in town, where Teco Julio had rushed him by canoe, said he would live, but *quiénsabe* if he would ever ride again. People said, "How do they say he will live if he can't straddle those ponies any more? If he lives he'll be back in the saddle." They also said, "Why does he leave us all alone, now that Don Chon is in town, sick; what will we do without those two old men?" The way they said it showed their fear and sadness; "Why did he leave us here all alone?" is what one says in the *pésame*, "the lament for the dead." But Don Panuncio is a tough old man, and could afford the best medical help—after a while we heard he was on the slow road to recovery.

THERE WAS MORE bad news. Don Juan Pereyra left Lomas Bonitas, left the *Columna Volante*. It was related that four men in citified dress, driving a big new car with an official State seal stenciled on the sides, came to Lomas to talk to him, and that he got in the car with them, drove away, saying farewell to no one. The incident seemed very mysterious—or the raconteurs deliberately made it sound that way. Then a tale began to make the rounds that someone knew someone who had seen that Pereyra was unarmed and wearing handcuffs when he entered the official car.

"We're going to miss Don Juan," Don Rodrigo said. He is Don Chon's eldest son, and has been filling in for his father since the old man fell ill.

"I don't think it will make much difference," Don Sebastián replied. "He was a good friend to us here, but even though he's gone, whatever happened to him, the *Columna* is still here."

"That's what I mean. I went to see the new *Comandante* when I was in town the other day—wanted to find out something about these new forms for the *guías*. He seemed pretty cold and unfriendly." *Guías* are permits for transporting livestock.

"Maybe that's part of their technique," I put in. "When I first met Pereyra I thought he was the unfriendliest type I'd ever seen."

"We'll know more about him after he's made a patrol or two," said my *compadre* Sebastián.

But there were no more patrols by the *Columna Volante*. The only people who saw the new *Comandante* were those who moved cattle out of the Xucuapan. Pereryra had been easy-going about brand inspections; the new *Comandante* was not, and he was reported to be very fussy about the documentation as well. And not at all friendly.

Some weeks later I stopped at Don Rodrigo's landing on my way home from town. He'd asked me to bring him a medicine for some calves that had the scours and some dress zippers and sewing-machine needles his wife needed. We had scarcely greeted when he asked me, "Did you hear anything about Don Juan Pereyra in town?" He seemed a bit excited—I knew he had been very friendly with Don Juan.

"No, I didn't. No one mentioned him. You know, it's been some time since he left, or since they took him away— people don't talk about him much in town any more. Why?"

"Well, this *muchacho* Ventura Ramos, you know him— he works for me sometimes—"

I nodded, of course I knew Ventura.

"He was in town—came back the day after you went downstream. He says he was in Don Adelfo's barbershop, waiting his turn, and picked up an old newspaper. He can't read, but he was looking at it. He says he saw a picture of Don Juan on the front page, Don Juan shaking hands with the Governor."

"The Governor? Does Ventura know what the Governor looks like?"

"He claims he does—and maybe he does. After all, there were pictures of him all over town around election time. Ventura was in town a lot then—he was working for Don Salomón and Don Modesto, driving cattle from along the river."

"And he was sure it was Don Juan?"

"Yes, of course. He couldn't possibly be wrong about that."

"Well, I hope he's right. I'd rather think it was like that and not like that damn handcuff story."

"The *santísima* truth is that I never believed that story— and my *tata* doesn't either."

[244]

"Your *tata* and Don Panuncio know how to sort out the truth from the nonsense in the gossip that spreads along the river. I wish I did. Too bad Ventura didn't ask Don Adelfo or someone to read him the caption under the picture."

"Well, you know how he is—he'd be embarrassed, saying he didn't know how to read—afraid they'd laugh at him and say if he doesn't know how to read what is he looking at a newspaper for."

15

Pattern of Violence

A SCHOLARLY FRIEND of mine from the States who has a passion for antiquities used to tell a story about a trip he made in search of a little-known archaeological site somewhere amid the sloughs and lagoons along the Gulf of Campeche. This is really his story, not mine, but I trust he won't mind if I borrow it, for he made clear that the place, when he finally reached it, was an isolated little pocket of frontier, something like this one. Measured on a map, by airline, it was quite near long-settled regions and fairly up-to-date towns. But from the nearest town it was a long haul by muleback over a muddy trail to the village where a canoe could be hired to make the longer trip, winding through mosquito-infested sloughs and twisting channels in mangrove swamps, to reach the small lagoon. Across the lagoon were numerous islets of fairly high firm ground, many with thatched houses. Apparently the region was fairly well populated. Finally he came to the big island where the ruins were supposed to be. The canoe men took my friend to a landing in front of a village of fifteen or twenty thatched huts.

Curious villagers came toward the beach as he and the

canoe men disembarked. They were most cordial, and helped to unload the equipment. My friend began to question them about local antiquities. They knew nothing at all. Finally one had an idea: if the stranger wanted to learn about "old things," who would be able to inform him better than the oldest man in town? Don So-and-so, they told him with pride, was one hundred twenty-nine years old—he would certainly know about other antiquities. My friend asked to be introduced to Don So-and-so, though doubting that he would learn much. He felt sure, of course, that the oldster's age was exaggerated—a man can become a myth, as it were, where there are no written records. In a small community where life expectancy is short, a man outlives his few contemporaries. He has no birth certificate, or if he has no one can read it. Younger people begin to say of a doddering old man, "Don So-and-so looks as though he were a hundred years old." One hundred is a big round number in Spanish as in English. Then it becomes, "He must be a hundred years old," then, "He's more than a hundred years old." Soon he believes it himself.

To my friend's surprise, Don So-and-so proved to be a sprightly oldster, a little frail and a bit hard of hearing, but otherwise in full possession of his faculties. Though doubtless younger than his alleged age, it was obvious that he had been in circulation a long time. He stated that he knew the island as no one else did—he had been the first settler there. Antiquities? My friend explained. The old-timer hopped up from his chair, rummaged around in a great wooden chest, and produced a beautifully carved and painted vase—a masterpiece of the Ancient People.

"Is this what you mean? I found this forty-one years ago, while I was digging out an armadillo among some little hills on the far side of the island."

"Oh yes!" My friend's voice shook as he fondled the treasure. "Do you recall where you found it?"

"Of course! Didn't I tell you, over among the little hills across the island. That's where the people lived, the Old Ones, long ago—even before my time. It's very clear: there are pieces of broken *ollas* and cooking pots scattered about on the ground—I once saw a piece of a broken *metate*. They lived on the tops of the litle hills. Anyone can see it. These kids," he gestured toward the grown men, some middle-aged, assembled to hear the interview, "these infants, they don't know anything, they have no eyes to see things, or the sense to understand what they see. Idiots, the lot of them!"

The objects of his slur smiled proudly at each other. Their ancient was so old that he knew more than anyone else.

"Can you, or can someone, take me there?"

"It's too late today. Stay here in your house. Tomorrow one of my elderly grandsons will guide you—I can explain to him just where the place is. I'd take you there, but at my age I don't care much for long hikes—one hundred twenty-nine, you know."

Some appropriate comment was clearly indicated—my friend came up with the not very original query, To what did Don So-and-so attribute his longevity?

As all old-timers do, Don So-and-so had his answer to this question. "I have thought about it myself. I have lived so many years—" he paused dramatically "—so many years because I have never in my life taken a drink of *aguardiente*."

The pronouncement caught my friend off balance—he had expected something different (he says he had been thinking that he could use a drink himself, even of *aguardiente*, after the long day of being parboiled by the scorching sun). He mumbled something about, "Oh yes, of course . . . *aguardiente* . . . very bad for the health . . . especially for the liver . . . doctors say it sort of cooks one's liver . . ."

"Well, I don't know about that. I don't know about livers," pronounced Don So-and-so. "But what I've observed in my one hundred twenty-nine years is this: men who drink *aguardiente* go to *fiestas*. At *fiestas*, that's where there's always lots of *aguardiente*. So they go, and they drink. And then they fight—someone always gets stabbed or shot or hacked up with machetes at a *fiesta*. That's why they all die young. Me, I never drank, so I never went to *fiestas*—so here I am, one hundred twenty-nine."

Quod erat demonstrandum. He leaned back in his chair complacently.

The old gentleman's theory that drinking leads inevitably to bloodshed, with the corollary that all bloodshed is caused by alcohol, is generally accepted in southeastern Mexico, both in the remote backwoods and in the towns. There is an apparently commonsense logic to the idea. A self-satisfying sort of logic, because the basic assumption is that most people are fundamentally pacific and reasonable, resorting to violence only when their judgment is perturbed by the fumes of *aguardiente*.

To translate the theory into personal terms let us imagine a hypothetical Don X, a decent little man who spends his days at hard labor in his *milpa*, in his cacao or coffee groves, tending his animals, weeding his pastures. Don X is a man who meets his social obligations squarely, providing for his family, assisting his relatives and *compadres* when necessary, attending and occasionally giving *velorios*, "wakes," which are, or become, *fiestas* in honor of deceased kinsmen and favorite saints. He has of course a host of *compadres* who have stood godfather to his children or he to theirs, and treats them all with proper respect, complying strictly with the norms of the special relationship of the *compadrazgo* that demand simultaneously a strict formality and a certain affection between *compadres*. He is, to repeat, a decent responsible member of his society.

But now, to test the theorem, let us invent for our Don X a *compadre* who is a twenty-one-karat scoundrel—mean, unprincipled, one who exploits the *compadrazgo* situation for his own ends. This person borrows Don X's fat, well-cared-for saddle pony, then returns it weeks later gaunt from hunger, its back a horror of saddle sores, without even an apology. Don X says nothing. Appealing formally to X, the wretch borrows money and maize, but does not bother to pay off his debts. Don X stoically chokes back his resentment. He cannot bring himself to be so crass and so heedless of the proprieties as to dun a *compadre*. Not even when the bad *compadre*, gloating over his vicious trick, addresses him disrespectfully in front of others by the familiar second-person *tu*, rather than by the formal *usted* that a *compadre* should use.

Then there was the time that the unprincipled *compadre*, walking into the house with the freedom that the relationship permits, when Don X was not at home, proceeded to make broad insinuations to the *comadre*, Don X's wife. Now while local standards tolerate some permissiveness in matters sexual, in the *compadrazgo* relationship the attitude is quite different. The very thought of sexual relations between a *compadre* and his *comadre* is shocking. It is vile incest. So Don X's wife broke free, ran out the back door and hid in the *acagual* behind the house. She knew the *acagual*, its trails and tracks, as she knew her kitchen. That's where she picked up old dried branches for firewood when her husband forgot to provide for the hungry maw of the kitchen fire. Squatting behind a thick clump of the thorny-leaved agave called *pita*, she watched. The beans in the pot on the fire scorched and burned; she smelled their acrid smoke. The baby wailed in the hammock. But she did not come out of the thicket until she saw her *compadre* leave the house, mount his pony, and ride away.

Don X came home to find her in tears. His first impulse was to beat her when she wept out her story. It is assumed that as a rule such situations are created by women—women through provocative behavior incite men to evil deeds. But he desisted. He remembered veiled references he had heard about his *compadre*'s behavior. Dinner was ready, but he did not want to eat. He squatted in the shade of the orange tree in the front yard, filing his machete blade to a razor edge, wondering why he had been so stupid as to become a *compadre* of such an unsavory character. The angry file in angry hands bit the mild-tempered steel. But anger dulled as he faced the fact that the *compadrazgo* was a sacred relationship, formed before God. And the next time he met his *compadre* he embraced him with the laying of his hand on the other's arm, which is the reserved Indian version of the effusive Latin *abrazo*, and said, "*Compadre*, how happy I am to see you again."

The *fiesta*. Pulses quicken to the rhythmic tinkle of the *jaranas*, throb as the cups or *jícaras* of *aguardiente* circulate. A feeling of euphoria as the alcohol entraps the senses. Then appears the *compadre*, swaggering, coarse, offensive. A careless slight. Euphoria transforms into a cold hard knot of rage in the pit of the stomach. The vast store of resentment wells up, its inhibiting bonds dissolved by the strong drink. Resentment that the fumes of alcohol spark to flaming hate. Don X draws his machete.

"Draw your steel, *hijo de la chingada*. Here one or the other of us, as God wills, shall die."

Steel rings on steel as they parry in the flickering light

of the kerosene wicks. Women scream, run to the shadows, turn to watch with sparkling eyes. Men catch their breath, finger the butts of their weapons, glance sideways to see who stands near. Each of the gladiators has his partisans, his kin. To try to halt the affray by detaining one of them may bring his people to his defense.

Steel blade clangs on steel blade as they slash and parry. Then one blade glances wide or misses and follows through too far, the other blade drives to bite deep into human flesh, to slake its thirst for blood. Jerks free, slashes and bites again. And again. The vanquished man screams or curses, collapses to the ground. The victor backs away, half crouching, his machete at the ready, the streak of blood on its blade gleaming black in the flickering light. Free of the crowd he turns to run to his horse, unties him, mounts, and the hoofbeats drum in gallop over the hard ground as the fallen man moans.

"The accursed *aguardiente* did it," people say.

That's the way it can happen. And does happen, sometimes. Of course, the participants need not be involved in the complexities of the *compadrazgo*—I used that circumstance to make a hypothetical case more striking. The theory recognizes that many things can trigger a conflict when strong drink inflames the baser passions. Thus, the old man was saying from the vantagepoint of his alleged one hundred twenty-nine years that the fumes of alcohol penetrate the mind's healing tissues of forgetfulness to awaken old rancor—memories of long-past, supposedly smoothed-over conflicts, of family feuds: "Your grandfather slew my great-uncle, damn you!"

The trouble with this theoretical explanation is that, like most folk sociology, or folk psychology, whichever it may be, it oversimplifies the picture. True enough, drink appears at times to melt away the learned social-behavior controls we call inhibitions. But cold-sober men as well as drunken ones resort to violence. Affrays do occur at *fiestas*, true enough. The *aguardiente* is blamed; folk sociologists do not consider that men who have had conflicts try to avoid each other ordinarily but at the *fiesta* inevitably meet face to face. Patently there are various factors at work.

One such force is the *machismo* concept, the theme of maleness, of virility, a vestige of medieval chivalry, which pervades Mexican—perhaps much of Latin American—thought. *Machismo* involves many things, including an emphasis on sexual virility. More pertinent to our present discussion, it involves a supersensitivity to insult and requires a violent reaction to the most minor slight, the least offense. A man who is *macho*, as, according to the standard, all good men should be, is duty-bound to avenge in blood any affront. There is no parity of "an eye for an eye"—the formula requires death for the least slur. "You can't say that to me and live—I'm *muy macho*," he says, reaching for his weapon.

Then there is the pattern of violence itself, which calls for use of weapons in any conflict. *Machismo* standards of chivalry require that one may slap or kick a dog or a woman, but a human male adversary must be dignified by attacking him with a weapon: machete or knife or gun. As a corollary, a blow with the hand is the bitterest offense one man can give another; only blood will vindicate it. The effective force of the corollary has weakened considerably in the towns in recent decades as younger men have been indoctrinated in the manly art of fisticuffs by movies and television. But in the country the standards are rigid.

There is the story of Don Adolfo, better known by his nickname El Hicotea, "the Painted Turtle," just why I never knew, unless his short, stocky frame—he was heavier-set and more heavily muscled than is usual hereabouts—suggested the thick round shell of a turtle. I can tell his story without compromising him in any way, because he is dead. He drowned four years ago over on the other river during a tremendous freshet. When the news spread, people said with sad little smiles, "How could he drown, if he was El Hicotea?" They did not say it in a mean way. People liked Don Adolfo.

When I first knew him he was working for Don Panuncio and living in the riverbank pasture on Arroyo Verde, a couple of miles by water above the mouth of El Ixtal. One wild stormy night my outboard motor broke down upstream from his house (I still had not learned that the better part of valor is to tie up at dusk—not to try to run the river at night). Paddling and drifting, I got the sluggish, heavily laden canoe to the landing in front of his house and called out to ask for shelter for the night. He came out in the pouring rain with a *candil*, a kerosene dip, to light my way—he had no flashlight (nor did I—mine had fallen over the side). He helped me to tie up the canoe and took me to his house.

The house was small, with palm-thatch roof and pole sidewalls in usual local fashion, with an adjoining similar but smaller structure that was the kitchen. It was very neat and tidy, the well-swept dirt floor so clean that I felt embarrassed that my wet clothes dripped water over it. It was plain that Don Adolfo was desperately poor—there are obvious signs that one learns to note. Not only did he have no flashlight, but I saw a stone *metate*, the old-fashioned grinding slab for corn, in the kitchen. The *metate* is infinitely slower and more laborious for grinding the leached corn into meal for *tortillas* and *pozole* than the cast-iron mills that most people use nowadays. But the mills cost more, frequently break down and must be replaced. On a rack in the smoke above the fire was a great stack of *jícaras*, but there were only a couple of plates and one large cup of the cheap enamelware most people use. The pole-framed beds on which the flock of youngsters slept had no mosquito nets, not that there would be mosquitos in a howling *norte*, but the close-meshed nets conserve some of the sleepers' body heat and fend off the gusts of raw chilly air that whistle through the spaces between the poles of the wall. Hence they are usually used in bad weather as well as in good—in good weather down at El Ixtal nearby swamps breed myriads of mosquitoes. Without a net one sleeps poorly, even at Don Panuncio's house.

While I changed to dry clothes in a dark corner of the living house, Don Odolfo's wife made coffee in the kitchen, coffee hot and black and so strong that it penetrated the enamel of the cup. I could taste the raw sugarcane juice with which it was sweetened. Apparently there was no sugar. Then I slept in a homemade hammock spun and woven of *jolocín* bark. Two or three times during the night Don Adolfo got up to bail out my canoe lest the rain squalls fill it enough to soak the cargo. I should have done this myself, of course—I intended to, but, wearied by the long trip, could not wake up in time.

It was not long afterward that Don Adolfo left El Ixtal to move upriver with his family, far up, above Don Amaranto's place. There were still new lands up there, unclaimed, unsullied by the ax. I did not see him for some time. Then he came to visit his "niece"—he was a cousin-uncle or something of the sort of our *comadre* Chana, Don Candelario's wife—and on the way stopped at our house. It turned out that the purpose of the trip was less avuncular socializing than business. He was, it turned out, an expert at alligator hunting and wanted to plan a campaign with Don Candi and Don Rufino against a big 'gator that lived part of the time in the narrow but deep pools of the Arroyo del Jó in my pasture. It was a big animal; Candi and Rufo had shown me his tracks where he had pulled his broad body up onto a little sandbar in the creek to sun himself—they estimated him at close to ten fcct long. Alligators have been hunted so assiduously for their valuable hides that big ones are rare hereabouts. And this one was wary, which probably is the reason he had lived long enough to grow to his huge size. Candi and Rufo had tried time after time but had never been able to take him, so they had called on Don Adolfo to aid them with his expertise.

Don Adolfo asked, most formally, for permission to hunt "my" alligator. He certainly wasn't mine, I replied, if they could kill him they were welcome to do so. I asked permission, in my turn, to go along to watch the process.

They didn't get him. The big saurian outguessed them, lying quietly in the pool while they waded about chest-deep searching for the mouth of his burrow, then driving stakes across it to close it off. Then as they poked withes between the stakes to see if they had trapped him, the reptile swam unseen, underwater, to the lower end of the pool, scuttled across the little gravel bar that separated it from the pool below, a long greenish-brown bulk that moved with amazing agility. Don Rufino, waist-deep in water, snatched his shotgun from the inclined bamboo he had hung it on and fired, but if the buckshot hit at all at the low angle they glanced harmlessly off the horny back scutes. While we searched vainly for blood sign, we heard the beast splash as he surged over the bar and into the pool below—he was on his way to the river.

Some time later, on a visit to El Ixtal, Don Panuncio

proudly showed me a near-seven-foot alligator hide hung up in the storeroom. He had encountered the reptile sunning itself by one of the ponds in his lower pasture, shot it with his pistol just behind and below the eye. The hide, well salted and moist, was hung up with some twenty pounds of scrap-iron oddments neatly sewed to the tail with numerous stitches that made small holes that would not show—alligator hides are sold by length. Then I told "Uncle" Panuncio about the 'gator that got away.

He laughed. "That Adolfo doesn't usually lose them. He's a good hunter—a good little man at anything. He's also good with a machete—do you know about his big fight?"

I shook my head as I poured myself another drink.

"Well, he doesn't talk about it himself—he's not one of those loud-mouthed types. But he's a tough man, very *macho*, when the chips are down."

Then he told me.

Years before, Don Adolfo, then a young man, was working at El Ixtal. He lived back up the *arroyo* with his young wife and their three or four small children. He felled the big jungle to plant his maize, interplanted grass for Don Panuncio, harvested his crop, turned over the land to the *patrón* with the grass clean weeded. In return he got days' hire weeding pastures when not busy with his own work and liberal credit for necessities at the store. He worked hard, supported his family adequately; he was, as Don Panuncio said, "a good little man."

There were three brothers of the Alor family, who lived down below La Laja, downstream from El Ixtal. They were a rough lot—troublemakers, boozers, fighters. They were *muy macho*. Among themselves they had some sort of peck order: they did not fight one another and stood by one another in time of stress.

The eldest of the three was Don Gilberto, a big, rangy-built, machete-scarred man. Most of his left ear had been sliced off by a machete slash long ago, there was a scar across his right cheek and several on his hands and arms. When wounded, it was said, he become more savage, fought his way through—he was reputed to have slain three men in fair fights, steel to steel, and have wounded several others. Don Adolfo, El Hicotea, was terrified of him. Don Adolfo was no coward—this was one of those peculiar interpersonal relationships. Where I grew up we would have said that Don Gilberto "had the Injun sign on him"—recalling ancient Indian superstitions to explain such a peculiar situation of dominance. Don Gilberto knew this, delighted in it, and sadistically exploited it. At *fiestas*, at the store—until Don Panuncio objected, and after that he waylaid his victim on the trail homeward—he slapped Don Adolfo in the face with open hand or whipped him with the flat of his machete, in the presence of others to make it worse. He made him kneel to beg pardon for imagined slights. Don Gilberto once had an inspiration for a stunt he repeated many times: machete in hand he obliged Don Adolfo to strip, then roll naked on a nest of the tiny red ants called *azucareras*, nasty-tempered little insects that sting with venomous hatred. The pain of the stings passes away soon, but for a brief time it is excruciating. Don Gilberto's cronies, watched and snickered. No one tried to repeat the torture—somehow they sensed that Don Adolfo would fight back against anyone else, that it was only Don Gilberto he feared with a craven terror.

One day Don Adolfo came home early from his work. From the hammock he called to his wife, "*Vieja*, bring me some coffee!"

She brought in a *jícara* of steaming black brew. It was bitter, strong-coffee bitter.

"What, no sugar?"

"There is none left."

"Why didn't you tell me? I'd have gone to the store to get some. What's the matter with you, don't you think of anything?"

Gaze downcast, she mumbled, "I- I- I didn't want to tell you—" Then she raised her head defiantly. "My *comadre* Juana told me that *cabrón* Don Gilberto has been hanging around the store for two or three days, boozing. If I told you we needed sugar and you went to get some, he'd have maltreated you again!" She burst into tears and ran from the house. Her bare feet pattered lightly on the dry ground.

Don Adolfo sat there in the hammock, amazed. It was as though his shadowed world of drudgery and fear had burst like an eggshell to let light pour in. His wife cared for him. It had never occurred to him before that she might.

She had been a slip of a girl, barely adolescent when he married her—married her in the old-fashioned way, by an arrangement with her father in which she was not consulted at all. He had spent his savings—the money a young man who works hard and has no family to support can scrape together—even gone into debt to buy the heifer her father demanded, and the turkeys and *aguardiente* for the small *fiesta* at the house of an aunt (his parents were dead) that served as the wedding celebration. She had been a good woman. Silent, patient, she prepared his food, washed his clothes, and mended them with neatly stitched-on patches. When there was no money for soap, she gathered nuts of the *coyol* palm, cracked them with a river cobble on a stone anvil, and ground the nut meats on the *metate* to a paste, which she cooked with wood ashes into a homemade soft soap. She kept the house tidy, satisfied him sexually, bore his children.

He on his part considered himself a good husband. He provided for her and their children to the best of his ability. He had built her a house. He bought her a *batea*, a great deep mahogany tray to wash clothes in. He planted and harvested maize and beans and rice for them to eat, worked at pasture weeding to make money to buy matches, kerosene, salt, cloth and thread and buttons for clothing, soap, and luxuries like sugar. He ran through the woods with the dogs hunting *tepescuinte* and armadillos for meat—he could not afford a gun—and fished in the river. He was not mean to her—struck her but rarely. But he had never thought of her with affection—she was just there, like any piece of useful furniture—nor had he thought of her as a source of affection. Now that he suddenly realized that she cared for him, his whole world changed. A vast wave of shame deluged him as he thought that the woman who loved him wept because he was a cowardly poltroon, the submissive, whining butt of a bully.

He got up. The baby in the bed began to cry. He picked her up, tucked her neatly in the hammock, swung her a few moments until the movement and the fresh air pacified her. Then he climbed the notched log ladder to the *tapanco* to get the new machete and file that he had bought and stored away for the coming time of clearing the forest for the *milpa*.

He found a corncob, broke it, jabbed the rattail handle of the file into it. Usually he cut and fitted neat hardwood handles to his files, but now he was in a hurry. Tip of the blade jabbed low into a doorpost, machete butt against his belly, knee under it to steady and give it tension, he filed the blunt, steep-beveled factory edge—useless for cutting—down to long sloping bevels glinting silvery to a razor edge.

His wife was still hiding in the brush behind the house.

He was glad. He did not want her to see what he was doing, nor did he want to talk to her. He rummaged in the clothes chest until he found his best—a starched white shirt and trousers—went to the *arroyo* to bathe hastily, put on the clean clothes. Like most men he gave his wife what cash money he had, but he knew where she kept it; he counted out the centavos for a kilogram of sugar, tucked them in his pocket. He took the old, worn machete from the scabbard, shoved it into a space between the wallpoles, fitted the new one in the sheath, belted it on. The new wide blade did not go quite all the way down into the scabbard, but it drew cleanly—did not stick. He tested it several times. Then he set out to Don Panuncio's store to buy a kilogram of sugar.

Don Adolfo was scarcely halfway to the store when a lanky figure rounded a curve in the trail ahead of him. It was Don Gilberto.

"*Hola*, little man! How good to see you!" Don Gilberto had been drinking but was not very drunk. Just drunk enough to be mean. "It's been a long time since we've met."

Adolfo went cold with the old fear that he always felt toward this tall rangy man, scarred, vicious, ruthless. "*Hola*, Don Gilberto. It's good to meet you."

"*Amiguito*, I just saw a beautiful ant hill a few steps back. It's too bad our friends aren't here to see you give our little ant-sisters a hearty meal. Take off your clothes and lie on the ant hill."

"No."

"Do what I say or I'll beat you with the flat of my machete."

"No, Don Gilberto." Why did his voice creak and squeak so? "Not any more. The time has come for one of us to die—draw your weapon." Don Adolfo's newly filed blade slid from the scabbard into his hand.

As he too drew, Don Gilberto frowned, noting the heavy new blade. His own machete was an old one, a *rabón*, filed to a thin point, but shorter, so that his advantage of reach was diminished. But he entered the fray boldly, confidently—he had fought before. He parried skillfully and with caution—the heavy new machete could snap his old thin one were he careless, leaving him defenseless.

Fighting with machetes is not just a wild swinging and slashing with blades, any more than boxing is just a haphazard swinging of fists. Machete fighting is a technique, with cuts, thrusts, parries, and counters, like fencing with sabers though perhaps less refined. I once, long ago when I was just learning about these things, sat horrified, watching two youngsters practice with sticks cut to resemble machete blades. They were working on a complex attack: a forehand feint, lightly parrying and disengaging the other blade so as to follow through, then crouching and leaning boldly to make a low backhand slash at the opponent's knees or shins. It could be worked the other way also, the feint backhand, the crippling low cut forehand. Obviously the crippled opponent could be dispatched easily. The counter consisted in jumping with extreme knee flection, tucking the heels up against the buttocks to clear the blade, and lashing out with an overhand slash at the unguarded head or neck of the adversary. The kids worked out very seriously for nearly half an hour. One, I knew, was twelve years old. His brother and coach was a little over thirteen.

Now the steel blades flashed, parried clanging, disengaged, slashed. Don Gilberto's shorter machete was a disadvantage, but he overcame it by pressing closer, constantly closer, making his enemy retreat. Its slim tapered point and lightness made it quicker for thrusts. One thrust just touched Don Adolfo's forearm. A sheet of blood flowed; in hot weather a person bleeds freely from a slight cut. A bit more and it might have severed a big vein or immobilized the muscles of the hand. Don Gilberto crowded. Another thrust—the point just touched Don Adolfo's left temple. Blood trickled into his eye, blinding him on that side.

Don Gilberto leered. "*Hermanito*," he panted, "I think this—is where you—die!"

A vicious slash. Don Adolfo parried precisely, twisted his wrist to flip his foe's blade wide. There was the opening. Adolfo slashed through with the cut that experts say is the most dangerous—an upward backhand, a long reaching backhand pulled through with all the strength of back and shoulder. The point of the machete caught Don Gilberto deep in the throat, the tip jerking the blade as it ticked on a cervical vertebra and slid free to cut through to the other side. Blood spouted wildly, like water from a broken garden hose. Don Gilberto dropped his machete, raised his arms in a helpless gesture. He gurgled, trying to scream. Then he fouled himself noisily and collapsed to the ground.

The vividness of bright flowing blood, the stench of blood and excrement drove Don Adolfo crazy—he went berserk. He hacked the prone body until it was a mess of bleeding wounds and haggled guts. For that little while he was insane. He saw the bloody deadly cut at the throat, hacked at it, hacked through the vertebra until he completely severed the head, then clutched it by the hair, walked to the bank, down to the water's edge, threw it into the river. Still dazed, he squatted at the water's edge.

Streaks of blood reddened his machete blade. He washed them off in the flowing water, saw the nicks where the thinned edge had struck bone, numbly took his file from his hip pocket to file them smooth. The routine activity calmed him, soothed him back toward sanity. He took off his blood-spattered clothes, rinsed the stains from them, wrung them out. Then he bathed, bandaged his light wounds with strips torn from his shirttail, dressed, sheathed his machete, and climbed the bank. When he passed the mutilated body he turned his head away. He struck out across the pastures toward a little-traveled trail that ran back into the jungles.

"It was pretty awful," Don Panuncio told me. "The body, I mean. It was a mess. Of all the things I've seen, and I've seen a lot in my time, that was the worst. A little boy found him—one of my *compadre* Humberto's—as a matter of fact, it was Emilio, the one that just married Don Margarito's daughter, and who lives upriver from you on the Arroyo Guanacaste."

I nodded. "Of course I know Emilio."

"He was just a kid. His *mamá* had sent him to buy a box of matches or a spool of thread or something. He'd been hanging around the store instead of going home, first because Don Gilberto, who was some relation to his mother, the late Doña Dionisia, kept buying candy for him, then because some other kids came along and they started playing. I finally shooed him home. He was riding a bony old goat of a gray pony, bareback. There must have been a bit of a northerly breeze, so the pony didn't smell the blood until he came round a little crook in the trail where the corpse was—then he shied, spilling the kid off, and bolted. The youngster got up, saw Gilberto's body, turned and ran back down the trail to the store, screaming. It took a lot of candy and crackers and soda pop to calm him down, so he could tell us what happened. We knew it was something serious—he'd rolled over some blood-stained ground and there were smears of blood on his little shirt."

The old man grinned. "Now I would pull Emilio together with *aguardiente*. But in those days soda pop was all he drank. It's a wonder he didn't die of bellyache, as much as we gave him. Finally we got some sense out of him. My *compadre* Chon was there, and some other people, so we saddled up to go see what had happened, to collect information for the death certificate so the relatives could recover the body. When we got there, I understood why the little boy had come screaming.

"I sent somebody to take him home on horseback, to break the news to Doña Dionisia, and to tell her not to wallop the kid for being late but to get a *curandero* to cure him of the fright. And we sent someone else, Don Petronilo, if I remember rightly, to notify Don Eduardo and Don Anastacio, Gilberto's brothers. It was well along in the afternoon, but there was still plenty of light to work out the tracks to find out what had happened. That's when I knew El Hicotea wasn't a real killer—of course we knew right away he'd done it. He'd kicked off his *guaraches* when the fight started—you have better footing barefoot, you know—so there were his tracks all over the place. The middle toe on his right foot crooks over to the outside in a peculiar way—you must have noticed it. To me it was clear what he had done. He'd killed because he had to. Then he went out of his mind for a little while—that's when he savaged the corpse. Real killers—professionals and those who become professionals—cut them down or shoot them and walk away from them, or maybe hide them to give themselves more getaway time. They don't savage them that way—"

"Wait a minute," I interrupted. "Seems that I remember being told that the late Don Chucho hacked up Don José's corpse—wasn't he a 'real killer,' then?"

"Well, you know, somehow I never made that comparison. Let's have a drink. All this talk dries out the throat."

He poured, gulped, passed me the glass. "That is quite true, Chucho did a pretty brutal job on his first victim. But there was something different about it. The difference between cold-blooded sadism and complete insanity. Chucho maltreated the corpse to make the relatives feel badly. Adolfo was crazily trying to destroy his corpse. Perhaps knowing the people involved in both cases makes me see a distinction.

"Anyhow, we buried Don Gilberto without his head. His brothers dove for it and paid some others to help search— we tracked Adolfo to the river by the blood drippings— but never found it. Maybe the catfish rolled it downstream. At the wake, and at the funeral too, the brothers cried and swore vengeance."

Soon after the *velorio de los nueve días*, "the wake of the ninth day" after the death, Don Panuncio sent for El Hicotea, having learned where the fugitive was hiding. Don Adolfo came in the night, slipping stealthily through the dark like the jungle-thing he had become. The dogs yapped and barked as he approached; Don Panuncio called them off, let him into the house, closed the door and barred it.

"I wanted to talk to you, Don Adolfito. How have you been?"

"All right. Well, not very well, really."

"I thought as much. How about a drink, Adolfito?" He poured *aguardiente* in a water tumbler, and they drank. "You're in pretty big trouble, you know."

"I know that, Don Panuncio."

"At the wake the brothers of the late Don Gilberto, Don Eduardo and Don Anastacio, swore they'd hunt you down and kill you, or if they couldn't find you, take revenge where they can. You know what they meant by that—you have a brother and a sister up on Arroyo Bravo. And your uncle Don Rosario. And there are your wife and kids."

Don Adolfo said in a small choked voice, "I understand, Don Panuncio."

"Your children are small, just babies."

Adolfo nodded. Tears glinted in his small closeset black eyes. He foresaw what the old man was going to say.

"They can't defend themselves. The Alor family is a hard lot—Don Eduardo and Don Anastacio would have no compassion."

Adolfo jumped to his feet, almost upsetting the glass of *aguardiente*. "I'd hunt them down and kill them like dogs if they—"

"Sit down and be quiet. Take a drink. Here, *salud*. That would be after it happened. Besides, you couldn't. They'd kill you instead. The Alor family is a long family—lots of cousins and uncles and nephews. Many of them don't like Don Eduardo and Don Anastacio much, but they're relations nonetheless. You've done well to have stayed alive this long."

"I was well hidden."

"*Qué joder.* I knew you were hiding in the jungles back behind your Uncle Rosario's place the day after you got there. They would have found out soon. Then there is your brother—he can't stand up to them, he with that crooked leg from the time the tree fell on him. And your sister. What can she do?"

"What can I do? I'll go face them, let them kill me. Then they won't murder my people." His face darkened in anger. "But I'll take at least one of them along."

"That's what I don't want to happen. That's what I want to avoid. Here, have a drink—*caramba*, looks like you've been out in the woods so long you don't appreciate good drinking liquor." Don Panuncio wiped his mustache with the back of his hand. "I've been talking with Don Eduardo and Don Anastacio. Talking pretty tough. Finally they've agreed to accept your going to jail as recompense for the killing—they'll take no revenge either on you or your family if you surrender to the law and go to jail."

"To jail? You mean in town, where they put men in cages like animals?"

"To jail. In a cage. I hear it's pretty bad. But it's better than being dead. And probably it's better than being alive to think about your children and your brother and sister and your uncle who have died for your fault."

"To go to jail!"

"To go to jail. For a while. I have a cousin in town, Don Serafino, who is a good lawyer. He can get you off with a short sentence on a self-defense plea. We'll go see him."

"But how do I know the Alor family will keep their word? While I'm caged up they can butcher my children, my brother and sister, my uncle!"

"You have my word. I'll see that they don't. They won't touch a one of your people, I promise. I've told them what I'll do if they don't keep faith."

"If you give me your word, Don Panuncio, I'll go." He was pallid, sweating with fright.

"Of course I give it. That's why I'm talking to you. We'll go in tomorrow. Drink up, and we'll get some sleep— we have to start early. You can sleep in that hammock in the back room. And that pistol in your waistband, the one your *compadre* Clemente lent you, let me have it—I'll see that he gets it back."

Don Adolfo was sentenced to five years and released in just less than four, for good behavior.

I twiddled the empty glass round and round on the counter as the story ended, trying to understand it. "You went away out on a limb, Uncle, on that deal. The Alor, if they were as bad characters as you say, could have taken offense at your protecting El Hicotea. Or if they had broken their word, when he got out of jail he might have held you responsible."

"I thought about those things a lot. But you see I *knew* all the people concerned. I understood what Adolfito had gone through—I didn't consider him a criminal, really. And the Alor—well, they were a bad lot, but there was one thing about them: they were *machos* in one of the few better senses of the term—I was sure that when they gave their word they'd keep it. So it seemed like a good time to work on my program of civilizing and trying to bring the law to the Xucuapan. Maybe it helped a little. And I don't want to presume about my motives, but I felt that there was a certain humanitarianism involved. I had to put up the money for legal expenses, of course."

"You were still taking a gamble."

"It worked out all right. Adolfito came back from jail quiet, pacific, not full of hate like some of them. The Alor brothers were dead by then—Don Eduardo died of snakebite, stepped on a fer-de-lance while picking coffee, and his brother died of dysentery soon after. The other relatives were not close enough to want to make trouble, and I warned Adolfo to keep away from them."

MY COMPADRE SEBASTIÁN and I were planning a trip to town. Both of us had a few fat hogs and some poultry to take in—a joint operation, sharing expenses, would be to our mutual benefit. The planning done, we were chatting. I mentioned Don Panuncio's story and how impressed I had been at the old man's altruism.

I didn't know that my *compadre* was annoyed: he had borrowed money from Don Panuncio to buy a couple of new bulls, then was charged interest on the loan. He hadn't expected, as a friend and *compadre*, to be charged interest. Five per cent—per month, of course. Well, it could have been worse: the usual country interest rate is ten per cent per month. But just then—eventually he got over it—my *compadre* was bitter.

"Altruism!" he laughed sourly. "Your uncle made it pay, as he does everything. El Hicotea really did eight years of time, not four. Four in jail, and four more working to pay off what Don Panuncio said he owed for legal expenses. Wasn't he living on Arroyo Verde when you first moved in here?"

I nodded.

"Well, he was finishing his sentence. Cleared and planted forty or fifty hectares of pasture in the second four years. Don Panuncio got every *centavo* back from him and more."

Later it occurred to me that I'd have preferred my *compadre* not to tell me that.

16

Profit and Loss

PABLITO AND ROSAMARIA were building a miniature corral and chute out of twigs and string under the shade of the *guásima* tree. They planned to spray their herd of toy cattle with make-believe tick killer. Downriver the throb of a motor sounded as a canoe rounded the point of the Playas pasture. They listened.

"That's Don Julio," Pablito said to his sister. "Go tell *Mamá* he's coming—I'll get a basket for the fruit and vegetables." *Mamá* was washing clothes by the well.

"It sounds to me like Don Alejandro's motor."

"Don Alejandro! It's the Teco Don Julio, I tell you! Go tell *Mamá*."

Teco (for Juchiteco) Julio and his teen-age son Juan usually save some goods for us on their fortnightly vending trips along the river—a few fresh tomatoes, a head of cabbage, exotic fruit like apples, pears, or grapes, or bakery rolls, which we always buy at briskly marked-up prices, for things like that break the monotony of the daily diet. (I bring such items from town on my trips, of course, but only in small amounts that can keep until consumed.) This may sound like a strictly cash-and-carry, or better, carry-for-cash, proposition but it is not. Teco and his son are men who don't mind doing a favor—carrying a message or bringing the spools of thread I forgot to buy last trip. So our relationship is more than a purely commercial one. They often climb the riverbank to the house for a coffee, a meal, or, if night overtakes them, for shelter.

Don Julio finished his drink, set the glass on the floor, lay back in the hammock. From the kitchen came sounds of cookery—the slap! slap! of *tortillas* being pounded out, and odors as well: Maria was preparing a spicy stew for supper. Juan was helping the kids bring in the milk cows— he likes to ride horseback but has few chances to do it. He and his father make good money at their canoe-borne merchandising, but it's a tough life—most of the time during their voyages they live on *totopos*, the durable baked *tortillas* that Doña Domatila, Don Julio's wife, makes in the Tehuantepec fashion, washed down with river water. They sleep curled up and cramped in their canoe.

"Don Concho sent you a message," Julio said. "He's coming to see you next week, probably Wednesday or Thursday. He sent *saludos*, of course."

"Thanks," I replied. "Which Don Concho, Concho Contreras?"

"No, the other one, from over on Arroyo Bravo—you know, the *papá* of Carmen and Andrés."

"Oh, Don Concho Gomez. That's good. I want him to repair the cedar canoe. It has a flaw in the bow that leaks a lot—needs to be reamed out and plugged."

"He's good at that sort of work. And he'll be glad of a chance to make a few pesos."

"Who isn't?" I picked up his glass, began slicing a lime. He had brought the bottle from his canoe; I was providing the limes and brown sugar.

"But he needs it. He's hard up."

"Don Concho? How is that? He has four or five cows, and I thought he was fattening some hogs. Last time I saw the boys—three months or so ago—they told me they'd made a good harvest."

"Not any more. Not since he took his wife to town for that operation. He got the money from Don Domingo— with what he already owed Don Domingo for provisions he had to turn over his cows, there were four, three with calves at foot. And the hogs—he'll have to turn his hogs over to Domingo as well, to finish paying off."

"Sounds as though he's in bad shape."

"He is. He wanted to buy some things from me—a sack of sugar and a few other things—on credit. He had no money. I hated refusing him, but I just couldn't give him credit—he's too much in debt to Don Domingo."

"That must have been an expensive operation his wife had."

"I guess so. Maybe. As I understand it, he never saw the money—Domingo made the arrangements with the doctor, paid him, then told Don Concho how much it had cost."

"Hm-hm. You mean Domingo made a big profit on the arrangement?"

"*Quiénsabe.* That's plainly what Concho thinks. He's pretty bitter about it. But there isn't a thing he can do but pay off. He used to be his own man—now he's Don Domingo's *peón.*"

"Hm-hm." I was thinking. I'd intended to drive a fairly hard bargain for the canoe repair job—now perhaps I shouldn't.

Don Julio continued. "I don't know what's happened to Domingo since he moved to town. I've known him for years, and he didn't used to be this way—what's the word: avaricious. He has the people on the *arroyo* by the short hairs—they all owe him money and he makes them turn over their produce: poultry, hogs, cacao, to pay off their debts. They have to pay his high prices and sell to him cheap. He's really squeezing them—milking them dry."

"What annoys you is that they don't buy from you," I jeered.

He chuckled, then turned serious. "No, that's not a fact. They wouldn't buy much from me anyhow. They live too far inland, and I can't operate on an exact schedule, so it's only by chance that I meet them along the river. They don't think it's good, what Domingo's doing. I hear there's a lot of bad feeling. Your neighbors are different from people down in the towns—they won't take too much squeezing."

"Well, I don't know. Just between the two of us, Don Panuncio always squeezed pretty hard. And he did it for forty years. People fuss a little, sometimes, but they get over it."

"Yes, but when he is a pirate, he does it with grace. He multiplies the bill by two, pays half price for the steer or fat hog the debtor brings him to settle the account. Really gouges him. But then he pours his sucker a few free drinks, talks about the good old days, slaps him on the back, gives him some candy to take home to the kids, and sends him home thinking old Panuncio has done him a great favor. Domingo doesn't do it like that. He threatens them—says he'll throw them in jail if they don't pay."

"How can he do that? Nobody goes to jail for debt."

"He can do it, all right. Files a charge of 'abuse of confidence'—something like fraud. But it's not good to do that to neighbors."

"I wouldn't think so."

"Not on this river. Not with men like Don Benito, Benito what's-his-name, the one who calls you 'Uncle.'"

"*Pa' su mecha*, hasn't Benito settled up with Don Domingo yet? He's been working for him all this past year."

"He never will, the way Domingo works it—he charges interest on the debt. Benito's hooked. You know, a *campesino* can make only so much in a year from his *milpa* and the animals he fattens, and what he can make in wages by the day or by contracts on the working days left. When he gets in debt over that amount he's had it."

"He can always run."

"Your nephew Benito isn't the kind to run—not from a few pesos of debt, anyhow. But now he's in trouble."

"How is that?"

"He had five fat hogs that he was supposed to turn over to Domingo on the debt. About six hundred kilos altogether on the hoof. Sold them to Fidel Márquez for cash. Don Domingo is in a rage about it."

"Why?"

"Why? Because Benito pocketed the 2,200 pesos. Domingo, who would have given him maybe 1,800 or 2,000, figures he lost a lot of money. The hogs were worth 3,300 at least, in town. They're bringing five pesos fifty the kilo. Domingo hurts all over."

"Don Domingo, with his good ranch and cattle—it's hard to see why he'd make a fuss for a few pesos."

"He has always liked to make a peso. But since he moved his family to town he's changed—now he wants to make it in a hurry."

"It's been a long while since I've seen Benito. If you happen to meet him, tell him I want to talk to him."

"I will if I get the chance."

17

The Owl in the Tree

THERE WAS NOT much coal oil left, and the wick of the coal-oil dip was trimmed so short that the flickering flame shed but a tiny light in the barren little kitchen. The two men sat at opposite ends of a table whose top was a slab hewn from a buttress root of a great *vari* tree. The night darkness leaked in through the spaces between the poles of the wall. Tree frogs chirped outside. Down along the *arroyo* the ugly toads boomed their chorus.

Benito sat, elbows on the table, tousling his red hair, which looked dark in the scant light. "*Cuñado*, I'm through. I'm at the end of the trail, with no way out. You know I had to give that money to the *curandera* Doña Josefa, who cured Clara when she was sick. Most of it anyhow. She's been dunning me for months. She might do something to your sister Clara."

"Do something? You mean witchcraft?"

"Witchcraft. One shouldn't even say the word. But people say she knows many things. I was afraid for Clara."

"Hm-hm."

"Today Don Arnulfo told me that Don Domingo is saying that if I don't pay him the money he'll send me to jail. I don't have it to give to him."

"Don Domingo! Always Don Domingo! What he did to me! I told you to keep clear of him—now he has you for his slave, trapped for a few miserable pesos!" Felipe's voice was a *nauyaca's* hiss. "That son of a bitch! Let's kill him, *cuñado.*"

Tree frogs chirped in the night, toads shouted. In the top of a nearby tree a tiny owl, the kind called *primavera*, hooted.

"Hear the owl, *cuñado?*" Benito said. His mouth stretched in a wide humorless grin. "You know the proverb: 'When the owl hoots, an Indian dies.'"

THE BRASSY SUNDISC was well past the meridian when they came out to the river, Benito's spindly sorrel pony swinging his legs in a rippling running-walk, Felipe's buckskin jogging along behind.

"I want a drink of *aguardiente*, a good stiff drink. Maybe two," said Felipe.

"We'll buy a bottle. On credit." They laughed. Their mounts' hooves raised tiny puffs of dust on the hard dry trail.

"*Buenos días*, Doña Dolores. And Don Domingo?"

"*Buenos días*," she snapped. She did not like them. "He's not here." She was Domingo's cook, mistress, and storekeeper—he had taught her to read and write to be able to keep accounts of credit sales.

"Where is he?" Benito asked. "I have to see him; I aim to settle accounts with him."

She brightened a little—she did not read the second meaning in the words. "He's branding some calves, in the other corral—the new one."

"Back in by the *ceiba* tree, where Don Antonio lives?"

"That's the place."

"Let's go give him a hand, *cuñado*. There's nothing like doing a man a favor before you settle with him."

"There's where you'll find him. He can probably use some help. He has only Don Antonio and his boys."

"Sell us a bottle of *aguardiente*, Doña Dolores. We'll pay for it with venison," Felipe said.

"With venison?"

"With good red deer meat," Benito grinned. "There's a great tall deer that comes out in my *milpa*, and we're going to kill him. Let us have a bottle."

"I can't. I don't have the key to the storeroom—Don Domingo forgot to leave it," she lied. She said later that she lied on an impulse, a vague fear that she did not understand. Perhaps she sensed danger—she believed, as all do, that alcohol sparks trouble.

"Ah, Doña Lolita, don't be mean! There must be a bottle around somewhere, or even part of one. We might even let you have the whole carcass, if you treat us right." Benito leered at her, till she felt he was looking through her plain dress.

"I tell you there isn't any!" she snapped. "Not till Don Domingo comes back! He can sell it to you if he wants to." She turned back to her kitchen. To herself she thought, "I'm going to tell Domingo about that insolent red-headed *hijo de la chingada!*"

The two men reined their horses around and set off inland, the bald-faced sorrel shuffling along at his running-walk, the buckskin jogging behind.

In the corral Don Domingo was slaving. Don Antonio and his two younger sons were not very good at handling cattle. The oldest boy, the only one who has a bit of talent for cowpunching, was in his bed with a fever. (There are those who can handle animals and those who cannot—psychologists have spent much time investigating less important things but have not solved the question why this should be.) Domingo roped, and often he had to tie, and he handled the irons and the castrating pincers. All his helpers did was to keep the branding fire going and wrestle down the smaller calves.

So Domingo was glad when Benito and Felipe rode up to the gate to ask if they might help. He slapped them on the back, joked with them as in the old days. Benito hung his .22 single-shot rifle on a branch of a *cocuite* tree outside the corral; Felipe unstrapped the .38 automatic from his waist, hung it close by. They went into the corral, shaking the kinks out of their lassos. They roped head and heel, rarely using the snubbing post but stretching the big brawny calves out on the ground so Domingo could stamp them with the hot iron, castrate the males. In a little over an hour they worked more animals than Don Domingo had been able to handle with his incompetent help since morning.

"That's the lot," he said, wiping his sweaty forehead with his hand, leaving streaks of grime. "Turn 'em out, Don Antonio. I wish you two had got here earlier—it's pleasant to work with good *vaqueros* for a change. Maybe you'll come to help me another time."

"All you'll have to do, Don Domingo, is to let us know. If you can do that, we'll be here," Benito answered.

Felipe laughed loudly, liking the jest. "That's right, Don Domingo. All you'll have to do is to let us know."

"There's a few fingers of *tequila* in a bottle in my *morral*," Domingo said. "Let's dry them up. Which way are you headed? Are you coming out to the river?"

"We'll go along with you for a short way, anyhow," Benito answered. He tilted the bottle, just moistened his lips, passed it to Felipe, who took a hearty drink. Don Antonio, returned from opening the corral gate, took another, and so did Domingo. A couple of inches of the pungent liquid remained in the bottle. Don Domingo worried it into the *morral*, along with the bottle of screw-worm dope, some other veterinary medicines, and his pistol, which he had taken off to work in the corral. It was the .38 Colt with the gold-chased butt plates. There were two rounds in the clip, none in the chamber. For a man brought up in an environment of violence, Don Domingo was very careless with his weapons. He hung the *morral* with bottles, medicines, and pistol on his saddlehorn, on the left side because his lasso was slung on the right, and mounted with a great jingling of the big spurs he liked to wear. His glossy-fat black horse, a big handsome horse for a big tall man, minced sideways a few steps, then trotted out the gate after Benito and Felipe, who were recovering their arms from the *cocuite* tree. Don Antonio and his sons trudged toward their little palm-thatched house to the right of the gate.

The trail from the corral gate skirts the edge of a small but deep pothole of swamp filled with *apompo* trees behind Don Antonio's house. The dense stand of trees screens off the trail, so that twenty-five or thirty yards along nothing can be seen from Antonio's house. The three horsemen jogged along in single file, Don Domingo first, then Don Felipe, Don Benito in the rear.

Felipe had insisted that he would do the killing. About sixty yards from the corral he drew his pistol. But his nerve evaporated, his hand shook so that he dropped his weapon. Benito kicked the spindly sorrel pony so it lunged past, unslinging the rifle from his shoulder and flipping the safety over. Somehow he did not want to shoot Domingo in the back. He kicked the pony on to come abreast to the right; as Don Domingo turned at the sound of the hoofbeats he reined up and fired.

He shot for the heart, as he would at a deer. But he held a little low. He hit Domingo in the right side, in the next to lowest rib.

Years ago a .22-caliber rifle was a toy, just slightly more dangerous than a BB gun, useful for plinking at tin cans and paper targets so one could learn how to use a real rifle. But modern .22's and their ammunition have been so improved that they are deadly weapons. As the hollow-point bullet passed through Domingo's rib, it shattered into hundreds of tiny razor-sharp particles that, given a downward vector by the curvature of the rib, churned his liver into bits.

The black horse stopped and stood firm as Domingo clapped his left hand over the gushing wound. Yellow sheets of pain flamed up behind his eyes, blinding him. "*Cabrón!*" he screamed. "You killed me!" His right hand flashed across into the *morral* for the pistol.

"What you've had coming to you!" Benito shouted, clamping his legs tight as his pony shied away from the gunshot. He yanked the bolt back to reload—the worn extractor slid over the casing, leaving it stuck in the chamber.

Domingo rocked back and forth in his stirrups. Amid the vivid flames of agony he remembered that the pistol was not loaded. He took his left hand from his wound to try to haul the slide back and jack a cartridge into the chamber, staining the slide with his blood. No one can know if he saw Benito shift the useless rifle to his left hand to draw that cut-down dirklike machete to finish him off—a vast wave of pain exploded in his head, then flickered out into black nothingness as he toppled from his saddle. Flat on his back. Dead. His right hand loosed the blood-smeared, useless pistol.

The shot and savage shouts had startled Don Antonio and his two sons. They came running from the house to where they could see past the trees down the trail to the tableau: Don Domingo's black horse, riderless, nibbling grass to the left; Benito's sorrel, riderless too, wide to the right, head up in alarm; Benito, spraddle-legged, bent over, the late afternoon sun glinting on his short machete blade as he used its point to pry the stuck empty casing from the chamber of his rifle; Felipe on his knees clawing at the ground, then getting up with something that gleamed black—his pistol—in his hand; and the bulk that was Don Domingo's body on the ground.

"What happened?" Antonio shouted.

"Nothing," called Benito. "Wait there a moment—we'll come tell you."

"We're coming to kill you too!" Felipe yelled. He fired twice. The bullets hit the ground twenty feet in front of Antonio and his boys and whined off uselessly to the left. As they turned to run they heard Benito snarl, "*Idiota!* Don't shoot till we get close!"

They ran away from the house, so as not to lead their pursuers there, although their machetes and Antonio's old shotgun were in the hut. Like rabbits fleeing mad dogs, they sprinted for a stand of thick brush north of the corral.

In the house the sick boy got out of bed. He was nearly sixteen—he knew what to do. He unhooked his father's shotgun from the nail it hung from, broke it to make sure it was loaded, locked it again, and cocked the hammer. He stationed himself behind the doorway, motioning to his mother to crouch lower behind the big wooden chest that held the family clothing. She clutched the three smaller children in her arms, cursing them in a flat whisper lest they attract attention by crying. The boy with the shotgun trembled as though he were about to fall apart, not from fear but from the malarial chill that seemed to be congealing the marrow in his bones.

Once the excitement of the slaying had passed, Benito and Felipe did not really want to kill Antonio and his boys. They searched the edges of the thicket desultorily for a while, shouting threats. Javier, the youngest, lay bellydown, heart thumping, peering from behind a clump of brush to watch Benito finally pry the jammed casing from his rifle, reload, sheathe his machete. Then the killers went away to catch their horses.

Antonio feared an ambush. He and his sons were witnesses, he realized. Only live witnesses can testify. They stayed hidden in the brush until dark. Cautiously he took his youngsters to the lightless house. Then, machete in hand, he set out at a trot to inform my *compadre* Sebastián, the Auxiliary Judge, the nearest representative of law and order; he trotted nearly a mile through the night before he turned on his flashlight.

18

Pursuit

MY COMPADRE SEBASTIÁN is a man who organizes his
tasks. He told his hired hands Fernando and Isidro to bring
in and saddle the horses, then sent one of them upriver and
the other up the lower course of Arroyo Bravo to notify
Don Faustino and other Auxiliary Police. Don Antonio,
on horseback despite himself, he sent downriver to sum-
mon other neighbors to come armed to the trail crossing
at Arroyo del Tigrillo, where the two groups would assemble. While waiting for the upriver people, Sebastián
readied his outboard motor and fuel, put them in his canoe.
If Domingo were wounded but still alive he could be
started to town to a doctor with no loss of time. Fernando
would take the canoe down to wait at Don Macario's
house, the nearest place on the river by trail from the corral by the *ceiba* tree. Don Sebastián packed a tablet of
ruled writing paper and some pencils in a plastic bag, a
couple of extra flashlights, and some spare batteries, readied
a shotgun and a rifle should anyone need them, checked his
own pistol. Don Antonio had insisted they would find the
killers at the scene of the crime—an unlikely notion, but
then one never knows.

The men from downriver were waiting at the stream crossing; the combined group numbered ten. My *compadre* Sebastián and Don Antonio rode in the lead, shining their flashlights ahead.

"Let me know when we get close, Don Toño. We don't want to ride all over the tracks with all these people."

"We're nearly there. Look, you can see the bulk of the *ceiba* against the sky."

A group of men riding these trails is often noisy, chatting, laughing, and shouting—this group was silent. Saddle leather creaked, spurs and bit chains jingled softly, horses' hooves thumped the hard ground in walk or jog-trot rhythms, and Don Sebastián questioned Antonio in low tones—those were all the sounds.

After a short while Don Antonio stopped his horse. "There!" He gestured with his light. "There he is! The white of his shirt shows through the grass and weeds."

"Let's move up where we can see a little more. Where were Benito and Felipe when you saw them?"

"Benito was standing to the left of the body, a little over two meters." He jiggled his light a bit to direct attention. "There, see that seedling *cornizuela?* He was standing just on the far side of that."

"And Felipe?"

"Maybe five or six meters farther on, there in that weed patch, to the left of where Benito was. The trail sort of angles back from where we're looking—back to the edge of the *apompos.*"

"Let's move in—carefully."

"*Compadre* Sebastián," Don Faustino called, "wouldn't it be better to wait till daylight? We might mess up some important tracks—it isn't the same looking for tracks by flashlight."

"We have to find out if Domingo is still alive. Let's go."

"Don Domingo is dead," said Antonio.

My *compadre* stopped, stared at him in the penumbra of the flashlight. "How do you know? I thought you said you didn't go near him."

"Well, he himself said so. That's what we heard him yell after the shot: '*Cabrón*, you killed me!' "

My *compadre* muttered a curse, then called, "Dismount, everyone. Tie your ponies. Don Macario, Don Mario! You two track deer by flashlight—come walk ahead of me here, checking the ground for sign."

They walked forward slowly, crouching, shining their lights close ahead of them. "Benito's sorrel pony crossed here. These are his little hoof prints," Mario said.

"Put your hat by them so the other people don't trample them out." Sebastián played his flashlight about. "Don Toño, is that the *cornizuela* where Benito was standing?"

"That's the one."

"Stay here shining your light on it, so no one goes near it. We may want to see where Benito dismounted."

They closed in on the body. Sebastián squatted beside it, touched the cold forehead, turned his light on the open eyes that glistened but did not move. Tears welled, trickled down my *compadre*'s cheeks. He had been fond of Don Domingo.

"*Ave Maria Purísima*, he's dead, he's cold dead! Those filthy murdering bastards!"

Mario bent over, gingerly moved the outstretched arm. "He's stiff! *Al carajo!* He's been dead for hours!"

"Since they shot him," put in Don Faustino. "Don Toño was right—when he shouted he knew he had been killed."

Don Sebastián wiped his eyes with his sleeve. "Let's see the wound. Don Mario, cut his shirt above the bloodstain." Mario tautened the shirt with one hand, slid his machete over the cloth to cut a neat right-angled flap.

"Small hole. Perhaps it was the .22 that made it after all," Faustino said.

"Of course it was the .22, Benito's .22!" Don Antonio exclaimed angrily. "I told you it was the .22! We heard the shot! *Caramba*, one knows what a .22 rifle sounds like. Then Felipe shot at us with his .38—twice—the sound was very different. Are you doubting my word?"

"No, no, that isn't it, Don Toño," my *compadre* interjected hastily before Faustino could answer. Don Faustino is a good man in any situation except that he is quick to take offense. This was not the time for squabbling. Don Sebastián gulped, wiped his sleeve across his eyes again. "The thing is that I have to make note of everything, to write the report for the authorities in town. My *compadre* Faustino knows that I have to check all the evidence."

Don Antonio turned away, growling in his throat. It had been a bad day—a day of shock, of fear, of shame at being caught unarmed and made to run and hide in the presence of his sons, and having to urge them to run and hide too. Don Antonio is no coward, but what can an unarmed man threatened by armed killers do—then running, lungs dry and aching, through the dark to bring the bad news—and now Don Faustino was insinuating that he had lied. He did not like Don Faustino much—there was the time that Don Faustino, mean drunk at a *fandango*, had reached under his shirt and he, wrapping his fist around the handle of his machete, had faced him down. At close quarters a drawback slash of a machete can be even faster than a pistol draw. Don Faustino had disliked him since; he was trying now to embarrass him. Don Antonio stamped off with his flashlight.

"There's his gun, where it fell out of his hand." Macario pointed with his machete.

"Look, it isn't cocked."

"Maybe it had a bad round in the chamber—didn't fire when he snapped it." Sebastián leaned over to pick the weapon up. He pressed the latch releasing the clip. "Only two cartridges!" he exclaimed as beams from several flashlights converged. "Domingo certainly wasn't expecting trouble!"

"Isn't that dried blood on the slide?" Mario asked.

"Looks like it."

"Why should there be blood there?"

Don Faustino played his light about the body. "His left hand is all blood-smeared. He must have grabbed at his wound, then tried to work the slide with the same hand."

"Don Toño says the pistol was in his *morral*," Don Sebastián muttered, trying to grasp the slide where there were no bloodstains. He ran it back. "The chamber is empty! *Dios Santo*, the man was unarmed! Chamber empty, hammer down."

"Could *they* have known that?" Faustino wondered.

"Don Antonio might know—"

"Don Sebastián! Don Sebastián! I've found it! Come look!" Antonio shouted.

"Wait a minute, Toño. Tell me first, could Benito and Felipe have known Don Domingo's gun was unloaded?"

"Was it unloaded? No, I don't think they could know. He had his gun in his waistband while he gathered the cattle, put it in the *morral* long before they got here."

"Could they have looked in the *morral*, or even have unloaded it?"

"No. He had the medicines in there too—you know how he was, kind of fussy about medicines for the cattle—he wouldn't have let them poke around in it. Now come over here—look, here's the mark of Felipe's gun—the butt end of the print is messed up where he picked it up, but the muzzle shows plain."

"It looks about right." Sebastián held the muzzle of the victim's gun—both weapons were Colt .38's—over the impression in the soft dirt. They matched.

Don Toño was excited. "This proves it! Felipe somehow dropped his gun! I thought that's what he was picking up when we came out to the trail, but couldn't be sure. He was riding behind Don Domingo when they left the corral, so he was going to do the killing, but he dropped his gun. Then Benito did it with the .22."

Don Mario broke in, "Why should Felipe have dropped it?"

"Maybe he was scared," my *compadre* suggested.

"Why? If he was going to shoot Don Domingo by treachery, in the back, what did he have to be scared of?"

"*Quiénsabe*. Maybe thinking of what will happen to him. We'll find out when we catch him. Now let's get busy. Don Faustino, have the people load the body on the old gray horse, the one Don Antonio rode. Isidro and Don Macario can take the deceased to the river by Don Macario's house. I'm going to take the body to town, to my *comadre* the widow."

"I don't think we can pack it on a horse. It's very stiff."

"In a hammock, then. Don Toño, get us a hammock from your house. Somebody cut a pole to sling it on. Isidro and Don Macario can carry it on foot."

Isidro grumbled, "We're the two smallest men here; and Domingo is big and heavy. You ought to—"

"Don Macario has to go—he knows the shortest trail to his house from the edge of the pasture. And you're the same height, so you two can carry easily together."

The fact was that almost any of the men could have found the trail—Don Sebastián felt he must send Macario, who had liked Domingo, but also was a kinsman of Felipe's.

"Don Faustino, you and Don Mario take everyone but

Toño and go to Felipe's house—it's nearest—then to Benito's. Surround the houses and arrest them if they're there."

"Not very likely—"

"Well, we have to start somewhere. I'm going to stay to write down Don Toño's statement, and those of his boys."

"Don Benito and Don Felipe were at Don Domingo's store this afternoon—my oldest boy saw them talking to Doña Dolores," one of the men from upriver said.

"Is that so? I'd better see if she has a statement to make, after I finish here."

"None of us will get much sleep tonight," Faustino said over his shoulder as he turned to untie his horse. "Mount up, *muchachos*, let's go."

News of the murder flashed up and down the river. Carlos Sanchez told me when he passed by at dawn; he was on his way in to the Arroyo Bravo, to inform his two brothers. They were among the many people heavily in debt to Don Domingo. His death would certainly affect them in some way. I didn't want to believe the tale—sometimes wild rumors flood our communications network. Then came Isidro with a note from my *compadre* Sebastián and the packet of pencil-scrawled papers in a cellophane bag. The note asked me to type out the declarations of the witnesses and his own report so Isidro could take them to town by next day's train. My *compadre*'s brawny hands, callused by lassos, machetes, and axes, do not grasp a pencil gracefully. His orthography—he had little formal schooling—is remarkable. From practice, I can decipher his cramped scrawl and strange spelling. Ordinarily one doesn't mind doing a *compadre* and good friend a favor. But this favor I disliked. It made me feel bad to write that tall Domingo, Domingo with his wide white-and-gold-toothed smile, was dead, and that Benito had killed him.

THE THREE MILK COWS knocked down fourteen posts and broke the top strand of wire in the fenceline across the swale behind the house. The posts were old and rotten— the fence was really pure sham. As the cows poked their heads between the wires straining to get at the lush grass on the other side, the weakest posts creaked and snapped. The wise old cows, who know as much about fence as anyone, feeling the tension eased, lunged. More posts snapped, the stretch of fence collapsed, and the cows withdrew their heads and blithely hopped over. So I had a chore to do, repairing the damage.

You don't dig post holes in soggy, soft mud. You cut a post, put the butt end on a length of tough wood that serves as a chopping block, holding the middle of the post against your left thigh, and chop tapering cuts off the butt with your machete, turning the post slightly after each cut until you have trimmed it to a long tapered point like that of a well-sharpened pencil. Then you grasp the post just above the center of balance, point down, lift it high over your head and slam it into the mud. You wiggle it loose, lift it again, and drive it down a little deeper. And again and again, until its tip is two feet deep and firmly set in the soggy ground. It is good work on a warm day. Shoulder and back muscles tense and strain as you lift the post, relax as your triceps tighten to slam it into the ground. Sweat dribbles from under your hat brim, trickles pleasantly down your chest and belly. You don't have to think about anything except how to balance the post's weight so that the tip drives into the center of the hole. You don't have to think about a friend who died before his time, a friend vilely murdered by another friend.

My fugue was interrupted by the tak-takety! of hoof-beats of a cantering horse on the dry hard ground to the river side, the house side, of the swale. Pablito came bareback on the old buckskin—his *mamá* had sent him to tell me Don Amaranto was waiting to see me at the house.

I left the tools, woke the blue pony who was dozing standing up under the shade of a *nanche* tree, and mounted to ride the short distance to the house.

There were two saddled horses tied under the *guásimo*, Don Amaranto's bay gelding, almost as lank and bony as his master, and a chunky handsome roan mare that I did not know. I looked toward the house and saw Don Manto sitting on the porch with his eldest son, twenty-five-year-old Fidencio. It struck me that Fidencio had much better taste in horseflesh than his father.

Don Amaranto set his coffee cup on the floor, rose to come striding out to meet me. "Don Pablo, I'd like to speak to you in private," he said, after formal greetings.

Pablito had slid off the buckskin and was tying him up. "Pablito, go tell your mother I've arrived. Stay there at the house; visit with Fidencio. Don Amaranto and I have to talk." He trotted off obediently.

"Don Pablo, this is a bad situation, a dangerous situation, this killing of Don Domingo."

"It's bad, for sure. I feel terrible about it, for I liked Don Domingo. But dangerous?"

"Dangerous. Don't you see, it's a start, a precedent, of a conflict—a war between peasants and cattlemen, between the poor and the rich."

The idea was shocking. I had never thought that there were rich and poor on the Xucuapan. There really were no rich, except Don Panuncio and Don Margarito. We cattlemen are all small operators who work hard to make a modest living. There are few of the really poor, by Mexican economic standards, aside from a sprinkling of very improvident people. Even Chepe Joloche eats regularly, and sufficiently—he's been putting on weight lately.

But "rich" cattlemen and "poor" peasants, we all live in the Xucuapan—we work together, we are welcome in each others' houses unless we have had personal difficulties, we go to *fiestas* and drink together.

"Do you really think so, Don Manto?"

"Of course I do. You're a newcomer, but I've lived most of my life on the Xucuapan. I can tell you that blood has been spilled, blood has flowed like water on these river banks." (I thought to myself, "For Christ's sake, think up a new metaphor!") "Good men have died by machete, by gun, by knife, but never before like this." His eyes glittered. Mentally I pictured him dressed in somber black instead of in faded khakis, so that he would look, as he sounded, like the Raven of evil augury. "Men have killed each other when crazed by drink. Men have killed for vengeance. Men have killed for troubles over women. Usually it was the *aguardiente* that made them do it. But this is the first time here on the Xucuapan a man has killed to avoid paying an honest debt."

"I don't think it was that simple. I think there was more behind it than the money owed."

"There wasn't. It was a purely commercial murder. Remember it next time some *fregado* wants to borrow a few hundred pesos to cure a sick baby or a sick wife. Wonder whether he'll pay you off in money or a bullet in the gut. Or a load of buckshot in the back from behind a yellow-wood tree."

I stared at him, appalled. He was earnest, intense. Don Amaranto is a man who has stood his ground in some tough situations. He, as everyone here knows, worries but does not scare easily.

"Don Amaranto, do you really believe it's as bad as that?"

"I certainly do."

"What are you proposing?"

"I think we cattlemen should meet to agree on some sort of action—some way to capture the criminals, to show the rest they can't get off scot-free. I think that's what Don Panuncio and Don Chon would do if they were here with us—how we need those two!"

"When is the meeting to be?"

"When I see the people. You're the first I've talked to. Can we count on you?"

I took a deep breath. "For anything correct and legal, yes, of course."

"What was all the secrecy with Don Manto?" Maria asked, after he and Fidencio had made their goodbyes and ridden on.

"Nothing. He wanted to talk about the late Don Domingo."

I put some brown sugar in a tumbler, squeezed a couple of limes, poured four fingers of *aguardiente*. Sipped and pondered. What had got into Don Manto? Class war on the Xucuapan? Cattlemen versus *campesinos?* He was being silly. I finished my drink and went back out to the fence-repair job.

Don Concho came looking for me. Maria offered to send Pablito to call me, but he said he could find me himself. We chatted casually. He drew his machete, trimmed the points on a couple of posts that I had left off-center. "When they're crooked, Don Pablito, they work over to one side as you drive them in—get your fencing out of line."

I offered him a cigarette. We walked over to a patch of shade behind a young *palma de coyol* and squatted on our heels, so he could talk about whatever he had come to say.

I led off. "The plug in the bow of the canoe works marvelously, Don Concho. Hasn't leaked a drop."

"I'm glad. I did the best I could—of course, I don't

have much skill for that kind of work—" He went into the formal self-deprecating routine, putting himself in the role of the faithful *peón* serving his *patrón*, which meant he planned to ask me a big favor. I became restive, wishing he would get it over with. I wanted to finish fixing the damn fence.

"I'm in difficulties, Don Pablito," he said at last. "I came to see if you would help me."

"Oh? Is that so? What happened?"

"I owed some money to the late Don Domingo. He said I could pay it off in parts, some after the harvest of the *milpa*, some after next year's harvests, without interest." (Easy to say, hard to prove—Domingo is dead.) "But now they say the widow Doña Cristina is coming to collect all the debts, all at once, cash on the barrelhead, or send people to jail."

"Who says that, Don Concho? *Carajo*, Doña Cristina will have to collect the debts, obviously. But she may be considerate—she lived here on the river for years; she knows all us people. How can anyone know what she will do? It was just yesterday that my *compadre* took the body to town—no one could possibly get back with such news."

Concho went sullen. "Well, that's what they are saying over on the Arroyo."

I did not want this either. More than once Don Concho and his sons had given me a hand when I needed it. "You know I want to help you if I can, Don Concho."

He looked me in the eye, his face tight and hard. "I am grateful that you say that." It was obvious he wasn't. "I have to beg for a loan because Don Domingo—the late Don Domingo, may he rest in peace," he added mechanically— "he ruined me. He gouged me, he took the little I had from me, bled me dry as he did other poor men. That's why they killed him. If they hadn't, someone else would have."

For the second time that day I was deeply shocked. Was this a threat? Could it be that Don Amaranto's somber appraisal was right? I flipped away the stub of cigarette, rose to my feet. Being pressured puts my back up, but I didn't want to get upset, much less show it, when I didn't understand what was happening.

"Don Concho, I'm glad you came to tell me about this. I'll do all I can to help you, but we'll have to wait till Don Salomón sends me the money for those old barren cows I sold him the other day. Come over a week from today; I should have the money by then—if you can't come, send the boys. We can work out something." Ostentatiously I looked at my watch. "It's getting late and I have some calves to cure back in the far pasture, so I have to go now. It was good to see you—give the boys my *saludos. Hasta la vista.*"

We shook hands; Concho turned and trudged off glumly.

Three days later I went to the Jó pasture to tend to some baby calves I had staked out under shade trees there. I was painting screw-worm dope on one calf's umbilicus under the big *zapote mamey* tree on the knoll on the far side of the creek when I heard the *peya* jays making a tremendous fuss where the trail comes out of the woods. I looked. Soon I saw a yellowish dot that was a palm-fiber hat, then the head and shoulders of a man come up behind the hill in front of the pasture gate. It was much too far for recognition. In throwing the small but spunky calf, my pistol had slithered on the cartridge belt till it hung far back, almost over my left buttock. Automatically, with no conscious volition, I shifted it into place on my left hip, then cursed myself for a fool, for letting Don Manto's dire auguries frighten me. The person rode up the gradual slope, came out on top of the hill. I still could not identify him, but his mount was almost certainly the short-legged, paunchy bay

mare that belonged to my *compadre* Sebastián—in which
case the rider was probably Isidro. He reined up, shouted,
"Hu-u-u!" in the shrill falsetto that carries long distances
in the humid air. It was Isidro.

"*Hola*, Don Chilo!" I shouted as he came near.

"*Hola*, Don Pablito! *Buenos días!* Your *compadre* Sebastián is at your house, waiting for you. He sent me to tell
you."

"That's good. How did you find me?"

"Doña Maria told us where you had gone. But she said
you sometimes spend a lot of time with the cattle, so your
compadre sent me to let you know he needs you."

"Good. Help me with the calves—there are three more—
and we'll go."

MY COMPADRE LOOKED WEARY. His brown face was
lined, there were dark patches under his eyes. His scraggly
Indian beard—he usually shaves it close—accentuated the
worn-out effect; I was surprised at how much gray was in
it.

We embraced, slapping each other affectionately on the
back. "How goes it, *compadre?*" I asked.

"Well enough, now I'm back home on the Xucuapan.
But it was bad, bad, downstream, down in town."

"What happened?"

"Everything horrible. Those people in town! My *compadre* Cristina, *pobrecita*, she collapsed when I gave her
the news—I went into the *arroyo* right up in front of the
house. I was frightened for a while—thought maybe she
had died too, from the shock. Then I went to the *Municipio*
to report the killing. That's when my troubles began."

"How do you mean?"

"That *Comandante*—"

"Don Marcos? of the *Columna?*"

"No, no. The *Comandante* of the municipal police, Don Fermín, Fermín Something-or-other, I don't remember his surname. You know him." I shook my head. Some new police officers had been sent from the state capital. "He was nasty. He said where was the Act of Demise—I told him I'd prepared it and it would arrive next day. So he said it was a felony to move a corpse before the Act of Demise had been properly submitted."

"*Dios Santo*, doesn't he know you're the Auxiliary Judge here, competent to write the act?"

"He should have known it—I told him. He knew—he was just trying to make things difficult. I told him, not once but several times, that everything—all their stupid papers—was in order, but that I was not going to leave the body of my *compadre* in the hot sun until it stank while I wasted time on paperwork. *Ay Dios, compadre,* Don Domingo was beginning to swell and stink, just a little, when I got to town. It's a long way, as you know, and the sun was hot. It was terrible." Tears filled my *compadre*'s bloodshot eyes.

"*Compadre*, what a miserable situation!"

"I turned and walked out. Wondered if the *hijo de puta* would apply the *ley de fuga*"—law of flight—"shoot me in the back and claim I was running away."

"Why didn't you go see Don Martín, the *Agente del Ministerio Público?* He's a decent man—he'd understand."

"I went to his office first, but he was out of town. So then I went to the *Comandante*. When I walked out on the *Comandante*, I went to the Municipal President, Don Jorge. By good luck he was in. I gave him my resignation as Auxiliary Judge, but he wouldn't accept it. Then I told him my troubles—he called the *Comandante* in and straightened it out."

"That was good."

"But the *Comandante*, the *semejante cabrón*, won out, in a way. He insisted on an autopsy."

"An autopsy! On a man killed of gunshot wounds! *Jesús nos perdone!*"

"That's what I thought. They must enjoy poking around in dead men's guts. But that's how they found out that Don Domingo had been shot in the liver, not the heart as I had believed."

"What difference did that make?"

"One difference it made was that I had to write a special report—that's how that *cabrón* Don Fermín got even with me. Wouldn't accept it longhand, and I couldn't find anyone to type it. I went back and forth between the offices"—a grin lighted the tired face—"by way of the saloon across the street for a few jolts of *tequila*. By late afternoon I was pretty high—resigned three or four more times. Finally Don Jorge lent me one of his secretaries, the cute little Tehuana—the one with the glasses. That part was all right. I wouldn't have minded if he'd lent her to me for the rest of the week."

Maria came in from the kitchen, with coffee for him, *pozole* for me. She had been listening. "*Ay, compadre*, you know it's my bounden duty to inform my *comadre* of the Teca menace."

He chuckled at her jest. "*Ay, comadrita*, why should you add to your *comadre*'s sorrows?"

Getting to my feet, I said, "Wait a moment, *compa!* I'll bring some *aguardiente* to spike your coffee with— then maybe you'll tell us more about the cute Teca."

"You seem to be very interested in her," Maria grumped.

I brought the bottle, poured a splash into the coffee, another into an empty cup that I gave to Maria. "Put some coffee in this for Isidro—he's sitting out there on the porch. Then what happened, *compadre?*"

"Nothing much. The Teca wrote the report. I was too tight and too mad by that time to care what she wrote—signed it without bothering to read it. Then, they gave me another batch of papers—forms to fill out. That's what I came to bother you with, *compadre*. The Teca didn't have time to do them for me. It was late by then—I had to go to the wake, and to the funeral next day. My *comadre* Cristina was in terrible shape—they had to get a doctor to give her sedatives."

"What will happen to the ranch—the cattle—the store?"

"She has some brothers, one is a *petrolero*, two are cattlemen from down near Magallanes. I talked to them after the funeral. They plan to tend the cattle until they can be sold. They got an official order, and seals to close the store—and a new padlock too. I locked and put seals on the store door this morning, before coming to see you."

Maria put in, "And Doña Dolores?" I caught a faint harshness in her voice—the tone of a married woman speaking of a mistress.

"She's almost as broken up as my *comadre* Cristina. I took some provisions and other things out of the store for her before I sealed it up. I don't believe my *comadre* will be very compassionate with her, even though that baby she has is Domingo's."

I said, "*Pobrecita.*"

Maria sniffed.

GAUNT AND WITH the pallor of a prolonged lack of sun and wind and rain, Don Panuncio sat in his wheelchair, a step so new in his convalescence from his encounter with the Gyr bull that he still did not maneuver it well. As he listened to their tale he sipped a *torito*—the nurse had gone home. ("It's scandalous," he had proclaimed. "She steals every drop of my liquor that she can find. One would not expect to encounter such depravity in a nice-looking, well-educated girl. Worse, she snitches on me to the doctor.")

Serious now, he said, "Then we don't really know who that tough sergeant is?"

"I didn't mean it quite like that," replied my *compadre* Sebastián. "I meant he was someone we hadn't known before. According to the letter they sent me, he and his five policemen were sent on special assignment from that new state police center. The letter gives his name. Not the names of his policemen, though. He's a Jalisco, by his accent."

"Some would-be gunman that they ran out of Jalisco years ago," growled Don Salvador.

"There are some parts of this business I still don't understand," the old man went on. "The first is, what's the matter with Don Faustino? Has he lost his wits?"

He paused. No one answered the rhetorical question, so he continued.

"There he was, *Comandante* of Auxiliary Police, with ten men, with the obligation to obey and to assist the Regular Police—the sergeant and his people who'd been sent to capture Benito and Felipe. Instead of cooperating, he clashes with the sergeant, blocks him, or, as the sergeant would say, interferes with him."

"*Bueno*," broke in El Güero, "What else could he do? You want him to stand around letting that thug beat up women and old men because they wouldn't tell where Benito was? Anybody knows they wouldn't tell—they're Benito's people. If he was such a competent policeman he'd have looked for tracks, to see if Benito had been there recently."

"He's probably a town cop," said Don Panuncio. "Doesn't even know about tracks."

El Güero went on, heatedly. "So now old Don Pedro,

Benito's *papá*, is probably going to die from having his ribs kicked in, and they say Benito's younger wife Clara is in bad shape from being jabbed over the kidneys with the muzzle of a Mauser."

"Poor old Don Pedro," Don Panuncio mused. "He was a good, tough man in his day—"

Don Salvador broke in, "He's a good tough man till he dies. Old, sick, stiff and hurting with rheumatism—he wouldn't take the sergeant's nonsense. Stood up to him, called him all varieties of *hijo de puta* and *cabrón*. That's when the sergeant knocked him down and kicked him." Salvador paused. "I've been told Benito cried like a child when he heard about the beating."

"And that's when Faustino and his people faced the town cops down," Don Sebastián said. "For the second time. The first was when the cops were going to take Benito's wives back into the brush to rape them."

"At least that's what Faustino thought they intended to do—it can never be proved. Were the town police pretty drunk?"

"Not real drunk, just a little. They were drinking the whole time—came with their *morrales* loaded with bottles of *tequila*. That about the women was the first real trouble. The second time, in Don Pedro's house, they say was worse. Don Candelario and Don Mario told me they flipped the safeties off their rifles, and they and the rest moved back against the walls till they had the police surrounded. My *compadre* Faustino with his shotgun against his hip, the sergeant with his pistol in his hand. It must have been a close thing—any one of seventeen men makes the wrong move and they all start shooting."

"That's what I'm getting at," Don Panuncio insisted. "But after a showdown like that—"

Don Salvador interrupted again. "Don Faustino did the

right thing. Those cops must have thought that the times of the dictator Don Porfirio Díaz were back. I hear the cops did just the same thing in those days—going around drunk, beating up people who'd committed no crime, just for the fun of it. That's one of the things the Revolution was about!"

"*Compadre* Salvador, *caramba*, you don't let me finish what I'm trying to say. I'm not saying Don Faustino was not justified in objecting to the sergeant's brutality. Sure he was justified. And he had the guts to face the *hijo de puta* down. But he made the big mistake later. Didn't you tell me that in Don Pedro's house the sergeant said he was going to report him?"

"That's right, *compadre*," Sebastián said. "They all say the sergeant said that he would report my *compadre* Faustino's 'lack of cooperation'! That's when Faustino told him that to do it he'd have to get out of the Xucuapan alive, and that it was a long road to town."

"There you are. That's what I mean. Faustino interfered with what the sergeant will say was his interrogation of important witnesses. Faustino even threatened him. And he was warned that the sergeant didn't intend to let him get away with it. So what does he do? He gets home about daybreak, sleeps till noon, goes out to tend his calves that he has tied up. Next day, his cattle, his clearings. As though nothing had happened. He's no infant—he should know you can't lock horns with the police and get away with it, without doing anything to protect yourself. *Hijo de la chingada*, he should have got a canoe and outboard—yours, *compa* Sebastián, or Pablito's, to race to town before the sergeant got there, to file charges against the sergeant in his own name, and that of Don Pedro, of Benito's women, of Don Filemón—didn't you tell me the sergeant beat up Benito's uncle Filemón too?"

"Knocked out what few teeth the old man had left when he pistol-whipped him. There weren't many."

"That's it. Faustino should have charged the sergeant with everything he could think of—before the sergeant arrived. He could have got to town that same day—on horseback the sergeant couldn't have gotten there till the following one. That sergeant is probably an old hand who knows how to make out his reports—now his charges are on file and Faustino's are not. That's why I say Faustino lost his wits."

Don Sebastián pondered, "I wondered about that. The sergeant asked me to take him to town in my canoe—I told him the motor had broken down, wouldn't start. But he didn't mention having had trouble with my *compadre*. He and his men slept for four hours—he got them up with shakes and yells—then they saddled up and moved out fast. I didn't hear about the trouble till the next day."

"Didn't the sergeant say anything at all?"

"Just that they couldn't find the criminals. He was kind of ill-humored, but I thought it was because he'd lost out on the reward."

"Reward? You didn't mention that before."

"The widow, my *comadre* Cristina, offered a big reward for the capture of Benito and Felipe—that's what the sergeant was after."

"And now," said Güero, "there's a warrant out for Don Faustino."

"If Don Juan Pereyra hadn't left, this would never have happened," Don Salvador mused.

"I've heard a dozen people say that in the last few days," put in Sebastián.

There was silence for a moment. Then Don Panuncio spoke. "*A la chingada*, this is really a bad situation. Sebastián, let me have that letter, the one with the sergeant's name. We are going to need a lot of help to straighten this out—the right help from the right people. Güero, wheel me down the hall to the telephone—I still can't steer this thing straight on a long run. Then come back. When I need you I'll yell."

He spent several hours on the telephone. Twice he shouted for them to bring him a drink. Finally he wheeled himself back. "*Qué joder*, I'm getting the hang of this thing—only bumped into the wall three times on the way back."

"And once on the doorjamb, coming into the room," El Güero jibed.

"That doesn't count," Don Panuncio snorted indignantly. "It's a very complex maneuver, turning into a doorway. Well, I talked to a lot of people. They all said just what I did—if Faustino had used any sense, and had beat the sergeant to town to file his charges and could prove them, it would be simple. The sergeant and his men would be in jail. The authorities, the people that count, are all strong against such police methods—they won't tolerate such nonsense. But now it will be a little more difficult. We'll have to wait till tomorrow—some are going to call me back. Nothing else we can do for Faustino just now—*Compadre* Sebastián, stir us up another *torito*, and tell me what else has been happening on the Xucuapan—"

Next morning they sat waiting while Don Panuncio hovered over the phone. The nurse bustled in and out, glaring at the obviously bottle-holding parcels they carried. Now and then the phone rang, down the hall. It was past noon when the old man wheeled himself into the room.

"Some discouragement, some encouragement," he announced. "That sergeant really knows how to write a nasty report. There is an order for the apprehension of

Faustino and all his auxiliaries who were there, for interfering with police officers on lawful duty, for aiding the
criminals to escape through such interference, for threatening with words and weapons, and a lot more things I
can't remember at the moment. Anyhow, now we know
what we have to do. It's going to take some time and work,
and some money too, to straighten out this mess, but we're
going to do it, not just those of us here, but all of our
group. And we can count on other neighbors too. Since
he moved in five years ago, Don Faustino has been a
good neighbor and has worked well with us—now when
he's in a squeeze we're going to help him."

"I have the idea that almost everyone in the Xucuapan
will want to help," remarked Güero.

"That's the second reason. I didn't tell you, but I heard
about this before you people came here. That Feliciano
Ramirez, the one that works for Don Pablito, came by and
told me. I wasn't sure—he exaggerates a good deal—makes
a good story better or a bad one worse—but he says that
everyone in the Xucuapan believes Faustino did the right
thing in facing up to that sergeant for beating up old
Don Pedro."

"Feliciano's right, from all I've heard—the Xucuapan
is of one mind about this. I've even heard some of the
wilder-talking ones say that any police that come to arrest
Don Faustino might have a lot of trouble. He defended the
Xucuapan, they say, now the Xucuapan should defend
him," Don Salvador said.

"Crazy idiots!" snorted El Güero.

"That's the point. That's why we have to do something
about this. If there is more trouble with the police, or if
Faustino is arrested, jailed, and fined until he is ruined,
everyone will resent it. Law and order on the Xucuapan
will be set back thirty or forty years. All that Pereyra did

will be wasted. I haven't worked all these years to bring in law and order just to have some Jalisco tough wander in to spoil it all in a few hours."

"All right, Don Panuncio, what is it we have to do?" El Güero asked.

"We are going to have all the injured persons file charges against the sergeant and his men: Don Pedro, or if he dies, his daughters, Benito's wives, and Don Filemón. Tomorrow you'll take a young doctor with you—he will examine all the injuries. He likes gadgets—he'll take a camera to photograph the bruises and one of those tape-recorder things to take statements. You'll have to see there are witnesses to testify they heard Don Pedro say those words into the machine."

"To testify? *Pa' su mecha*, will this really go to trial?" Don Salvador asked worriedly.

"We don't know. But we have to be ready if it does. Get other people to help—"

"What if Don Pedro has died and is buried?"

"That's up to the doctor. If he says dig the poor old man up, you do it. As I was saying, get others to help— all of us and anyone else you can count on. You have to take depositions from everybody involved, including the Auxiliary Police. Make Don Pablito get to work with that typewriter of his. My lawyer cousin will have the papers for the depositions ready in the morning—he'll probably be here to explain them to you. Where's Don Faustino now?"

"I'm not certain," grinned Sebastián, "but I've heard he's on a little camping trip out in the woods."

"Tell him to stay there until we get everything organized. Send him some fish hooks and salt—the weather is fine for salting and drying panfish—he can prepare me a bale of them. That will give him something to do to pass the time."

"We'll need lots of paper and pencils, and ink pad for fingerprints—none of those people can sign their names."

"I have an ink pad, almost new," Sebastián proffered. "Let's take my *compadre* Pablo a typewriter ribbon—I know what kind he uses."

"What do we do about Benito and Felipe, Don Panuncio?" asked El Guero.

"Let them alone for now. We have to pull Don Faustino out of the fire first—then we'll decide how to handle them."

"What if they run? Clear out of this part of the country?"

"Then they're no longer our problem. But I don't think they will."

"*Compadre* Panuncio," Sebastián said slowly, thoughtfully. "Isn't there any possible way to get Pereyra back?"

"It would be very difficult. But after we resolve this Faustino business we might look into trying to arrange a visit."

TIME IS A RIVER that flows by from endlessness to endlessness, the one great reality for all its invisibility. One may scarcely be aware of its current flooding past. Only by noting incidents, swept along in its grasp as bits of flotsam—a sere yellow leaf, a twig, a faded blossom— sweep by in the rolling, rippling, swirling water of the river, does one come to think of it: "My, how swift it runs!"

Almost before we knew it, it was time to burn off the clearings and put the dry little kernels of seed corn into the ground where warmth and moisture, swept along by the current of time, would convert them into tall green maize plants; then there was weeding to do as the violent downpours of early summer turned to the short brisk thundershowers that punctuated the bright pleasant summer days. Time swirling by brought the sticky hot dogdays of late August-early September as the sun's shrinking declination brought its heat closer. The *milpas*, fading from green to the buffs and tans and purples of ripening, were doubled over, and, as a bit more of time's flood rippled past, the grain on the ears dried hard and sound, ready for harvest. That fall the first *nortes* began early—short, violent, drenching, wind-driven storms. We farmers harvested the maize in the breaks of good weather between storms, bringing it into the storehouses in sackfuls by tumpline, pack animals, or canoe. When the *nortes* blew, the cattle drifted around and around their pastures, heads low but not feeding, getting lean. When the storm passed, they gobbled the grass down hungrily.

I switched off the radio. The wind-driven rain hissed on the palm thatch, rattled on the corrugated iron of the porch. "Maria, I'm going to town tomorrow."

"Good," she said. "There are a lot of things we need. But will this *norte* be over? Tomorrow may be very wet."

"The Stateside radio says it's blown itself out in the Mississippi Valley—they had fine weather there today. It should taper off here tomorrow. But they're predicting another one by the end of the week. I'm dead-heading downriver—there's nothing to take—so I'd rather go down in the rain and try to catch the bit of good weather between storms to come back with the load of provisions."

"You know how you want to do it. You have three white shirts starched and ironed. Will that be enough?"

"Plenty. Let's sit down to work out a shopping list."

I left a little after six in the morning, as a sullen first light glowed under the black cloud cover and turned the river into a streak of silver mounted in black shadows. It was far from a bright light, but one could see the black fangs of the snags that menace canoe and motor. A little past five that afternoon—after about nine hours' running time with the ten-horse motor wide open, plus a couple of hours visiting *compadres* along the way—I nosed the canoe in toward the landing of a friend in town who lets me leave it there during my shopping trips. I was drenched to the hide, despite my crude-rubber poncho.

Doña Geronima, my friend's wife, was peering out through the dusk and rain. She is kin, some way, to Maria. "*Hola*, Don Pablito, are you traveling in this kind of weather?"

"*Buenas tardes*, Doña Geronima. Hunger is worse than wet and cold. When we run out of provisions I have to come in."

"And my relative Maria?"

"Sends you greetings. She also sent you a couple of fryers. Here they are, nice and wet."

"Many thanks. You're soaked—come in and have some hot coffee."

"Thanks. I'll unload the motor and gas cans first."

"Put them on the porch in the usual place. Aren't you going to change to dry clothes? You'll catch an awful cold."

Dry, with a bellyful of hot coffee, I walked downtown; I always go to the post office first, if I get to town before the six o'clock closing time. The rain had slackened to a fine drizzle. Tomorrow the weather would be good.

"Don Pablo! *Hola*, Don Pablo!" The shout came from the doorway of Don Luís's saloon across the street. I turned to see a bulky figure, but could not identify it in the dusk.

"Don Pablo! Come over here!" I angled back across the street. A bit closer, I recognized him—it was Don Juan Pereyra.

We embraced, with shouts and much backslapping.

"*Qué milagro*, Don Juan! How good to see you! When did you return to this place?"

"Couple of days ago. What a lucky chance! I was hoping to see you. You're looking well. How's the family, Doña Maria and the youngsters?"

"They're fine, thanks. You're looking in good shape—put on a little weight. The good life, eh?"

"That's right. Let's go in out of this drizzle."

The saloon was as it always is from dusk to midnight, in cold weather as in hot—a big underlighted bare-walled barn of a place, floor cluttered with small, square, roughly nailed-together plank tables, around which the customers sat on similarly roughly made stools, shouting at each other to make themselves heard over the bellowing of the juke box—what the place lacks in decor and hygiene it makes up for in decibels. A long plank bar, behind which Don Luís presides, runs partway along the left side—once, long since, it was whitewashed but is now stained and blotched with spilled drinks and other things. The atmosphere is compounded of odors of stale beer and rank black tobacco. In the far right corner is the *mingitorio*, "urinal," a tiled rectangle along the wall with a pipe from which water sometimes dribbles into the shallow concrete trough at the base, the source of a miasmic stink of stale urine that makes its presence felt at nearby tables. Don Luís's is the best saloon in Lomas. There are others, but in comparison they are rather shoddy.

In the middle of the room four tables had been pushed together end to end to form a single long unit, about which sat a group of men. I recognized them—or most of them—as persons of local importance. They had already been there for some time, judging by the accumulation of liquor glasses and empty beer bottles on the table (in these places waiters use the empties in their bookkeeping—when a client requests the bill they count the empties to get the total. Then they clear the table for a new start).

Don Juan steered me toward the joint table. I greeted the men I knew; he introduced me to those I didn't. Then he said, "You'll excuse us for a few minutes—I've been wanting to talk to Don Pablo. He comes to town so seldom—I want to make the most of this chance. We'll join you shortly."

We walked to an empty table near the end of the bar. "It's good to see you, Don Pablo," he said as we sat down. "People said you hadn't come into town for more than a month—I hoped I might find you." He hammered his fist on the table and shouted, "Waiter!"

"It's been nearly six weeks. I'd no idea you'd be here. It's been quite a while since you left."

A waiter shuffled over. "I'll have a *tequila* and a beer— Corona. What'll you have, Don Pablo?"

"Rum—no water, no ice. And a small Dos Equis."

"There's no Dos Equis," the waiter shouted over the din.

"Superior, then," I yelled back, hoping he might hear me.

"I went to see Don Panuncio a few days ago," Don Juan said as the waiter turned away to the bar.

"Oh? How was he? It's been a couple of months, or a bit more, since I last went to see him."

"He's improving a lot. Drinking *aguardiente*, of course, and spinning around in that wheelchair. I asked him if he was about ready to start roping Gyr bulls again, and he said he is going to buy a dozen of the red *cabrones* just to practice on." We laughed at the typical retort.

"It's good he's getting better—I think he probably will be back roping before too long. Maybe even Gyr bulls. He's tough, that old man," I said.

"If he weren't, he'd be dead. What he went through, from the way I heard it, would have killed an ordinary man. By the way, he said he wanted me to talk to you if I had the opportunity—I would have, anyhow, of course, but he mentioned it specially."

"Oh? What about?"

"About this business of the late Don Domingo, and Don Benito and all. He said he thinks you're a little upset about it."

"Well, I was—" The waiter finally brought the drinks. We toasted, "*Salud,*" sipped. Then I continued. "I was upset, I guess I still am. It was a shock, in the first place. Especially since I knew the people involved so well. Then all the mess afterward, with that Sergeant What's-his-name—"

"Fernández."

"That's it, Fernández."

"You know he's all finished, don't you? When that old man he beat up died, they gave him and his men tough sentences on the homicide charge. They're in for a long time."

"I heard so. I also hear that he's appealing."

Don Juan shook his head. "He doesn't have a chance. We want to keep him for an example of what happens to his kind of policemen." Then he said, "I talked to Don Marcos, too."

"What Don Marcos?"

"The *Comandante* of the *Columna,* the one who succeeded me."

"Yes. You know the story, I suppose. Some people got nervous because the story went around that Benito and Felipe were hiding somewhere away up the other river, and had joined with a couple of fugitives from Chiapas. People said it was the start of a gang—that they would terrorize the whole region, and a lot of things. So some people decided to go talk to your Don Marcos to see if he would take the *Columna* and go get them. The way you used to."

"You went with them, didn't you?"

"Yes. I didn't want to have any part of it, but Don Panuncio wanted me to go along. So I did. That was another shock, in a way. Don Marcos had not the least interest in law and order on the Xucuapan. In fact, he was almost rude, the way he told us it was none of his concern and that he had no intention of going. I'm afraid I was almost rude too."

Don Juan finished his *tequila*. "It's too bad. He should have explained the setup to you—trouble is, he's sensitive about it. The truth is he can't make patrols. They've changed things so it isn't a *Columna Volante* any more— it's just a brand-inspection station. He's a good police officer, but his hands are tied—they gave him the job as a promotion, then cut down his personnel, his authority, his transportation. He's bitter about it, and all mixed up."

"Well, he might have told us."

"He thinks it looks like a reflection on him. His pride is hurt. He hates being just a brand inspector—was going to quit, until they promised him a transfer early next year."

"That makes a difference—if I'd known that perhaps I wouldn't have been so perturbed. But you see how it was: after all you'd done, getting law enforcement to work on the Xucuapan—people seemed to be accepting the idea. Then you leave, and it all falls apart. Worse than it used to be."

"Worse? How do you mean?"

"*Caray*, before you came in there, there were troubles. But a killer could surrender to Don Panuncio or Don

Chon or somebody, or let the Auxiliary Police take him in, or run for it. Sick old men and pregnant women didn't get beaten up in the name of 'law and order.' " I became a little heated. "I'm not the only one who's worked up about it—there are many people who very seriously talk this foolishness about not letting a police force come in to the Xucuapan. 'We'll ambush the bastards,' they say. 'We don't need them or want them. Don Faustino showed us they can be run out.' "

"That's just big talk."

"I think so too. But a bad kind of talk. It shows how they think about law and order. It shows their attitude. I don't think that's progress, myself."

I gulped the rest of my drink and my beer. My mouth was dry. Don Juan pounded and shouted to get the waiter's attention, then made the gesture that means "two more of the same." Then he leaned close. "*Por Dios, hombre*, you do take this hard. No wonder Don Panuncio wanted me to talk to you. Here is what will happen—" He looked over his shoulder—the waiter, rapid for once, was headed toward us. "Wait till he serves us; have you a smoke? I seem to have lost mine."

We lighted up, then drank the newly served drinks.

"Here's the story—it's confidential, but I think it will be good for you to know it. I'm coming back to take charge of this thing myself, and I'm in a position to get anything I want in the way of men, equipment, transportation. I'm going to do it for one reason; can you guess?"

I pondered. "Well, you and the late Don Domingo were good friends."

"We were, but that isn't it. It's not kindly of you, really, to suggest it. And it's not because you and Don Panuncio and Don Sebastián and Don Roberto and the rest are my friends. It's because I feel I must finish the job I started. I think this is the key case. If it's cleared up, the law will mean something in the Xucuapan—if it isn't the clock will go back years and more years. So I myself am going back in there and get Don Benito and Don Felipe."

I looked into those pieces of glacial ice he has for eyes and saw that he meant what he said. I thought of not-very-valiant Felipe and the fool redhead Benito hiding back in the jungles and I shuddered. Then I thought of Domingo's wide cheerful smile turning into a skull's vapid grin two meters underground, and knew Don Juan was right: law and order *had* to come to the Xucuapan.

Epilogue

As I, FROM THE VANTAGE POINT of a different time and place, look back on those troublous days along the Xucuapan, I realize that it was all part of the predictable stress and tension and explosiveness of the frontier situation. A frontier is transition itself, not a stable condition in which man is in equilibrium with himself and nature, but a continual flow of pressures and strains far stronger than anything known to the relatively static phases preceding or following it. The wilderness condition lasted for thousands of years, its massive quiet not really disturbed by the small bands of ancient hunters, nor even by their descendants who girdled a few trees to make space for their tiny maize plots. It was not until the first of the modern pioneers moved into the region to begin their ruthless onslaught on the great forest that imbalance occurred, and with it the pattern of violence. At first the conflict was with the jungle itself, and with its denizens: the jaguars, the snakes, the poultry-eating small felines, hawks, opossums, the host of maize-devourers—peccary, raccoon, coati—and the innumerable individuals of many species of birds. In the early days of pioneer settlement—the period when Don Chon moved in to the Xucuapan, the time of Don Procopio (he whom the jaguar snuffled)—clashes of man against man occurred as well, but infrequently. Only in relatively recent years is human blood often spilled on the ground. This, it seems, is an effect of the change of the ephemeral frontier into civilization. With many more people than ever before in the frontier community, there are more frequent occasions for interaction. "Good" land—good in the sense not only of fertility but of accessibility—is becoming scarce. Some men have more of it than others. Familiarity with the town—all we have of civilization—increases. The rise in production causes the town to take more notice of the isolated pocket that is the frontier, and to be more concerned with the maintenance of law and order there, among other things.

The local Cattlemen's Association had been established long since, for it is a semigovernmental institution required by federal law to be established in livestock-raising regions. As part of a national antimalarial campaign, teams of technicians traversed the region spraying houses with a high concentrate of DDT to kill mosquitoes. Our neighbors complained that the DDT killed their cats, so that mice became a great nuisance; but for a time, at least, the prevalence of malaria in the region decreased. Our *compadres* write that a federally supported school has been opened on the lower section of the river, with two or three more being planned. Eventually a highway will be built into the Xucuapan, so that the trip to town will be a matter of an hour or less; fat steers will be loaded out in trucks rather than being fought out with ropes through their swollen bleeding noses, as they are now. As entry is facilitated, many more settlers will come pouring in. The present holdings of two hundred, three hundred, five hundred, or a thousand hectares of land will be broken up into parcels of twenty-five hectares—sixty acres or less. Then, densely populated, productive, policed, and taxed, the Xucuapan will become just another part of modern rural Mexico. Such is the normal destiny of a frontier. But some of us will feel a twinge of nostalgia for the old free-and-easy days, troubled though they sometimes were.

GLOSSARY OF SPANISH TERMS

abrazo: embrace

acagual: second-growth bush (after jungle cut)

acuyo: wild plant, leaf used in cookery for seasoning

adentro: within, inside

Agente del Ministerio Público: equivalent of District Attorney or Public Prosecutor

aguardiente: white sugar-cane rum

ahosh: a tree

al carajo: expletive, considered vulgar

amash: small wild chile pepper, very hot

apompo: a tree, grows in swampy areas

arroyo: creek, stream

azucareras: type of small stinging ant

batea: wooden trough for washing clothes

broza: tinder, dried leaves, brush, twigs in felled timber

cabrito: "little goat"; used for brocket deer

cabrón: swear word, offensive, not literally translatable, equivalent in usage to English "son of a bitch"

camalote: a thick-stemmed coarse grass

camino real: "royal road"; any main trail

campesino, -a: peasant

candil: small kerosene-burning lamp

carne con hueso: meat with bone

carnicero: butcher

cazuela: heavy pottery cooking vessel

cedro: Spanish cedar

chachalaca: gallinaceous bird

chalté: a hardwood tree

chaneca: mythical malicious dwarf of jungle

chingar (and derivatives—*chingada,* etc.): swear word, untranslatable, considered to be of sexual reference, with abusive connotations

cholina: large gallinaceous bird

cocuite: leguminous tree

cojones: testes, in sense of "balls"

Columna Volante: Flying Column

comadre: co-godmother

Comandante: Commander

compadrazgo: co-godparent relationship

compadra, compa': co-godfather

cornizuela: a spiny small tree

cotorra: a medium-size parrot

coyol: small hard-shelled fruit of a palm

cuñado: brother-in-law

cundeamor: a vinaceous weed

curandera: a curer, herbalist

diablo: devil

doblando: doubling (referring to *milpa,* doubling over the stalks)

en campana: "in bell"; house design with roof, no sidewalls

en falco: referring to canoes lashed together with cross-poles for stability

fandango: folk dance

fiesta: celebration, party

fregado: maltreated (vulgar)

fogón: raised firebox filled with earth and/or clay, for cooking

ganado mano: "gaining a hand"; trading work

garrabato: stick hook used in machete work

guapaque: a tree

guaraches: sandals

guásimo: a tree

guatope: a tree

guavina: wide-mouthed predatory tasty fish

guayabo: guava tree

guayacán: hardwood tree

guirina: a small parrot

hacendado: a member of the landed class

hermanito: little brother (affectionate)

hicotea: painted turtle

Hola!: Hi!

huachín: a blackbird, fond of seed

huapango: folk dance

jabalí: peccary

jarana: ukelele-like instrument

jícara: dish or cup made of tree gourd

jijole: son-of-a-gun (euphemistic)

jolocín: a tree

jolote: catfish

joder: to abuse; vulgarism with sexual connotations

loro real: a large parrot

macabil: trash fish

macayo: a tree

machismo: maleness, virility

macuile: a tree

majagua: a tree

mancuerna: two steers (cows, etc.) tied together

mano: hand; five of anything

marín: large white-jowled peccary

masa: lime-leached corn, ground to dough

mayacaste: large freshwater shrimp

mayoral: foreman

mazate: brocket deer

metate: grinding stone for corn

mierda: shit

milpa: cornfield

mingitorio: urinal

mojarra: panfish

mojarra azul: panfish very similar to bluegill

mole: sauce of bitter chocolate and chile peppers

morral: carrying bag of jute

muchacho: boy

mulato: palo mulato—a tree

Municipio: county seat

nanche: a tree, or its cherrylike fruit

naugales: witches that assume animal form

nauyaca: fer-de-lance (*Bothrops atrox*)

nixtamal: lime-leached maize

norte: norther

padrino: godfather

palencano: a blue-headed parrot

palma de coyol: a palm that produces oil-rich fruit

Pa' su mecha!: "By your mane (hair)!"

pata de cabra: goatsfoot weed

patio: yard of a house

patrón: boss

peón: worker

pepegua: a species of ill-humored ants

pésame: regrets, expressed to kin at death

petate: palm-fiber mat

peya: a big brown jaybird

pishishi: native duck

pita: string

plazo: set period of time

por Dios: by God

posada: shelter (for the night)

pozole: ground maize beverage

primavera: springtime; pygmy owl

puerco de monte: peccary

pulpa: boneless meat

querencia: home region, especially of cattle

Qué milagro!: "What a miracle!"

rabón: "big tail"; thin worn-out filed-down (narrow) machete

ranchería: loosely structured village

rozadera: leather guard in eye of lasso to prevent wear

sakwas: large bird of oriole family

salimos: first person plural, present or preterit, of *salir,* "to go out"

salvaje: savage; name of mythical monster

sanpedreño: a panfish

serete: large rodent, rabbitlike but short-eared

shish: sediment

siete-en-boca: "seven-in-mouth"; small sweet banana

silantro: herb used for seasoning

son: song, especially folk song

taco: tortilla rolled into tube around food

tamale: ground leached maize, cooked in leaves

tanai: a wide-leaved plant

tapanco: pole attic

tarima: plank dance platform

tata: father (affectionate)

tenwaiyaka: panfish

tepescuinte: agouti

tequila: beverage distilled from maguey

tilcampo: species of iguana

tocayo: namesake

toh: wide leaf, used for wrapping, etc.

tololoche: a tiny wild grape

tomatillo: a tree

torito: little bull: drink of *aguardiente*, lime juice, and brown sugar

tortilla: flat cake of ground lime-leached maize

totopos: hard dry form of *tortilla*

triste: sad

troja: granary

tronco de venado: big deer, a whopper

uña de iguana: a liana

varaprieta: a tree

vara: unit of measurement, about 32 inches

vari: a tree

velorio: wake, or festival in honor of a saint

viejo; vieja: old man; old woman —form of address, or term used by spouses

zapote mamey: a tree, or its large fruit

A NOTE ON THE TYPE

The text of this book is set in Monticello, a Linotype revival of the original Binny & Ronaldson Roman No. 1, cut by Archibald Binny and cast in 1796 by that Philadelphia type foundry. The face was named Monticello in honor of its use in the monumental fifty-volume *Papers of Thomas Jefferson*, published by Princeton University Press. Monticello is a transitional type design, embodying certain features of Bulmer and Baskerville, but it is a distinguished face in its own right. Composed, printed, and bound by The Haddon Craftsmen, Inc., Scranton, Pa. Typography and binding design by Kenneth Miyamoto.